Colonial Bureaucracy and Contemporary Citizenship

Colonial Bureaucracy and Contemporary Citizenship examines how the legacies of colonial bureaucracy continue to shape political life after empire. Focusing on the former British colonies of India, Cyprus, and Israel/Palestine, the book explores how postcolonial states use their inherited administrative legacies to classify and distinguish between loyal and suspicious subjects and manage the movement of populations, thus shaping the practical meaning of citizenship and belonging within their new boundaries. The book offers a novel institutional theory of "hybrid bureaucracy" to explain how racialized bureaucratic practices were used by powerful administrators in state organizations to shape the making of political identity and belonging in the new states. Combining sociology and anthropology of law and the state with the study of organizations, this book offers new knowledge to overturn conventional understandings of bureaucracy, demonstrating how routine bureaucratic practices and persistent colonial logics continue to shape unequal political status to this day.

Yael Berda is Assistant Professor of Sociology and Anthropology at Hebrew University and a non-resident fellow with the Middle East Initiative at the Harvard Kennedy School of Government. She is the author of *Living Emergency: Israel's Permit Regime in the West Bank* (2017) and *The Bureaucracy of the Occupation* (2012). Berda has worked as a practicing lawyer specializing in administrative, constitutional, and international law in Israel/Palestine.

Colonial Bureaucracy and Contemporary Citizenship

Legacies of Race and Emergency in the Former British Empire

YAEL BERDA

Hebrew University

CAMBRIDGE
UNIVERSITY PRESS

CAMBRIDGE
UNIVERSITY PRESS

University Printing House, Cambridge CB2 8BS, United Kingdom

One Liberty Plaza, 20th Floor, New York, NY 10006, USA

477 Williamstown Road, Port Melbourne, VIC 3207, Australia

314–321, 3rd Floor, Plot 3, Splendor Forum, Jasola District Centre,
New Delhi – 110025, India

103 Penang Road, #05–06/07, Visioncrest Commercial, Singapore 238467

Cambridge University Press is part of the University of Cambridge.

It furthers the University's mission by disseminating knowledge in the pursuit of
education, learning, and research at the highest international levels of excellence.

www.cambridge.org
Information on this title: www.cambridge.org/9781316511664
DOI: 10.1017/9781009053495

© Yael Berda 2023

First published 2023

A catalogue record for this publication is available from the British Library.

Library of Congress Cataloging-in-Publication Data
NAMES: Berda, Yael, author.
TITLE: Colonial bureaucracy and contemporary citizenship : legacies of race and
emergency in the former British Empire / Yael Berda.
DESCRIPTION: Cambridge ; New York, NY : Cambridge University Press, [2022] |
Includes bibliographical references and index.
IDENTIFIERS: LCCN 2022026119 | ISBN 9781316511664 (hardback) | ISBN
9781009054393 (paperback) | ISBN 9781009053495 (ebook)
SUBJECTS: LCSH: Bureaucracy – Asia. | Civil service – Asia. | Postcolonialism – Asia. |
Asia – Politics and government – 1945- | Asia – Race relations. | Asia – Colonial
influence. | Great Britain – Colonies – Asia. | Great Britain – Colonies – Administration.
| BISAC: SOCIAL SCIENCE / Sociology / General
CLASSIFICATION: LCC JQ32 .B47 2022 | DDC 351.5–dc23/eng/20220801
LC record available at https://lccn.loc.gov/2022026119

ISBN 978-1-316-51166-4 Hardback

Contents

vi

Contents

Figures

Preface

The origin of this study began with a practical problem. When representing Palestinians who were detained without trial after protesting against the Separation Wall in 2004, as a novice human rights lawyer in military courts, I could make arguments about the (il)legality of a military decree or invoke habeas corpus. I could make arguments about human rights violations. They mostly failed, but the arguments could be made, and even written into a protocol and addressed in the telegraphic, stenciled decisions of the military courts. However, most of the cases I represented were much more mundane. Those cases could not be argued about in court. They almost seemed to be "outside" or "beyond" the rule of law. Not because they were exceptional but because they were so routine and mundane. They weren't about "regulations," or "rights." They evaded the realm of "administrative law." They were about bureaucracy. They were cases of workers who needed documents to cross checkpoints and access their work in Israeli cities and were denied entry by Israel's civil military administration for various "security" reasons. One simply couldn't argue about their "rights" in courts. There were no formal laws that governed the permit system. The administrative regulations were unpublished and the military decrees hard to decipher. The Israeli legal system perceived the permits to move not as rights but as a system of privileges that could be granted or revoked with no obligations. I gradually discovered that, (alongside the workers themselves, employers, Palestinian and Israeli lawyers, and human rights organizations,) there was a massive system to regulate Palestinian mobility that had developed alongside the Oslo peace negotiations and was a feature of separation due to the promissory note of achieving a state at some unknown point. It was a mammoth bureaucratic system that was inefficient and yet managed to achieve its goals at the same time, slowing down population movement, enabling a system of surveillance and control, and preventing people from accessing land, their families, and options to choose their future. This "bureaucracy of the occupation" affected the daily life of millions of Palestinians in the West Bank, Gaza, and East Jerusalem and Palestinian citizens inside the border of Israel, as well as their Israeli employers. But there were no laws and no ways to challenge the bureaucratic system itself in courts. Legally, the system organizing the administration of the occupied territories was based on the inherited British colonial Defence (Emergency) Regulations of 1945.

The bureaucracy functioned nothing like one would expect from a model of administrative bureaucracy in a liberal state. Not that Israeli bureaucracy ever did, but the disparities with anything else I knew were striking. Human rights organizations called the system inefficient; some said it was contradictory and made no sense, others called it an arbitrary bureaucracy.

But it did seem to have features that, in their messiness, contradictions, and arbitrariness, remained consistent. Those features were the classification of people, not only according to their region, occupation, or political affiliations but also according to degrees of suspicion. They included various restrictions on mobility and the matching of those restrictions to the identity of different groups and their levels of risk and suspicion. They consistently differentiated the possibility for mobility based on a racial hierarchy, one that later turned into yet another set of classifications and differentiations. And one could rarely find the bureaucrat that made the administrative decision on any particular permit. Most intriguing was the way the bureaucratic system, which was in various stages of institutionalization and without a central system of coordination, was made up of many different bodies and yet agents created similar documents and categories without direct coordination.

All this mammoth bureaucracy that shaped the lives of hundreds of thousands of Palestinians every day was not addressed in the law; it was not part of political negotiations. The practical problem, then, was that there was no way to challenge these administrative decisions about mobility in courts. There was no right to movement, entry was a prerogative of the state, and the decision itself was formulated as being for "security" reasons, so judges read paraphrases of the secret service response based on their intelligence.

pertaining to national security denied to others based on their identity. Also, as a former litigator, I had the privilege to both decipher and choose to ignore the primacy of judicial and legislative documents, and focus on the very mundane, everyday bureaucracy and show how it shaped citizenship.

Acknowledgments

There is no way to thank all the people that have made this journey possible. I will start with a dedication to people working to transform the discriminatory legacies of conquest and partition into trajectories of equality, freedom, self-determination, and return in Cyprus, Israel/Palestine, and India.

The interdisciplinarity of this project, straddling law and society, sociology of organizations, legal histories, and postcolonial sociology, was both an immense challenge and a wellspring of fascination for me. Mistakes and blind spots remain my own, yet this book was made possible through the efforts of so many remarkable people over the course of the last fifteen years. I will mention only a fraction. My deepest gratitude is to my teachers for their guidance, deep engagement, and openness to the interdisciplinary challenges. Paul DiMaggio's support of my work, his patience, enthusiasm, and brilliance have been a wonderful blessing and also an inspiration for the kind of sociologist, scholar, teacher, and colleague I would like to be. His generosity with time and energy, unbending belief in the project, and willingness to engage with new subjects and archives were a great gift. Learning from Kim Lane Scheppele how to study, teach, and think law and society was invaluable. At LAPA (the law and public affairs program at Princeton University) she introduced me to an incredible network of law and society scholars, historians, social scientists, and legal philosophers who became my extended intellectual family. Bhavani Raman introduced me to law and society in colonial India, and also embodied a living, breathing example of the power of critical interdisciplinary scholarship. She is a role model I can only aspire to. I thank Miguel Centeno for his extraordinary support and enthusiasm for the project. Yehouda Shenhav – teacher, mentor, friend, and colleague – was the person that first interested me in the sociology of organizations and the study of colonialism. His guidance, mentorship, and generosity have been pivotal in my life (especially working with him on the model of hybrid bureaucracy and new concepts of sovereignty). It is such a privilege to collaborate intellectually and politically.

This transnational study would never have materialized without the nannies, teachers, and babysitters of my daughter Romi and later my son Adam and those who helped find them; in New Delhi, Kavita Tak and Anu Anand; in London, Maya Gelman; in Tel Aviv, Lia Ariel, Shani Rimon, and the staff at Gan Achva; in Jerusalem, Shula, Meir, and Lili from Kol Haneshama; in Cyprus, Anni, Maria, Eleni Pitsillidou, and Shosh Steinovitz; and finally, in Princeton, Claudia Marcano, Jamie Dorrance, Mrs. Adriano, Milta Crispo and Dorota, Mrs. Seasee, and the wonderful Lea Bulvik. Josh, Allison, and William Schnable were like family to us.

At Princeton's Sociology Department, I have countless people to thank: Viviana Zelizer, Delia Baldassarri, Andreas Wimmer, Paul Starr, Rania Salem, Christina Mora, Amir Goldberg, Gregoire Mallard, Hannah Shepherd, Pierre Antoine Kremp, Sophia Apetkar, Jeff Lane, LaTonya Trotter, Allison Youatt Schnable, Angel Christin, Sara Kaiksow, Stephanie Schacht, Elaine Enriquez, Cristobal Young, Maria Abascal, Manish Nag, Rene Flores, Denia Garcia, Yossi Harpaz, Michelle Phelps, Bart Barnikowski, David Pedulla, Erin Johnston, and Karen Levy. The department's administrative staff were wonderful in organizing the complex logistics of this project. Thank you, Donna DeFransisco, Amanda Rowe, Cindy Gibson, and magic grants manager Bobbie Zlotnik. At LAPA, Leslie Gerwin, Judy Rivkin, and Jen Bolton were a great help. LAPA fellows who read drafts or commented on my work over the years were Martin Laughlin, Ali Sulzberger, Malcolm Feeley, Teemu Ruskola and Jenine Bell. Fellow students and friends I learned so much from were Rohit De, Arudra Burrah, Kalyani Ramnath, Angel Christin, Intisar Rabb, Sarah Kaiksow, Radha Kumar, Lubna El Amin, Rotem Geva, and Vinay Sitapati. Thanks to Hendrik Hartog from History, Carol Greenhouse and Elizabeth Davis from Anthropology, Dimitri Gondicas from Hellenic Studies, Ezra Suleiman and Atul Kolhi from Politics, Anthony Appiah from Philosophy, and Mischa Gabowitsch and On Barak from the Society of Fellows, and the legendary librarians of Firestone. I am indebted to the institutions that provided me with funding and affiliations: Princeton University Center for Human Values, the

Princeton Institute for International and Regional Studies (PIIRS), the
Social Science Research Council for the DPDF grant, and the National
Science Foundation for the dissertation improvement grant (Award
#1061227), Programs for Hellenic Studies and Judaic Studies, and the
Emile Zola chair at the Stricks Law school; at Harvard, the Harvard
Academy for international and regional studies, the Weatherhead Center
for International Affairs, especially the cluster on comparative inequality
and inclusion, and the Middle East Initiative at the Harvard Kennedy
School. I am thankful for the institutional affiliations to the Van Leer
Institute in Jerusalem, the Centre for the Study of Law and Governance at
Jawaharlal Nehru University (JNU) in New Delhi, and Berg Institute for
Law and History at Tel Aviv University's Faculty of Law. Friends at the
Law and Society Association and the American Sociological Association
annual meetings gave valuable feedback: Binyamin Blum, Jothi Rajah,
Elizabeth Kolsky, Sandy Keidar, Itamar Mann, Mitra Sharafi, and Marc
Galanter; Ranisa Mawani, Jeenie Lokaneeta, Shreemoyee Gosh, Julian
Go, Claire De Couteau, Gurminder Bhambra, Issac Arielli Reed, and
Munira Charrad; Jeena Lokaneeta, Kalyani Ramnath, and Brenna
Bhandar; Asaf Likhovski; Lisa Hajjar, Nimer Sultany and Noura
Erakat. I am also grateful to the collaborative research networks (CRN)
of the Law and Society Association, the British Colonial Legalities CRN,
and the Law in South Asia CRN. Comments at workshops and seminar
talks were invaluable: at George Washington University, from Daniel
Nerenberg, Nathan Brown, Ilana Feldman, and Harris Mylonas; at the
Law and History Workshop at Tel Aviv Law, from David Shorr, Roi
Kreitner, and students; at the Legal History Workshop on Israel and
India at Stanford, from Ritu Birla and Elizabeth Kolsky; at the Van Leer
Jerusalem Institute research groups on partitions, and on the military
government in Israel, from Ornit Shani, Ayelet Ben Ishai, Mori Ram,
Arie Dubnov, Zeela Rubel, Benny Nuriely, Irit Balas, and Adel Mana;
the Empire research group at PIIRS; at the Center for Law and
Governance at Jawaharlal Nehru University, from Niraja Jayal and
Pratiksha Baxi; at the SSRC DPDF workshops on state violence, with
special thanks to Ivan Ermakoff and Stathis Kalyvas who suggested
adding Cyprus as a case study. Faisal Devji shared with me unpublished
chapters of his wonderful book *Muslim Zion*, which provided a creative
political framework for thinking about partition in a comparative
context.

I conducted research in Israel, India, Cyprus, and the UK and owe
thanks to the archivists and librarians, scholars and friends that helped

with the research, but also welcomed Romi and myself into their life. In Israel, I am grateful to Helena and Michal at the Israeli State Archive, Batya Leshem at the World Zionist Archive, Yifat at the Israel Defense Forces Archives, and the staff that runs the Al Muqtafi database at Birzeit University Institute of Law. Adam Raz, Lior Yavne, and Akevot for their incredible work. Conversations with Adriana Kemp, Ronen Shamir, Bashir Bashir, Avishai Erlich, Muhammad Jabali, Ron Harris, Asaf Likhovski, Raif Zreik, Gadi Elgazi, On Barak, Moshik Temkin, Merav Amir, Eilat Maoz, Hila Dayan, Lana Tatour, Irit Ballas, Omri Greenberg, and Rivi Gillis are woven into this text. My close friends gave support and brought joy: I thank Anat Rosilio, Betty Benbenisti, Khulood Badawi, Yulie Chromtzenko, Ronen Eidelman, Lin Chalozin Dovrat, and my sister Tal.

In Cyprus, I thank Effi Parparinou at the Cyprus State Archives, the amazing Alexis Rappas for all the wonderful contacts and incredible scholarship, Avishai Erlich for putting me in touch with scholars, and Yannis Papadakis, Nicos Trimikliotis, and Costas Constantinou for sharing their knowledge, contacts, and razor-sharp insights. I also owe thanks to Mete Hatay for all the contacts in North Cyprus and his inspiring work and the amazing Rebecca Bryant for her support and sending me her manuscripts in preparation, which were critical to the project. Thanks to George Georgalides for all his time and the books on Ronald Storrs, to Diana Markides for pointing to the importance of district commissioners, to Fiona Mullen for setting up interviews and for helping to release post-independence files at the Ministry of Interior, to Andreas Mavromatis for his time and knowledge, to Helena Vassiliou, my research assistant, translator, and friend, to Mustafa Erogan and the staff at the Public Information Office (PIO) of the Turkish Republic of Northern Cyprus (TRNC) for helping me find the retired administrators, to Shani Cooper Zubida for her friendship and help, and to Vathoula and the staff at the Cyprus American Archaeological Research Institute where we stayed every trip. In India, many thanks go to Jaya Raman and Mr. Subramanian at the National Archive in New Delhi, to Mahesh Rangarajan and the staff at the Teen Murti Archive, to the Centre for the Study of Law and Governance at JNU, to Niraja Jayal Gopal and Pratiksha Baxi for their support and insights, to Ujjwal Singh for his brave scholarship, to Besharat Peer, Sanjay Kak, Stephen Legg, Manika Goswami, Collin Gonsalves, Aparna Balachandaran, Rohit De, Arudra Burrah and family, to the Vajpeyi family, to Achia Anzi and Chana Zalis for their friendship and help, to Khinvraj Jangjid for being amazing, to Murad Khan, Ratika Kapur and Kisho, Shreyasi Jha and Aarohi for being our playmates, and to Aarti Bartholomew for lovely times. Orit Shani gave me intellectual insights, much confidence, and invaluable tips on how to navigate life and the archive with an infant. In London, I thank the staff at the National Archives at Kew, and to Elian Weizman, Dimi Reider, and Nataly Ohana Ivri. I am grateful to my friends from Princeton who have become family: Rania Salem, Ronny Regev, Yiftah Elazar, Kalyani Ramnath and Hannah Louise Clark, Amir Goldberg and Gi-li Vardi, Cristina Mora, Gregoire Mallard and Eleanore Lepinard, Allison Schnable, Judith Mennasen Ramon, and Maya and Naftali Meshel.

At Hebrew University, I thank my department, especially Gili Drori, Areej Sabbagh-Khoury, Michal Frenkel, Vered Vinitzsky Sarousi, Nurit Stadler, and the administrative staff. Academia for Equality provided a political-intellectual home, with special thanks to Hila Dayan, Karin Levy, Zvi Bendor, and Matan Kaminer.

The Harvard academy provided an incredible space for intellectual engagement and facilitated an author's conference that changed the nature of this book. Many thanks to George Steinmetz, Chris Tomlins, Laleh Khalili, and Faisal Devji for their time and their insights, and to Ajantha Subramanian for chairing and for her support and to Bruce and Kathleen for all their help. Conversations with colleagues at Harvard were crucial to my work: Thank you, Naor Ben Yehoyada, Jeff Kahn, Arunabh Gosh, Raul Sanchez De La Sierra, Chris Gratien, Benjamin Siegel, Yukiko Koga, Cristina Florea, Natalia Gutgowski and Darryl Li. Special thanks to Michele Lamont, Kirstin Fabbe and Melanie Cammet, Steve Caton and Arne Westaad. The program for Judaic Studies generously funded a year of lectureship at Harvard's Department of Sociology, which welcomed me warmly thanks to Jason Beckfield, the late Tali Kritzman Amir, Shai Dromi, Cresa Pew, and Yuval Feinstein. The final year of revising the book happened at the Middle East Initiative at the Kennedy School – I am grateful to Tarek Masoud, Julia Martin, and Mikela Bennet.

The anonymous reviewers at Cambridge University Press provided important insights and suggestions. Thanks to my editors Sara Doskow and Rachel Blaifeder and the editorial and production staff at Cambridge University Press.

At the final stages, this book would not have come to fruition without the support, love, and critical comments of Yehouda Shenhav, Paul DiMaggio, the one and only Orna Ben Naftali, Ben Siegel, Rania Salem, Noura Lori, Cristina Mora, Khulood Badawi, and my mother, Elayne

Mahadevi, and Michael Bocking, the support of Michal Frenkel, my sister Tal, and the great editorial work of Kirsty Kay. Orna Ben Naftali and Ruthie Ginsburg found the cover photo of the book, a checkpoint in Umm Tuba, taken by Estie Tzal. The community at Botanic Gardens 2019–21 was a lifesaver and I owe you all.

Thanks to my teacher Joanna Macy, for the inspiration, and to Anita Barrows, whose love, poems, and beloved safe house in Berkeley are a blessing. Finally, I would like to thank my parents, Elayne and my late father Henri, for their big love. I also thank my sisters, Tal and Tamar, my daughter, Romi, the best travel companion and my personal sunshine, and my son, the amazing Adam. Their love and support make my life hopeful and full of surprises (and challenges) every day and remind me of my commitment to making another world possible in these uncertain times. I also thank Tomer, my ex husband and the Chen family, for their support for the transnational journeys we all made.

This book is dedicated to my father, Henri Berda Z"L, who never let the darkness of history dampen his hopes for the future.

Archive Abbreviations

CSA	Cyprus State Archive, Nicosia
SA	Colonial administration files
MI	Ministry of Interior files in Independent Cyprus
CZA	Central Zionist Archive
S19	Statistical Department of the Jewish Agency
IDFA	Israel Defense Forces Archive, Kiryat Ono
IOR	India Office Records collection at the British Library
L/P&J	Political and Judicial
L/P&S	Political and Secret
ISA	Israel State Archive Jerusalem
MASC	Princeton University Manuscript Collection – Nancy Crawshaw Papers CO881
NAI	National Archives of India, New Delhi
HD	Colonial Home Department
MEA	Ministry of External Affairs
MHA	Ministry of Home Affairs
MRR	Ministry of Relief and Rehabilitation
NMML	Nehru Memorial Museum and Library, New Delhi
TNA	The National Archives at Kew, UK
CO	Colonial Office documents
FO	Foreign Office documents
MED	Mediterranean Department of the Commonwealth Relations Office
WO	War Office documents
TRNC	State Archive, Kyrenia

Introduction: The Spectacle of Independence and the Specter of Bureaucracy

At the stroke of the midnight hour, as the world sleeps, India will awake to life and freedom. A moment comes, which comes but rarely in history, when we step out from the old to the new, when an age ends, and when the soul of a nation, long suppressed, finds utterance.[1]

On the eve of India's independence late on August 14, 1947, India's first prime minister, Jawaharlal Nehru, narrated the moment of transition from colonial rule to national sovereignty in front of the Constituent Assembly. It was a moment of great promise as India embarked on the most significant experiment with democracy in human history, the largest universal franchise in elections, and the formation of the longest-standing constitution in postcolonial history to date.[2] It was also the night before India's formal partition into the dominions of India and Pakistan, the night before waves of genocidal violence and forced migration shaped the new nations within the newly delineated territories.[3]

In national narratives, one rarely thinks of such a historic moment of independence and decolonization as also a moment of the transmission to the new states of colonial bureaucratic practices and routines and the politics embedded within them. The spectacle of independence, when subjects of the empire were to become future citizens of their own newly partitioned states, tends to eclipse the dimmer side of that which resists change in political life. But that very same night of Jawaharlal Nehru's legendary speech on India's awakening was also a deadline for bureaucrats – the civil servants of British India – to decide which new state, on which side of the partition line, they would serve. Would they continue their work for independent India or join the civil service in Pakistan?[4] Would they move their families with them to the uncertainties of partition or leave them behind until it was safer? These were dramatic decisions. Many did not know just how dramatic it would be, as it was hard to anticipate the scale of violence and displacement that would ensue.

Muslim civil servants who would opt that night to serve in Pakistan but who later changed their mind would be labeled "suspicious people." They would be closely followed by intelligence departments, their loyalty to India doubted. That suspicion and classification as "those of doubtful loyalty" would overshadow their life and work. Further, that very same night, some of those who crossed over to Pakistan were to lose their right to citizenship in India. Muslims who tried to come back would spend years applying for return permits, navigating a labyrinthine bureaucratic regime that had been established to control such movement.[5]

This book investigates the legacies of colonial bureaucratic practices in two of the most fundamental state-building arenas: the delineation of citizenship and the identity of civil servants. Using the framework of partition, it traces a set of bureaucratic practices – similar across space and time – in three very different colonies designated for partition as a condition for their independence from colonial rule: India, Palestine, and Cyprus from the last decades of colonial rule to the first decade of the new states of India, Israel, and Cyprus.

Partition in all three states was conceived as a method to maintain British imperial domination and as a solution to ethnic conflicts in an era where national self-determination had legitimized population transfer (later called ethnic cleansing). It produced violence and displacement on unprecedented scales in each of the territories.[6] Separating territory and population meant that population classification and the governing of mobility to create partition were critical elements of defining citizens and "others" within the new borders.

Taking a cue from Hannah Arendt's insight on how we can understand political membership through those excluded from it, this book tracks the way the new states – India, Israel, and Cyprus – used the colonial bureaucratic routines and forms that they inherited in the delineation of political belonging and the making of the civil services in the wake of partitions. This study thus revolves around the bureaucratic fates of "citizenship's others," those denied full participation in the political community who nevertheless remained roped to the state through their designations as residents, refugees, intruders, and infiltrators (Arendt 1951; Macklin 2007; Bhambra 2015; Tatour 2019).

It is necessary to focus on the role of bureaucratic practices in the making of the new states from an organizational perspective. Drawing conceptually from three wells of scholarship – the cognitive/cultural accounts of the state in sociology and anthropology (Bourdieu 1994; Steinmetz 1999; Mitchell 1991a; Corrigan & Sayer 1985; Sharma & Gupta 2009; Joyce & Mukerji 2017); new institutionalism in organizations (DiMaggio & Powell 1991); and historical institutionalism's recent focus on incremental change (Mahoney & Thelen 2010) – it seeks to answer some major questions relating to the impact of colonial bureaucratic legacies in new states following partition: How did the bureaucratic organizing principles and administrative scripts of colonial rule shape political status in the new states? What role did colonial bureaucratic practices, classifications, and documents, developed to control and subdue subject populations across the British Empire, have in shaping the relationships of the new postcolonial states to the populations that had become political minorities? And how did colonial bureaucratic practices shape the aftermath of violent partitions that continue to shape the political life of the new states to this day?

LEGACIES OF COLONIAL BUREAUCRATIC PRACTICES

The transmission of bureaucratic practices from British colonial rule to the newly independent states might seem entirely unremarkable for at least two reasons. The first is that the institutional scaffolding of postcolonial states was erected during colonial rule, while imperial subjects, those who were relegated to the "waiting room of history" (Chakrabarty 2009), both negotiated with and fought against the colonial administrations for independence. Thus, as Timothy Mitchell observed, "colonial subjects and their modes of resistance are formed within the organizational terrain of the colonial state" (Mitchell 1991b: ix). In the aftermath of the British Empire, the new states inherited "readymade administrations" including the civil services (Chatterjee 1993: 204) that had been trained in and served colonial rule through years of intense anticolonial and intercommunal conflict (Burra 2010). Indeed, the inheritance of colonial bureaucracy has been perceived as both an asset and a burden for the new states, depending on one's epistemological standpoint on the impact of colonial rule and the way it continues to shape the present.[7]

The second reason it might seem unremarkable rests on Max Weber's assertion that in any regime change "the bureaucratic machinery will normally continue to function just as it has for the previous legal government" (Weber 1978: 143); that the operating rules of bureaucracy are fixed and remain stable over time and space. This idea generated the subsequent assumption that perpetuation also meant that legacies of

British colonial bureaucracy bore semblance to Weber's imaginary model of a rational organization concerned with efficiency and guided by the rule of law (e.g. Halliday et al. 2012).

This assumption is problematic: any study concerned with historical institutional continuity and change cannot assume continuity without a close examination of the kind of bureaucracy at issue (Hacker, Pierson, & Thelen 2015). The bureaucratic practices, routines, and forms that were inherited on that night of independence from British colonial rule developed under the conditions of a regime of conquest, which operated within a political system of pronounced racial hierarchy, otherwise known as the "rule of colonial difference" (Chatterjee 1993; Steinmetz 2008b), a perpetual state of emergency, uncertain domains of jurisdiction justified by that racial difference, and the perceived threat it posed to the maintenance of colonial rule (Hussain 2003; Stoler et al. 2007). The same observation applies to Palestine/ Israel and to Cyprus, where both the practices that created a hierarchy between populations and the significant periods of rule by emergency were ordered through bureaucratic classifications, forms, and procedures.

How did these features of race and emergency shape British colonial bureaucracy? Bureaucracy was the hub of power in the colonies that was both concerned with juridical normativity and claimed to rule by law, but in which there was limited political representation for subject populations and where, for the most part, administrative and executive actions were beyond the reach of courts (De 2012). If race was the relational marker that made the colonies "safe" from the "dangers of universalism" by enabling the differentiation between citizens and subjects, as Laurent Dubois writes (2005; see also Go 2018), then emergency was the method by which the differentiation was maintained through the decoupling of an aspirational legal liberal discourse from everyday bureaucracy that operated to manage populations and repress struggles for equality. Departing from how the symbolic power of the state was acquired by the extension of administrative reach in modern nation-state formation, where the extension of the powers of population enumeration, classification, and registration rendered the state more legitimate in the eyes of its population (Loveman 2005), the paradox of the colonial state was that the more formal its administrative reach and the more elaborate its monitoring and management of subjects' lives, the less it managed to achieve the acquiescence of its subjects, leading to further repressive laws and to the delegitimization of authority (Comaroff 1998).

While colonial emergency laws have been previously investigated as counterinsurgency – that is, in their role in quashing anticolonial struggles and labor disputes – they were also tools that afforded colonial bureaucrats wide power and discretion, shaping the organizational practices, templates of action, and categories they used to classify people and the spaces they could move in (Hussain 2007; Legg 2008). Bureaucratic discretion and administrative reach grew in the epoch between the two world wars, as a grid of emergency laws proliferated throughout the British Empire to quash anticolonial struggles, consolidating powers of classification and identification, policing, and the monitoring of mobility within the bureaucratic administration.

Considering the above, my focus on bureaucracy serves three main objectives. First, it calls attention to the pivotal role of colonial bureaucracy and everyday administrative practices in shaping political outcomes following regime change; second, it provides a synthetic model of British colonial bureaucracy to facilitate research on the organizational legacies of colonial rule; and third, it shows how these everyday practices shaped the making of citizenship for minorities and the making of the civil service in the aftermath of violence and partition through a comparison of bureaucratic practices across space, between colonies, and across time from the colonial government to independent governments. This legacy has had long-term effects. It still does.

Placed in a broader scholarly discourse, this focus serves some additional objectives. First, it extends an invitation to rethink the primacy given to law in studying colonial legacies: the legal and political afterlives of empire are of intense interest across disciplines ranging from those that perceive them as legacies that have shaped postcolonial nation-states to those that view them as the histories of the colonial present. Law has been the constitutive and most enduring element of British imperialism (Brown 1995), producing a spatial and temporal colonial order (Mawani 2014) and being perceived as the core carrier of its legacies. At the nucleus of existing scholarship of British colonial legacies thus stand legal systems and courts. Bureaucracy, or administration, has been subsumed into law, or treated as a "neutral" variable, explicitly or implicitly assuming it followed the Weberian model of rational-legal bureaucracy (Halliday et al. 2012; Lange 2009). The principled decision of this study is to give legal rulings and legislative deliberations a back seat and station in the driver's seat bureaucratic practice: the routines, forms, classifications, and documents for managing populations employed across the three colonies that shared the transitional framework of partition.

Second, comparative research on the chronotope of bureaucratic colonial practices also expands the anthropologies and histories that investigate state bureaucracies: after the cultural turn in the sociology of the state and the rise of anthropologies of the state, the study of bureaucracies in the colonial aftermath turned to the "everyday state" and to the study of the materiality of bureaucracy, particularly of documents, files, and forms that shape political relations, populations, and organizations (Hull 2012; Mathur 2016; Kim 2016). Yet this rich literature has mostly focused on national or regional bureaucracies. The present study uses a connected transnational framework to compare bureaucratic practices across colonies and successor states.

Third, most, though not all, studies of colonial bureaucracy separate between the classification practices of registration, immigration, and census enumeration, on the one hand, and practices of security or counterinsurgency, including monitoring of mobility, on the other. This study, like a few others (Khalili 2012; Legg 2008; Singha 2000; Mawani 2018), resists this separation: it couples the bureaucratic work of population classification according to suspicion with the bureaucratic work of ordering mobility through spatial-legal means, reflecting these intertwined preoccupations of the central hubs of British late-colonial governments and the manner in which they informed each other. It thus looks at how a set of bureaucratic practices developed during the last decades of colonial rule across three connected cases of colonies designated for partition. Tracing how they affected access to citizenship and the making of new civil services through regimes of classification and the monitoring of mobility, it culminates in disclosing their effects following independence on both the minority populations and the colonial civil servants themselves.

FRIENDS, FOES, AND THE MAKING OF POST-PARTITION CITIZENSHIP

The Classification Nexus of People and Mobility

This study's empirical focus is on bureaucracy from the last decades of British rule into the nascent years of the new states in India, Palestine/Israel, and Cyprus. It investigates how bureaucratic practices, routines, and documents developed and affected two core elements of modern state power: the classification of populations through the census and other administrative categories (Loveman 2014; Cohn 1989; Anderson 2006) and attempts at the monopolization of the legitimate means for mobility (Torpey 1998).

Classification was necessary to render populations legible as an object of governance for alleged forms of development (Scott 1998) but also to satisfy the constant, anxious hunger to dissect populations, viewing them as a source of threat and undesirability, for the sake of surveillance, policing, and forced migration (Singha 2000). The production of rules for social classification was based on uncertain knowledge and was in constant flux (Stoler 2010b). On the one hand, the categories created were alleged to indicate that "states not only naturalize certain distinctions and not others, but they also help constitute particular kinds of people" (Loveman 2005: 1655); on the other hand, census categories were forged by social struggles and negotiations between population groups and administrators over definitions of group boundaries, allocations of resources, and the perpetual lack or limiting of representation in the colonial state (Emigh et al. 2016). In the colonial context, this gap between categories and classifications and the colonial social world was greater than elsewhere because the legal, bureaucratic, and ideological superstructure was imported from the metropole (Gupta 2013).

Torpey (1998) argues that modern states have always monopolized legitimate means of movement across and within their borders by identifying populations and differentiating between members and nonmembers. Emerging South Asian histories, however, point to the imperial origins of mobility restrictions based on identity, demonstrating that racialized restrictions of mobility and migrations in the colonies serve as alternative origins of modern nation-states' attempts at monitoring mobility through identification and documentation (Mongia 2003, 2018; Zamindar 2007).

These intersections of forms of state power – population classification and the ordering of mobility – also correspond to two features of British colonial rule: racial hierarchy and governing by emergency, usually used as a set of restrictions on mobility covering the whole gamut from preventative detention and confinement of suspicious or dangerous individuals to designation of large territories as dangerous or disturbed, requiring permits for the movement for entire populations.[8]

OF PEOPLE AND TERRITORY: THE EXTREME CASE OF PARTITION IN THE MAKING OF CITIZENSHIP

It is well established that colonial distinctions between populations, particularly those based on racialized religious categories, created ethnic conflicts in the aftermath of the British Empire (Wimmer 1997;

Mamdani 1996; Goh 2008). Scholars from a range of different theoretical traditions further agree that colonial legacies of differentiation shaped citizenship (see, e.g., Brubaker 2010; Sadiq 2017). Partitions were the extreme cases in which conflict led to the design of a territorial separation of populations.

The study investigates this legacy from a dual perspective: first, the cultural accounts of the state concerned with the cognitive and material methods of power engendered by everyday practices, routines, and documents of population management that create the powerful metaphysical effect of making the state appear to exist as a separate entity (Mitchell 1991a; Corrigan & Sayer 1985), as well as its spatial and legal limits (Ferguson & Gupta 2002; Das & Poole 2004). Second, it presents new institutionalist accounts of organizational change (DiMaggio & Powell 1991) that view administrators not as "conduits for the diffusion of preexisting laws, but as those that shape the law, and organizational practices as carriers of scripts and schemas" (Suchman & Edelman 1996). The study tracks the material forms of classification and enumeration, as sites of both colonial domination and negotiation with local elites; the ways that forms and applications designated categories of loyalty and suspicion; and the consolidation of documentary regimes to restrict mobility in the colonial states. It then traces how these elements of colonial classification and mobility restriction shaped the violent aftermaths and the strikingly similar methods the new states used to deal with population movement within their new boundaries to prevent the return of those that had become refugees. Return was prevented by their classification designation as "intruders" and "infiltrators" when they "illegally" crossed newly minted "borders" to enter the new states' territory.

The transnational framework of partition, the territorial separation devolving authority over local populations newly defined as national, was both produced by and affected the British imperial bureaucratic repertoire that anxiously classified populations and attempted to control mobilities as its fundamental elements of the power to colonize and create social order by administrative means (Mitchell 1991b; Stoler 2010b). Once introduced, partition accelerated the preoccupation with demography, as population numbers and classification would create "majorities" and "minorities" that had material consequences for the territories to be partitioned (Devji 2013: 51). Yet, as Arie Dubnov and Laura Robson show (2019: 3), partition was a transnational phenomenon and a consequence of the interwar era, and not the inevitable outcome of incompatible primordial identities.

Across the three colonies studied here, the bureaucratic practices of classification and mobility monitoring were similar but the legal, political, and demographic trajectories of partition were not. To be sure, partition was not only an imperial plan to maintain control of its former colonies but was also a grand political project of national elites (Chatterji 2012) and the product of minority national ideological movements and anti-colonial struggles – an observation to which we will return shortly. But partition was also a massive bureaucratic project of population transfer and management. The macro historical project of partition was formed through the micro processes of what Ian Hacking (2007) has called "making up people" through lumping together, separating, and designating population classification schemes. Vazira Zamindar has shown, through the experience of partition's survivors, how classification schemes were deeply intertwined with managing the mobility of people across the new borders, which in turn shaped political belonging (Zamindar 2007; see also Jayal 2019). Documents that enabled mobility did not only mediate between classification schemes and actual people but also became the means through which people would be classified on the continuum of citizenship, delineating citizens, residents, refugees, infiltrators, intruders, and enemies of the state.

COMPARISONS AND CONNECTIONS: THE TRANSNATIONAL HISTORIES OF PARTITION IN INDIA, PALESTINE, AND CYPRUS

Comparisons of colonial "origins" are never simple. On the one hand, one might assume that the commonality of legal origins and the existence of shared imperial policies and strategies create what Julian Go (2011) has called the "patterns of empire" on a macro level, leading to similarities in outcomes. On the other hand, how technologies of rule varied within and between colonies is a consistent feature of imperial power and of uncertain jurisdictions and differentiations (Stoler, McGranahan, & Perdue 2007; Steinmetz 2008a, 2008b). As Steinmetz (2008a) aptly writes, variance in violence and technologies of rule is important inasmuch as how it affected subjects in the long-term legacies of colonialism. The challenges of comparison across colonies are further amplified by the political and scholarly controversies over the definitions and trajectories of ethnic strife, and whether they were created or exacerbated during colonial rule.

To make use of the variation while exploring the commonalities and connections between colonies, this study, inspired by Gurminder Bhambra's approach of connected sociologies (2014), compares the micropractices and organizational routines in three colonies against the connected macropolitical framework of their designated partitions. The study of mundane organizational routines within the transnational framework of partition is inspired by Julian Go's approach of "Global Fields and Imperial Forms" (2008), which combines Paul DiMaggio and Walter Powell's conception of organization fields with Pierre Bourdieu's field theory as an effective way to connote the relational connections, effects, and diffusion between metropole and colony, as well as between colonies.

Present-day India, Israel/Palestine, and Cyprus were all formerly British-controlled territories that shared legal structures in which the British sought to solve intercommunal conflicts through partition and in which, during the years before planned partitions, there is evidence of a concentrated effort on the part of the British to quash political opposition to their rule and control the population through an array of emergency laws. The anticolonial crises were instigated by demands for political representation against a system of colonial rule that purported to subsume power to the rule of law, declared commitment to liberal politics, and consistently failed, as a feature of its rule, to provide equality to its subjects.

Partitions, proposed as ad hoc solutions to local and imperial conditions, were carried out by mass violence and utterly failed to solve the intercommunal problems. This point is underscored by the fact that they continue to perpetuate violence, displacement, and dispossession of Palestinians and prevent their return, alongside causing communal violence and the systematic erosion of rights for India's Muslim minority and the exclusion of Turkish Cypriots from the Republic of Cyprus due to the suspension of its constitution.

This commonality should obscure neither their differences from each other nor the uniqueness of their political trajectory. Israel, Cyprus, and India differ not only in their size, geography, and economy but in their contemporary political regimes. Israel is a settler colonial state of a unique type; it is for settlers without a "homeland"; and it is built on the scaffolding of the British mandate that provided the Zionist movement with the political framework for including the Jews in Palestine while dispossessing Palestinians (Pedersen 2016). It is the only case in which settler colonialism was officially recognized (Seikaly 2015: 5). India is a quasi-federal constitutional republic, increasingly defined by ethnoreligious majoritarianism (Chatterji et al. 2019). The Republic of Cyprus was founded as a consociational democracy, which since 1964 has suspended those parts of its constitution that afforded Greek and Turkish Cypriots shared power and representation through a judicial state of emergency (Constantinou 2008; Bryant & Hatay 2020).

Further, Israel maintains a militarized colonial structure of rule over Palestinians in the Occupied West Bank, the Gaza Strip, and East Jerusalem, and each is differentiated by its residents' political status and mobility. Beyond majoritarianism toward the Muslim minority, India's rule through an array of security laws in Kashmir and parts of northeast India is highly contested. Cyprus is partitioned: the Turkish Republic of Northern Cyprus is a de facto state, recognized only by Turkey.

Prior to British colonial rule, all were governed for centuries by Muslim empires: the Mughals in India and the Ottomans in Palestine and Cyprus. These empires' legal and political legacies continue to shape both scholarly debates and contemporary policies. This is also the reason for the choice not to include Ireland, the first partition in the interwar era, despite its pivotal role in the diffusion of practices of imperial counterinsurgency and policing. The classic comparison of partitions has been Ireland, Palestine, and India (Fraser 1984; O'Leary 2007; Dubnov & Robson 2019). Studies of counterinsurgency and policing have focused on Ireland and Palestine (Khalili 2010; Hughes 2009) or Ireland and Cyprus (Sinclair & Williams 2007; Anderson & Killingray 2017). Moriel Ram (2015) has compared settler colonial geographies in Israel and Northern Cyprus. British rule in each of the colonies differed in form and duration: over two centuries of the British Raj in India with parliamentary oversight; eighty years of the Protectorate and then the Crown Colony in Cyprus; and three tumultuous decades of the Mandate for Palestine, created and overseen by the League of Nations.

Partitions were the political outcomes of the British attempt to maintain domination while devolving powers for self-rule to the colonized subjects (Dubnov & Robson 2019). Victor Kattan (2018) argues that partition created a paradox – it entrenched a majority rule yet provided a basis for minorities to claim statehood only if they formed a majority in each territory. In the competition for political power, the leadership of minorities in the colonies – the Muslim League in India, the Zionist organization in Palestine, and the Turkish Cypriot leadership in Cyprus – favored partition plans as a means to overcome minority status and claim the right of self-determination in independent, self-governing states. The Indian National Congress and the Palestinian national movement favored a republican system throughout the territories. Greek Cypriots favored *enosis*, unification with Greece.

The plans and preparations for partition shaped political life in the colonies, but their violent aftermath was unforeseen even by those who fiercely opposed them. The partition of India into India and Pakistan led to horrific violence, including the killing, forced migration, and displacement of millions. The partial partition of Mandatory Palestine led to Israel's establishment and the Palestinian Nakba, the forced exile of 750,000 Palestinians, a population replaced within a few years by a similar number of Jews, both European Holocaust survivors and Mizrahi Jews from Muslim countries (Cohen 2002). In Cyprus, the attempt to avoid partition on the one hand, or *enosis* on the other, led Greek and Turkish Cypriots to establish a bicommunal republic that collapsed into violence and divided the population in 1963 when most of the Turkish Cypriot population fled to enclaves, creating an early version of partition. The island's de facto partition by force occurred in 1974 when Turkey invaded Cyprus to protect Turkish Cypriots who feared Greek nationalist violence, later creating the Turkish Republic of Cyprus.

The historiographic debates on the reasons for partition are beyond the scope of this book. Nevertheless, each chapter recounts the histories of partition that are relevant to the bureaucratic practices and the negotiations between administrators and subjects that it addresses.

BUREAUCRACY AND "CITIZENSHIP'S OTHERS"

Delineation of political belonging in new nation-states is perceived as an emancipatory moment of national self-determination – a moment symbolizing the realization of political aspirations and linking the new borders of the nation to its citizenry through political will and representation. Membership is thus conceived as construed by political struggles, consecrated by law, and administered by state agents. It is rarely thought of as being created through bureaucratic practice.

This perception is essentially the classic European story of the making of citizenship as gradual inclusion: from mobilizations and political struggles to defined rights and membership in a political community (Marshall 1950; Bendix 1964/2017; Turner 1990; but see Somers 2005 for critique). This story, alas, obfuscates rather than illuminates the transition from imperial subjects – an enforced status of subjugation – to citizenship in the new postcolonial states. The incompatibility between stories indeed goes beyond the fact that the European story excludes the racialized imperial and colonial histories of the making of citizenship in the new states (Lowe 2015; Bhambra 2015; Go 2013). Postcolonial citizenship is a different story because formal citizenship had to be defined to include the rights and duties that subjects of an explicitly racialized system of government never had before in the differentiated framework of imperial citizenship (Jayal 2013; see also Goh 2008). The definitions, in turn, were not created by law. In the very first years of the states, prior to the enactment of formal citizenship laws, those definitions were created by bureaucratic practice and emergency measures that cemented the violent aftermaths of war and partition (Chatterji 2012; Jayal 2013; Roy 2010). Group identity and nationality were fused together, creating a layered citizenship as a preferential status of membership and as the aspirational possibility for exercisable rights (Sadiq 2008). This was thus not a binary process of inclusion and exclusion but was a designation of status that enabled continued domination over those with graded forms of citizenship that have been called "citizenship's others" (Macklin 2007; Bhambra 2015). This form of continued domination was enabled by bureaucratic practices.

This study investigates these practices across the colonies during imperial rule through the lens of classic new institutional theory in organizations. It draws on Paul DiMaggio and Walter Powell's (1983) reformulation of Weber's "iron cage" metaphor, not as created by the drive for efficiency but rather revealing that organizations operate within a juridical and cultural field; a field in which they are constrained and tend to become similar by incorporating policies and practices through isomorphic processes that both diffuse across the field and constrict the ability for future change. The unit of analysis is the organizational practices themselves and not the structures of the bureaucracy or the negotiations of power between administrators.[9] For the transition from colony to independence, this study loosely employs concepts from historical institutionalism to explain the divergent use of population classification repertoires and the monitoring of mobility by the new states against their respective minorities. Because postimperial citizenship was not gained through mobilization but was distributed by the state, the continuities of bureaucratic practices and emergency laws played a pivotal role in shaping the citizenship of minorities.

LOYALTY AND SUSPICION: BUREAUCRATIC PRACTICES TO CLASSIFY POPULATIONS IN THE COLONIAL STATE

In India, Cyprus, and Palestine, bureaucrats attempted to understand and control both imagined and material aspects of identity by classifying populations, matching identities to resources and allocations through the forms, templates, and applications they handled. There were two main axes of population classification. One thoroughly researched as the hallmark of colonial rule by racial hierarchy and the baseplate for its forms of knowledge was categorizing populations according to what we may call demographic traits: race, religion, caste, and gender. The other, much less studied in this context, was based on the feature of perpetual emergency, ensuring classification according to the level of security threat that a person or a type of population posed to the state. Suspicion upended other types of classification, shifting constantly according to changing political or economic needs in each location, or in the wake of an agenda of the Home Department or the emergence of new technologies to evaluate the level of suspicion.

In the second axis of classification according to suspicion, the colonial state cataloged people according to their relationship to the government: from loyal citizens, collaborators, and cooperators to suspects, enemies, and those of doubtful loyalty. These were not only used as counterinsurgency measures to quash uprisings or strikes but were central in the administration of the everyday, particularly in applications for identity documents that enabled movement. Clerks recorded the different categories of suspicion in the rubric marked "recommendation" on official forms. Sometimes these categories were explicitly stamped in the box for "evidence of good character" on the forms that people used to apply for posts as civil servants or to request special status as British nationals or British-protected persons.[10] They were noted in the endorsement letters for people applying for passports, travel permits from state to state, and on applications for permits to travel to sensitive areas.

Examination of hundreds of applications and reports across the three colonies discloses that there were largely three possible grounds for including someone in the suspicious population category in the final decades of colonial rule: classification based on identity and belonging to a community (political groups or constructions of native criminality such as "criminal tribes," a remnant of the earlier criminalization of tribals and "dangerous classes" that were categorized as backward yet unrecognized as indigenous; see also Brown 2001; Nandi 2010; Singha 2015; Major 1999), suspicion based on actions known through intelligence, and suspicion based on the evaluation of mundane applications for a post or a service such as requests for licenses or passports.

These practices became ingrained in the bureaucracy. In the aftermath of partition, classification according to loyalty and suspicion determined access to identity documents for mobility and, in turn, for citizenship. The axis of suspicion was a conceptual grid that bureaucrats in the new states used to distribute documents enabling and restricting mobility for those attempting to return, once the overt violence accompanying partition subsided. Documents were distributed based on categories of identity and a graded scale of suspicion, founded on perceived loyalties, belonging, and trajectories of movement. The identity documents disseminated for the purpose of mobility in turn, either enabled or prevented their holders' claims to citizenship.

In the transition of the civil services in both Israel and India, the categories of loyalty and suspicion were central to the process of shaping the civil services in formal and informal processes – purification committees in Israel and organized campaigns in India to determine if those that had served the British were too corrupt or not devoted enough to the new nation. In Cyprus, the identities and appointments of civil servants were an intercommunal battleground and became one of the factors that led to constitutional collapse and descent into violence.

THE BUREAUCRATIC TOOLKIT OF EMERGENCY

The vast scholarship on colonial emergency laws has focused on counterinsurgency, policing, and surveillance, addressing their effects on the daily lives of subjects. The role emergency laws had in shaping mundane bureaucratic practices, methods, and documents has, however, remained a blind spot. The ministries of home affairs and governors' offices were the hub of bureaucratic activity that relied on emergency laws and shaped the practices, routines, documents, and lists of administrative actions to manage populations in times of crisis, mostly through the monitoring and restriction of mobility. States of emergency in the colonies were used as an elastic category, stretched mainly to encompass the preservation of colonial capitalism as well as to crush riots and insurgencies. But emergency laws also formed an administrative toolkit, a set of forms and classifications that could be drawn upon to promulgate decrees and restrict movement in areas declared "dangerous" and "disturbed." I call this spatial-legal repertoire the "bureaucratic toolkit of emergency."

Given that imperial occupation generated a legitimacy crisis and effected perpetual negotiation between political exigencies and rule-based law with high rates of enforcement on infractions (Hussain 2019: 7), colonial governments relied on state violence and biopower, on a scale far greater than that used in the disciplining projects of their colleagues in the metropole. Coercion and the fear of both physical violence and "withheld violence" (Azoulay & Ophir 2009: 101) defined relations between the many organizations that made up the colonial state and its subjects. Governance by emergency meant the British intervened violently to restore order, through the "civilizing" legal vehicle of "Peace and good government acts" (Tomlins 2006). Because they had neither the resources nor the need to govern the entire population through direct threats of violence, it was critical that they define the "dangerous population" (Berda 2020) who would be the target of enforcement.

These definitions meant more regulations for colonial officials as they classified populations and matched population categories with rules and administrative practices (Hussain 2007). From the mid-eighteenth century, British colonial officials justified emergency legislation on the grounds of security, economic instability, or the hostility of the subjugated population. Through a process of "civilizing" and legitimizing martial law as police power, emergency powers were incorporated into the peacetime administrative systems, effectively routinizing emergency both as a form of governance and as a tool of law enforcement (Neocleous 2007). In the epoch between the two world wars, emergency laws proliferated, stemming from the Defence of the Realm Act 1914, across the British Empire. These were used in India, Palestine, and Cyprus to manage the movement of civilian populations, affording wide discretion to bureaucrats, magistrates, and district commissioners to confine people to particular spaces, designate territories as "disturbed" or dangerous areas, institute curfews, and enable mass preventative detention. Blacklists, various permits that authorized movement despite restrictions, preventative detention, and the empowering of military personnel to govern civilians became central features of everyday population management. The bureaucratic toolkit of emergency transported the universally worded emergency laws into the local, racialized practices of everyday population management, primarily concerned with managing mobility according to status and perceived level of suspicion.

The continuities of emergency laws played a crucial role in the adaptation of the bureaucratic toolkit of emergency following independence. Israel and India both retained the colonial repertoire of emergency, although differently. Cyprus's bicommunal constitution deliberately excluded the possibility of the use of emergency laws during internal unrest. That decision was a critical juncture that shaped how each of the three states used their inherited axis of suspicion and bureaucratic toolkit of emergency. Most significantly, the continuity of emergency laws was a determining factor in the bureaucratic response to the violence and displacement of partition: the establishment of regimes to monitor mobility and prevent the return of those who had fled or were otherwise exiled.

MOBILITY REGIMES IN THE AFTERMATH OF PARTITION

Partition was not an event. Vazira Zamindar shows through the experience of its survivors in India and Pakistan that the "long partition" was a process that shaped the experience of political belonging, status, and mobility in relation to the border for decades (2007). Similarly, scholars of Palestine use the "long Nakba" to denote the partition project, including the defunct promise of a Palestinian state, and its long-term effects that have defined Palestinian status and mobility along the lines of partition (Rouhana & Sabbagh-Khoury 2019; Feldman 2018). In Cyprus, the de facto partition represents an ongoing fluctuation between normalizing partition and a continued state of exception, in which Turkish Cypriots have citizenship in a state they cannot reside in and so reside in an unrecognized state.

In the aftermath of partition and independence, both Israel and India developed mobility regimes to prevent the return and control the movement of Muslim and Palestinian refugees and returnees who had fled in the wake of war and the violence of partition. The same practices, documents, and methods used by the colonial bureaucracy to designate suspicion and prevent mobility were in turn used against returnees who had become minorities in the aftermath of partition. The use of similar bureaucratic routines in a new context has been called the "hidden face of institutional change," as the maintenance of institutions held in place in a different context alters their effects (Hacker, Pierson, & Thelen 2015).

These bureaucratic mobility regimes and spatial systems of surveillance and control, established to manage subject populations, acted as institutional mechanisms that shaped boundaries of belonging by administrative means, enabling bureaucrats to exclude minorities from the political community while still maintaining control over them. Although the forms and routines of the permit regimes, from the designation of "disturbed areas" to the proliferation of various types of permits and evidentiary procedures, were nearly identical to those used during colonial rule, their significance changed: they now designated the form and content of political belonging.

The permit regimes instituted three categories for classifying the population: first, the category that bureaucrats assigned to people (i.e., citizen, resident, intruder, or refugee); second, the identity document a person carried; and third, the physical location of a person on the crucial date of partition, which determined one's legal status. The permit regimes also gave rise to ad hoc administrative structures and practices, such as forms and internal regulations, which were intended to be temporary. The documents of the mobility regimes were later used to differentiate claims for citizenship and residency through a graded axis of suspicion.

In both Israel and India, the continuity of emergency laws was a crucial component of the transitional governments, a critical juncture that enabled the use of instruments of the colonial era, mostly in managing the movement of citizens, residents, refugees, "infiltrators", and "intruders". In India, colonial emergency laws were legislated by parliament and incorporated into the constitution (Kalhan 2010; Singh 2007). In Israel, which has maintained a state of emergency since its inception, colonial emergency laws were the baseplate of a military government that imposed authority on the part of the Palestinian population that had remained in what became Israel during the war. The situation in Cyprus was different: upon independence of the bicommunal republic, the emergency regulations were annulled. That absence of colonial emergency laws from the toolkits of the state – brought about an entirely different outcome when the republic collapsed into violence in 1963, and Turkish Cypriots fled to enclaves that were under siege, eventually forming the territorial line of Turkish invasion that would partition the island from 1974 until the present.

The striking similarities in administrative legacies across varied regimes cannot be explained solely by the continuities of law or administrative personnel, explanations that could be suitable for a study of each of the states individually. The similarities invite us to probe the kind of bureaucracy that affected them, the organizational structures and practices that are the carriers of legacies despite the high variation in the political conditions and conflicts in each of the new states.

HYBRID BUREAUCRACY

Organizational theory has generally turned a blind eye to imperial and colonial histories.[11] This lacuna hinders our understanding of colonial bureaucracy and its administrative legacies. Torn between the attempt to conceptualize it within the Weberian rational-legal model of organization (and ergo as race-neutral) and the critical insistence that such a model "never existed anywhere" (Mbembe 2001: 44) neither in the colony nor in the metopole, generates a theoretical challenge.

That challenge has not escaped the critical eyes of scholars of colonial rule. Ann Stoler notes the misrepresentation in many scholarly accounts of the colonial state, particularly those preoccupied with colonial governmentality, which implicitly paint it as reflecting the Weberian model of "rationally minded, bureaucratically driven states outfitted with a permanent and assured income to maintain them, buttressed by accredited knowledge and scientific legitimacy and backed by a monopoly on weaponed force" (Stoler 2010b: 57–58). Other scholars, having observed that the British colonial administration did not operate on a basis of a systematized institutional theory, contend that it was rather an array of improvisational practices and failed attempts at achieving order and legitimacy. This absence of a particular model of governance stems from what John Comaroff (1998) calls "the essential paradox of the colonial state" that was both ordered and incoherent, rational and absurd, violent and inefficient.

Sociologist Ivan Evans grounds his monumental investigation of the Department of Native Affairs – the bureaucratic hub that cultivated the authoritarian South African Apartheid state – on the proposition that "imperial Britain failed to generate blueprints or theories about colonial administration" and that colonial bureaucracy was a localized affair, a paternalistic model of administration based on the ad hoc prerogative of the "man on the spot" (Evans 1997: 9–12). In a somewhat similar vein, legal historian of imperial sovereignty Lauren Benton proposes that imperial administrators had "no official handbook" to explain which forms of the law were best to institute in colonial settings; rather, she depicts what new institutionalists might call administrative entrepreneurs and adopters: they treated European legal traditions as a "useful collection from which they might draw selectively in crafting colonial legal systems" (Benton 2002: 261).

In line with Hannah Arendt's characterization of colonial rule as a "bureaucracy instead of government," Ilana Feldman suggests that the separation between bureaucratic authority and state legitimacy lends itself to a distinctive mode of operation she calls "tactical government"; that is, a set of practices of everyday life (Feldman 2008: 11, 16–17). Rather than "messiness" and "incoherence," she shows how "tactical government" is the means of governing that shift in response to crisis and presumes little stability in governing conditions (Feldman 2008: 23).

It is indeed Arendt who points to what amounts to a nascent theory of colonial bureaucracy, a conception that was articulated in the writings of a prominent colonial official, Lord Cromer, proconsul of Egypt (Shenhav 2013; Shenhav & Berda 2009). Cromer is a central figure in her compelling

Origins of Totalitarianism, his writings serving as a key in her analysis, linking the imperial bureaucratic rule of racial differentiation between citizens and subjects to the rise of totalitarian regimes. Framing the role of empire as a constitutive process in the making of modernity and the imperial career of the modern nation-state, Arendt claims that the interrelated categories of race and bureaucracy were the pivotal tools that consolidated British imperial order (Mantena 2010: 85). She describes the juxtaposition between modern bureaucracy and "race-thinking" as a major political moment in modern domination that Max Weber had overlooked:[12]

Two new devices for political organization and rule over foreign people were discovered during the first decades of imperialism. One was race as a principle of body politic, and the other bureaucracy as a principle of foreign domination. Without race as a substitute for the nation, [and] ... without bureaucracy as a substitute for government, the British possession of India might well have been left to the recklessness of the "breakers of law in India." (Arendt 1951: 65)

Still, despite the fundamental role that race (as a substitute for nation) and bureaucracy (as a substitute for government) play in her analysis of the legacies of colonial bureaucracy in the making of the catastrophic twentieth century, Arendt did not delve into the ways race affects bureaucracy.

Reflecting on Arendt's puzzle of race and bureaucracy, Nasser Hussain contends that she overlooked the role of emergency, central to the particular form of the rule of law in the colonies; "how law puts race in place, how it utilizes a system of categories and rules, and a general conception of types of people and of risk, to institute and maintain a conceptual and physical segregation" (2007: 521). Hussain proceeds to demonstrate how the state of emergency and necessity shaped the way the British colonial state governed, pointing to a particular form of bureaucracy. The British colonial bureaucracy, observes Hussain, was based on the systemic expansion of executive discretion that effectively collapsed the separation of powers, so officials, clerks, and commissioners made law in their daily and mundane decisions, consolidating the power of the colonial state while containing the semblance of the rule of law (Hussain 2019: 5).

Following Arendt's intuition that Lord Cromer's writings contain "what amounts to a theory of bureaucracy," the first part of this book traces a set of systematic organizing principles based on Cromer's correspondence addressed to a network of twenty-two colonial officials, some of whom he communicated with about the administration of "subject races." Cromer labeled this as a "hybrid bureaucracy." While these subjective administrative stories are masculinist, racist, and self-aggrandizing, at times to an extreme state of self-delusion, they are nevertheless precious: they offer the possibility of gauging a set of shared understandings of administrators about the organization of late British colonial rule and producing a synthetic set of organizing principles.

"Hybrid bureaucracy" implied that bureaucrats and administrative officials employed sovereign-like powers, made extensive political decisions, created laws, and defined the limits of their own discretion, particularly when the authority over the territories they ruled was contested and controversial. Cromer and his compatriots describe separate administrative practices and regulations for racial groups that were formally defined as "subject races." They legitimized differentiation in two ways: explicitly, through concepts around the racial inferiority of colonized peoples who were not considered full-fledged citizens, and implicitly, through decoupling law from administration to enable the universal wording of laws while allowing the bureaucracy to carry out the explicitly racialized practices that matched official action to classifications of subjects (Esmeir 2015: 32, 41). The state of perpetual emergency – characterized by excessive legalities and extraordinary measures – made that inversion of the "rule of law" both possible and necessary, for in the colonies it was impossible to maintain juridical order without exceptional measures (Esmeir 2012).

The writings of these interconnected colonial officials disclose a synthetic model based on five organizing principles: racial hierarchy, secrecy, wide discretion and administrative flexibility, personalism, and the systemic creation of exceptions. The systemic creation of exceptions did not exclude colonial subjects from the law but roped subjects into the patchwork of decrees and ad hoc arrangements that engendered procedural violence and permeated social life through a grid of emergency laws (Esmeir 2012).

The constant creation of exceptions had two consequences. The first, unsurprisingly, was that "hybrid bureaucracy" had very little to do with the imaginaries of the Weberian rational-legal model of bureaucracy. The latter, as is well known, was guided by precision, speed, predictability, coordination, reduction of friction to raise efficiency to its optimal level, and the expectation to function according to universal considerations of competency in order to achieve the "very calculability of results" (Weber 1978). It was equally far from a "rule of experts" or the calculations of risk that are otherwise depicted in accounts of colonial governmentality (e.g., Mitchell 2002).

The second consequence was that systemic exceptions offered bureaucrats multiple opportunities for moments of decisionism, in which discretion exceeds legal authority while magically remaining within the bounds of legal normativity. Exception and decisionism as prerogatives of sovereign power have been closely associated with Nazi jurist Carl Schmitt's critique of the liberal rule of law but have more recently been used to describe the discretionary and law-making power of administrators (Honig 2009: 63).

We live in an age characterized by the politics of emergency, where decisionism and bureaucratic discretion merge across the globe (Honig 2017; Li 2018), in which critiques of liberalism question the very distinction between colonialism and liberalism/ Given that liberalism is implicated in colonialism (Lowe 2015), and given the way race is used to justify the tension between illiberal methods and liberal discourse in counterinsurgencies (Khalili 2015), immigration, and policing, a major critique of a hybrid model of colonial bureaucracy might be that all modern state bureaucracies are hybrid.

This book, tracing the chronotope of change and making use of the concept of "administrative memory," makes a more modest claim: the value of extracting the organizing principles of colonial bureaucracy, through the eyes of officials themselves, is in providing a scaffolding for the systemic examination of continuity and change of colonial bureaucratic practices across space and time, without assuming the existence of the rational-legal model, or engaging the deviations from it.

ADMINISTRATIVE MEMORY: THE METHOD, DATA, AND STRUCTURE OF TRACING ORGANIZATIONAL PORTRAITS ACROSS REGIMES

Cultural and cognitive accounts of the state that view modernity as an imperial project (Mitchell 1991b; Steinmetz 1999; Go 2013) share some common critiques of rationalist accounts with new institutionalist accounts of organizations. Yet, despite the groundbreaking anthropologies of state bureaucracy that theorize the political life of documents and routines and how they mediate the experience of the state (Das & Poole 2004; Hull 2012; Navaro-Yashin 2007), sociological studies on the legacies of colonial rule have rarely employed an organizational perspective (but see Go 2008; Mathur 2016).

The general goal of new institutionalism in organizations was to "develop explanations of the way institutions incorporate historical experiences into their rules and organizing logics" (DiMaggio & Powell 1991), stressing the impact of normative cultural models and mythologies on organizational structures and practices (Suchman & Edelman 1996). Both these perspectives – the cultural and cognitive accounts of the state and new institutionalism in organizations – share the view that routines and practices are the carriers of politics – in our case, the scripts and schemas of the state. These scripts include representations of material artifacts and mundane routines as imbued with the abstractions of authority and legitimacy (Mitchell 1991).

Drawing upon the literature of new institutionalist studies on organizational memory, this study employs the concept of "administrative memory" as the dynamic agglomeration of processes, templates of classification, and strategies of action in an organization, which can be traced back to a previous regime in a specific locale, regardless of shifts in the regime's juridical framework or in its administrative personnel. Orthogonal to collective memory or "social mnemonic practices" (Olick and Robbins 1998), in which individuals remember historical events, or agents deliberately shape events to be remembered or condemned to collective amnesia as an orchestrated process, administrative memory involves automatic cognition, which is directed by schemas and scripts that exist within the routine of the organization. In their now classic study of organizational memory, Barbara Levitt and James March (1988) posited that routines accumulate the lessons of experience, despite the turnover of personnel and the passage of time. Rules, procedures, documents, and beliefs are conserved through systems of socialization and control: "These organizational instruments record history and shape its future path which depends on the processes by which the memory is maintained and consulted" (326).

This concept is particularly useful in the case of transition from colonial to postcolonial rule to detect the specific practices that were carried over from one regime to another, without assuming a priori that practices are inherited and transmitted. The method used for tracing continuity and change of similar sets of practices was the construction of organizational portraits at the bureaucratic hubs of population management: the Home Department in India, the General Secretary and Department of Immigrations in Palestine, and the governor's office in Cyprus, from the 1930s until the transition to independence. The organizational portraits of various corresponding departments and organizations in the new states were drawn from the interior ministries in India, Israel, and Cyprus, and the ministry of minorities and military government in Israel, from independence until the legislation of citizenship laws in Israel and India in the 1950s, and until 1968 in Cyprus.

Organizational portraits focused on three arenas: population classification for identification documents, especially for movement (forms, evidence, documents demanded from applicants, and decision-making processes); various forms of restrictions based on emergency laws; and the negotiations around census schedules. They were constructed from a range of documents, including organizational charts, office registers, minutes of internal debates, statistical tables, regulations, standing orders, and reports from district commissioners.

Sources were drawn from the following archives: India Office (British Library); Colonial Office (National Archives) in London; State Archives India and the Nehru Memorial Library in Delhi; the Israeli State Archive and Central Zionist Archive in Jerusalem; and the Israel Defense Forces and Defense Establishment (IDFA) Archive in Kiryat Ono; the Cyprus Republic Archives in Nicosia, the Turkish Republic of Northern Cyprus (TRNC) Archive in Kyrenia, and interviews with former Greek and Turkish Cypriot officials (due to gaps in the archives after the constitutional collapse in 1963).[13]

Through a parallel demonstration of theory (Skocpol and Sommers 1980), I traced similarities between practices that share similar characteristics but differ in one major factor and in the outcome of interest: while India and Israel retained the colonial emergency laws following independence, the annulment of emergency laws at independence in the Republic of Cyprus served as the divergent factor, where the colonial repertoire of governing mobility was not used, even when communal violence led to displacement and an eventual siege.

Tracing the political negotiations and controversies regarding population management practices within the bureaucracy, and between administrative officials and political leadership, highlighted two domains of administrative activity that exemplify the way administrative memory was transmitted from the colonial administration to the independent administration: while the intercommunal conflicts and negotiations within the administrations differ in each case, a similar corpus of population management technologies and templates of action emerged in all three cases, even when the political and historical conditions were significantly different, in the classifications of civil servants and, in the cases of India and Israel, in the mobility regimes.

The research on hybrid bureaucracy was based on the writings of a set of twenty-two interconnected colonial officials, who wrote most systematically and purposefully on colonial government and administration and who acknowledged or cited Cromer as a source of knowledge. These officials had served in India as well as in other territories.[14]

Structurally, the book comprises three parts and five substantive chapters that deploy different modes of comparison in addition to the introductory and concluding chapters. Part I provides the theoretical backdrop of hybrid bureaucracy. Part II focuses on the development of the bureaucratic toolkit in the colonial states. Chapter 2 compares classification regimes across the three colonial states, while Chapter 3 follows the development of the bureaucratic toolkit of emergency in India and its diffusion to Palestine and Cyprus. Part III focuses on the aftermath of colonial rule. Chapter 4 compares the classifications of civil servants according to loyalty and suspicion and Chapter 5 compares the restrictions of mobility and return of populations in the aftermath of intercommunal violence.

Part I, Hybrid Bureaucracy: How Race and Emergency Shaped the Organization of Colonial Rule, comprises one chapter. It stipulates the conceptual and theoretical underpinnings for the organizing principles of hybrid bureaucracy to challenge the view that British colonial bureaucracy did not have a set of distinct institutional forms and theories of administration. It proposes that "looking over the shoulder of the bureaucrat" from the perspective of colonial officials provides a set of organizing principles of hybrid bureaucracy that were not dysfunctional in and of themselves but rather served as sources of power. It generates a synthetic model of this type of bureaucracy to provide scaffolding for the analysis of how explicitly racialized practices and a perpetual state of emergency affect bureaucratic organization and practice.

Part II, The Axis of Suspicion: Classifications of Identity and Mobility in Crises, comprises two chapters that investigate how bureaucratic practices developed and diffused in the colonial states, focusing on population classification, through negotiations and the demographic battles over the census, according to the axis of suspicion, and the monitoring of mobility through emergency laws. This part tracks how in India, Cyprus, and Palestine, bureaucrats attempted – via forms and templates – to understand and control both imagined and material aspects of identity through population classification. There were two axes of population categorization: according to demographic traits and according to the security threat that a population posed to the state. Suspicion upended other types of classification, shifting constantly according to changing political or economic needs in each location. During times of crises, bureaucrats used the axis of suspicion to designate "dangerous populations" or dangerous spaces, and develop a toolkit of emergency comprised of different methods to monitor mobility.

Beginning with the transition from Mughal and Ottoman rule, **Chapter 2, Forms of Suspicion: Mobility As Threat, Census As Battleground,** focuses on the forms and schedules of the census as a site of negotiation and as a battleground infused by the axis of suspicion between administrators and communal leaderships, comparing bureaucratic negotiations and processes of separation in each of the colonies. It compares how hybrid bureaucracy deployed the census as a toolkit of government, in which categories of religion, language, and region gradually solidified into ethnonational identities. Through attempts to standardize, homogenize, and separate, communities were constituted as essentially different to justify the selective pairing of administrative practice with population. Division into majorities and minorities turned the census forms into a site for negotiation between subjects and officials, as well as an arena for rivalry between communities. Suspicion or embrace of enumeration techniques depended on one's proximity to the negotiation over resources, amid fears of control.

Chapter 3, The Bureaucratic Toolkit of Emergency, tracks how the bureaucratic toolkit of emergency developed between the two world wars. Focusing on India as the central case, it follows the making of blacklists and suspect lists, the proliferation of disturbed areas and closed zones, exit permits, mobility regimes, and the registration practices of foreigners. It then traces how these practices diffused through the horizontal circuits of empire to Palestine and Cyprus, in times of crisis, forming a conceptual grid of classifications of mobility according to suspicion.

Part III, Administrative Memory and the Legacies of Emergency, comprising two chapters, investigates the legacies of colonial rule in the new states: the classification of bureaucrats according to loyalty and suspicion, and the mobility restrictions on those attempting to return after the violence of partition.

Chapter 4, Loyalty and Suspicion: The Making of the Civil Service after Independence, compares how colonial classifications of identity according to loyalty and suspicion were used by bureaucracies in the new states to define the administrators themselves and to shape the making of the civil services. Purification committees to vet former civil servants of Mandate Palestine, campaigns that designated certain types of corruption as disloyalty, and the explosive fight over representation by ratio in Cyprus were all carried out along the graded axis of suspicion.

Chapter 5, How Hybrid Bureaucracy and Permit Regimes Made Citizenship, tracks the bureaucratic response to the violence of partition, war, and independence in each of the states, focusing on the mobility regimes established to prevent return in Israel and India, where the documents and evidentiary demands of the mobility regimes enabled claims to citizenship. Demonstrating how the transfer of bureaucratic practices governing mobility depended on the continuity of emergency laws, this chapter shows the divergent outcome in Cyprus, which relinquished emergency laws at independence.

The book's conclusion offers an alternative conceptualization of minority citizenship that remained after partition. It proposes that citizenship in these independent states cannot be conceived in terms of rights linking the nation-state to the individual. From the perspective of the minority, citizenship is a negative relationship of nondeportability: rather than political status, citizenship is a bureaucratic construction that prevents the state from deporting citizens, thereby turning citizenship for minority populations into a regime of mobility. Although this book confines the implications of such an analysis to the former British Empire, I further outline a path toward a door we are yet to open: research querying how bureaucratic population management shapes citizenship for minorities in the contemporary modern state. In other words, citizenship as a mobility regime.

PART I

HYBRID BUREAUCRACY: HOW RACE AND EMERGENCY SHAPED THE ORGANIZATION OF COLONIAL RULE

The Effective Disorder of Hybrid Bureaucracy

In 1908, Lord Cromer, the British proconsul of Egypt,[1] outlined the organizing principles of colonial administration in his essay on "The Government of Subject Races" (1908).[2] The text was published the very same year that Max Weber laid out his model of rational-legal bureaucracy in *Economy and Society*, a model that would become the foundational text for imagining modern state administration, even for its critics.

But rather than forming an exemplary model of Weberian rational-legal bureaucracy, Cromer and his essay became key to Hannah Arendt's analysis of the disastrous effects of racialized bureaucracy and the sphere of power afforded to administrators when they ruled over populations that were excluded from political representation. Arendt theorized the ways that racialized bureaucracy in the colonies produced the political possibility for the organization of the systematic genocide of the Nazi regime, based on the initial gap between the legal status of citizens in the metropole and that of subject races in the colonies (Shenhav 2012). Sociologist Yehouda Shenhav suggests that Arendt thought of Cromer's "government of subject races" as a sketch of "what one might call a theory of bureaucracy" (Arendt 1951: 310) and extended his analysis to constitute a paradigmatic case for understanding imperial bureaucracy (Shenhav 2013: 385).

Following up on Arendt's intuition, this chapter traces the effect of the perpetual state of emergency and the rule of colonial difference on the way bureaucracy was perceived in the British colonies, through the "theories" of the administrators themselves. Cromer believed that the only possible way to rule such a massive population over time was not "by the edge of a sword" but through a powerful bureaucracy that he termed a "hybrid form of government to which no name can be given and for which there is no precedent,"[3] well aware that his model of rule departed from the usual modes of administration of citizens. To be sure, Cromer did not produce anything close to a systemic theory of imperial administration but his writings and correspondence with a network of colonial officials (which will be introduced shortly), at a time when the heavy-handedness of colonial rule was challenged in both Britain and the colonies, offer a potential archive of what officials thought colonial bureaucracy entailed.

As we shall see, Cromer's "hybrid bureaucracy" was government by rules that included the adaptation of separate administrative regulations, practices, and possibilities for racial groups that were formally defined as "subject races." These separate practices and despotic methods of physical and procedural violence and coercion were justified through concepts of the racial inferiority of colonized peoples, who were considered not as full-fledged citizens but as potential threats to colonial rule. Maintaining the differentiated practices of hybrid bureaucracy required the use of martial law in various forms justified by the "lawlessness" of the natives (Hussain 2019: 102).

THE IMAGINARY RATIONAL-LEGAL MODEL OF BUREAUCRACY

Weber was the first to offer a systematic account of modern bureaucracy's ideal type, arguing that precision, speed, predictability, coordination, and reduction of friction raised efficiency to its optimal level and that pure bureaucratic organizations were expected to function according to universal considerations of competency in order to achieve the "very calculability of results" (Weber 1978). Weber formulated his rational-legal model in relation to liberal European societies that had undergone historical processes of "rationalization" in which "the rule of law" was increasingly considered a fundamental definer of legitimate rational action (Kalberg 1980).

Rationalization has been aptly described as "a grand meta-historical analysis of the dominance of the west in modern times" (Kim 2012). Rule of law was so significant because Weber warned against "instrumental rationality," when the action to achieve an end became a value in itself.[4] According to the rational-legal model that relied on the "rule of law" for its legitimacy, political participation is based on equal citizenship in which "people are no longer followers or subjects, but citizens who possess formal rights of participation" (Bendix 1956: xxviii) in a state.

For Weber, even though the liberal societies were imperial and colonial powers, the role of the "subject races" and how they were governed through racialized classifications were not considered significant to the developments perceived as endogenous and independent processes originating in Europe (Bhambra 2016: 335). Generally, Weber also believed that the category of race was superfluous, another form of social closure that, similar to ethnicity, was "unusable" as a category of analysis (Weber [1922] 1978: 394–395; Brubaker 2014).

Despite the epistemic exclusion of imperial and colonial histories from the rational-legal model of bureaucracy, it continues to occupy the imagination of scholars and publics who perceive modern state bureaucracy as firmly anchored in the rule of law (Go 2020).[5] Therefore, if one was to measure Cromer's colonial bureaucracy through the imaginary lens of Weber's rational-legal bureaucracy, they might mischaracterize it as mostly dysfunctional or broken:[6] instead of the "rule of law," colonial bureaucracy is ruled by a patchwork of laws and decrees. Stability, predictability, and hierarchy of command are replaced by administrative flexibility and secrecy; the clear boundaries of jurisdiction, discretion, and systematic, abstract guidelines are replaced by wide discretion and personalism.

ARENDT AND THE COLONIAL MODEL OF HYBRID BUREAUCRACY

Most scholars of British colonial administration and its legal scaffoldings contend that British colonial administration did not operate based on a systematized institutional theory or a particular model of governance, but was an array of improvisational practices, institutions, and attempts at achieving order and legitimacy. In "Reflections on the Colonial State," John Comaroff calls the inherent disorder of colonial rule the essential paradox of the colonial state that was "both ordered and incoherent, rational, and absurd, violent, and inefficient" (1998). Ilana Feldman, in line with Hannah Arendt's characterization of colonial rule as "bureaucracy without government" in which there is no government accountability to itself (Arendt 1970), suggests that one must distinguish between bureaucratic authority and state legitimacy, which lends itself to a distinctive mode of operation she calls "tactical government," as a set of practices of everyday life (Feldman 2008; 11, 16–17). For Feldman, instead of the "messiness" and "incoherence" of colonial government, "tactical government" is the means of governing that shifts in response to crises and presumes little stability in governing conditions (2008: 23). Ivan Evans foregrounds his investigation of the Department of Native Affairs, the bureaucratic hub that grew the authoritarian South African apartheid state, on the proposition that colonial administration did not follow a particular theory or model of government – "imperial Britain failed to generate blueprints or theories about colonial administration" – and that colonial bureaucracy was a localized affair, based on the ad hoc preroga-tive of the "man on the spot" (Evans 1997). Lauren Benton, a legal historian of imperial sovereignty, writes that imperial administrators had "no official handbook" explaining which forms of the law were best to institute in colonial settings; rather, as administrative entrepre-neurs and adopters, they treated European legal traditions as a "useful collection from which they might draw selectively in crafting colonial legal systems" (2002: 261). George Steinmetz suggests that most productive investigation of the colonial state, and its administration, is through analyses of social fields, of knowledge, power, and control, in which administrators are perceived as experts.

This chapter challenges the view that British colonial bureaucracy did not have a set of distinct institutional forms and theories of administra-tion; it outlines the organizing principles of colonial bureaucracy as they were articulated and understood by a network of British colonial admin-istrators in the twentieth century that revolved around Lord Cromer. It is a synthetic model of hybrid bureaucracy, to provide a scaffolding for the analysis of the ways explicitly racialized practices and a perpetual state of emergency affect bureaucratic organization and practice. It proposes that "looking over the shoulder of the bureaucrat" from the perspective of colonial officials provides a set of organizing principles of hybrid bureau-cracy that facilitates the interpretation of inconsistencies and contradic-tions of imperial bureaucracies that were not dysfunctional but served also as its sources of power.

These organizing principles are not an alternative model of bureau-cracy that seeks to include the effect of "race" as a category designating action and justification, and the way race has shaped organizations, as in some recent groundbreaking attempts to theorize how race changes the operation of organizations (Ray 2019; Byron & Roscigno 2019). Instead, it can serve as a conceptual tool to escape the rational-legal model of bureaucracy that continues to occupy the imagination of students of state organizations and serves as a primary tool of comparison. Despite inces-sant critique, the rational-legal model remains the primary template for the description, measurement, and comparison of bureaucratic structure and practice, even though, as Achille Mbembe provocatively suggests, it "did not exist anywhere" (2001). Mbembe's critique is not only against using the Weberian rational-legal model of bureaucracy as a measure of the efficacy of bureaucracy in postcolonies but also challenges the model itself because state bureaucracies everywhere are racialized and segregated, particular and incoherent, and in a constant practice to obtain and maintain legitimacy (Morgan & Orloff 2017: 18).

The organizing principles of hybrid bureaucracy are helpful for the study of institutional legacies of colonial bureaucracies following regime change (Mahoney & Thelen 2010: 4). Because they are not a neutralized "rational" model but embed the political conditions of colonial control in which they were formed,[7] they facilitate tracing the way institutional legacies have not only transferred bureaucratic routines and schemas to the new states but have also, through inherited bureaucratic practices, themselves shaped political outcomes. This chapter extracts from the discourse between the network of bureaucrats a set of recurring principles of action of a hybrid bureaucratic domination, where legal, traditional/despotic, and personal methods of domination were combined.[8] From the writings of a network of British colonial bureaucrats, five organizing principles can be outlined: racial hierarchy, personalism, secrecy, wide discretion and administrative flexibility, and the systemic creation of exceptions. From Cromer's writings and his correspondence with a network of twenty-two officials, I extracted these organizing principles of hybrid bureaucracy. The systemic creation of exceptions was both an organizing principle of the bureaucracy and the way the colonial state practiced a differentiated rule of law, justified by a condition of perpetual emergency (Hussain 2019: 113; see also Comaroff 2001) that did not exclude colonial subjects from the law but did the opposite; their inclusion in the patchwork of laws, decrees, and ad hoc arrangements was a colonizing force that engendered procedural violence through a grid of emergency laws (Esmeir 2012).

Cromer and his compatriots all wrote and corresponded during the era of British imperial expansion (1857–1922), when imperial ideology shifted from a universalist to a culturist stance, as the underlying assumptions of the imperial "civilizing missions" were questioned and repudiated during a crisis in liberal justifications for imperial rule (Mantena 2010: 9). British bureaucracy in Egypt during Cromer's term was described as "paternal," "despotic," and "absolute" (Berger 1957: 120). As mentioned, Cromer was the first bureaucrat to collate a theory of imperial bureaucracy in "The Government of Subject Races" (1908) and in *Modern Egypt* ([1908] 2010). Using the pseudonym Carthill, Sir Joseph Bampfylde Fuller served in East Bengal and provided a detailed description of the principles of British bureaucracy in India in his *The Lost Dominion* (Carthill 1924) and *The Empire of India* (1913). Sir Frederick Lugard, the governor of Hong Kong and Nigeria, provided a description of administrative indirect rule, which he labeled "the dual mandate" (1922). Edward Cecil, who served under Cromer, wrote *The Leisure of an Egyptian Official* and John Sydenham Furnivall, who served in Burma, wrote *Colonial Policy and Practice* (1948).

Although their analyses of imperial bureaucracy are biased, racist, and self-aggrandizing, at times to the point of delusion, underscoring successes and hiding failures, they provide a gateway into the administrative principles they perceived and created through multiple methods of physical and procedural violence and coercion, which were to form the "hybrid bureaucracy."

HOW COLONIAL OFFICIALS CREATED HYBRID BUREAUCRACY

In the racialized political systems Britain established across the globe to dominate nonwhite populations, there was "no question of signifying consent through electoral processes, [as] legality became the preeminent signifier of state legitimacy and of 'civilization,' the term that united politics and morality" (Hussain 2019: 4). Anticipating the uncertain future of the British rule of Egypt, in 1883 Lord Cromer suggested replacing laws with flexible decrees and additional despotic methods of domination like those that Weber observed in premodern imperial bureaucracy.[9]

Cromer and his compatriots recognized the growing challenge to the legitimacy of imperial rule in the twentieth century.[10] Government by rules represented the basis of moral legitimacy within the realm of the British colonial power, juxtaposed with the premodern despotic rule of their predecessors, the Mughal and Ottoman empires. Lord Cromer called it "sane imperialism" (Baring 1912: 307). Cromer believed:

Once we have to draw the sword, not merely to suppress some local effervescence, but to overcome a general of people of subject races, goaded to action either by deliberate oppression or by unintentional misgovernment, the sword will assuredly be perilous to defend this for long, and the days of our Imperial rule be numbered. (Baring 1908a: 6)

Three principles dominate Cromer's writings: (1) During emergencies, bureaucratic officials create exceptions to existing rules, which eventually become part of the administrative structure. (2) A select group of bureaucratic officials knows about and uses written but unpublished rules and internal regulations. This secrecy creates contradictory administrative decisions and expectations. Moreover, because they are not grounded in law, the authority of these administrative decisions depends on the status of the official who makes the decision and the identity of the person he administers – a principle of "personalism" that inculcates identity as a major predictor for which set of regulations or practices bureaucratic officials will use.[11] (3) The flexibility of official decision-making disperses authority and widens the scope of sovereignty of the officials, who effectively make law by bureaucratic means.

The growing sphere of bureaucratic sovereignty was created through a state of perpetual emergency. Nasser Hussain showed how rule through perpetual emergency, in which sovereignty was neither "despotic or democratic," was justified by the perceived "inferiority and lawlessness" of the natives (2019: 39–40). In turn, emergency powers were necessary to maintain racial hierarchy and differentiated legal and administrative practices for different populations. The state of perpetual emergency and its routinization enabled the justification and legitimacy of the hybrid model of bureaucracy that was neither lawless nor illegal and achieved domination not by exceptional measures that excluded its subjects from the law, but precisely by incorporating its subjects into its legal system through administrative practices (Esmeir 2015).

RACIAL HIERARCHY AS "SCORN AND BIAS": UNIVERSALISM AND IMPERSONALITY

The principle of universalism encompasses the rule of law (subordination of the official to the law) and equality before the law (the same law applies to all). The term "rule of law" has a peculiar history in the British colonies, where claims to the legitimacy of their rights through law were the very way the colonial state roped its subjects into the structure of domination and subjection to practices of monitoring and control (Esmeir 2012: 9).

Universalism is an idealized feature of rule in the modern state, which established a direct relationship between the administration of the state and the civil and political rights of the population (Tilly 1995: 229). Universality was a major legitimating feature of direct rule of state bureaucracy, and the neutrality and alleged benevolence of administrative expertise:

The best proof of the fact that the thought of the bureaucratic thinker is pervaded by the official representation of the official is ... the power of seduction wielded by representations of the state ... that portray bureaucracy as a "universal group" endowed with the intuition of, and the will to, universal interest; or as an organ of reflection and irrational instrument in charge of realizing the general interest. (Bourdieu 1994: 2)

Weber based his concept of impersonality in bureaucracy on the maxim *Sine ira et studio* ("without scorn and bias"), which he perceived as the condition for conducting "objective" scientific research and rational administration. Weber writes, "Bureaucracy develops the more perfectly the more it is dehumanized, the more it succeeds in eliminating from official business love, hatred, and all purely personal, irrational and emotional elements which escape calculation" (Weber 1978: 975). Official neutrality and personal disinterestedness in the outcome of an administrative decision were central to both economic markets and state organizations.

As Bourdieu shows, universalism in bureaucracy is a myth, yet it upholds the legitimacy of the civil servants through the belief that "There is no contradiction in fighting, at the same time, against the mystificatory hypocrisy of abstract universalism and for universal access to the universal" (Bourdieu 2000: 71–72). Indeed, legal scholars of colonial rule who view the rule of colonial difference and the perpetual state of emergency as a "contradiction" to the universal rule of law do not see this contradiction as effecting Weber's rational-legal model (Halliday et al. 2012). Indeed, the rule of colonial difference – that is, establishing different rules, standards, practices, and administrative routines within the state bureaucracy – shattered the performed principle of universalism, which prompted the British bureaucracy's incessant scramble to justify the judiciousness of its rule (Kolsky 2005).

BRITISH RULE OF INDIA AS TEMPLATE FOR GOVERNING "SUBJECT RACES"

Cromer based his articulation of hybrid domination on what he encountered during times of emergency in the administration of India as private aide to Viceroy Northbrook, his cousin. Warren Hastings, Governor General of India (1773–85), was one of Cromer's inspirations for his model of rule.[12] Hastings served the East India Company, which created a semi-sovereign state that collected taxes, took over the surveillance networks of the Mughal empire (Bayly 1999), waged wars, managed the lives of subjects, and administered justice in its local colonial offices, which were the locus of statecraft and knowledge production (Raman 2008).

Cromer was interested in Hastings's philosophy of administrative decentralization that relied on "the man on the spot . . . who [knows] the natives [and represents] the forces of 'law and order'" (Cohn 1989: 135). Sovereignty in practice in racial India "could mean nothing but despotism" – a despotism that was inherited from the Mughals because only the power of the Leviathan, in a perpetual "state of necessity," could keep the permanently rebellious population in order and prevent the imminent threats to security and order in the state (Hastings quoted in Mukherjee 2010: 17). The British must therefore "modify and adapt the old, to fit English ideas and standards" and "produce a piece of machinery that English officials could operate and English opinion tolerate" (Cohn 1989: 136). As Bhagavan (2003: 20) summarized: "In colonial India there were to be no citizens, only subjects of the empire and 'traditional' princes." This preposition of the Indian model of administration inspired Lord Cromer, who produced a simplified and selective semblance of the rule of law. He advised against codification and chose to incorporate selective European laws into local Indian customs and institutions to produce an artifice of justice.[13]

Hastings admitted that British domination "exceed[s] the rule of law" (Hastings quoted in Mukherjee 2010: 29). After the dissolution of the East India Company, the government of India produced wide-scale codification that was to become "the colonial rule of law" (Hussain 2019: 60). Colonial governors frequently resorted to martial law, which bases its authority on the legal maxim *Salus populi suprema est lex* (i.e., "the safety of the people is the supreme law"). The necessity of martial law in India and later in Egypt, as well as other British colonies, was condoned by racially based justifications rooted in the "inferiority and lawlessness" of the natives (Hussain 2019: 102).

In 1858, after the great revolt that challenged the legitimacy of British Company rule, sovereignty passed from the East India Company to the Crown. The first Government of India Act established the India Office and the early version of the Indian Civil Service. Queen Victoria's proclamation granted amnesty to the rebels, recognized Indians as British imperial subjects, and promised to ensure "that all shall have the equal protection of the law." The proclamation produced a semblance of an imperial rule of law, a myth of universalism, but despite the project of a universal codification of law and an end to the corrupt and direct violence of the despotic Company rule, subjects and administrators alike were acutely aware of the racial hierarchies of legal protection and implementation (McClure 2018; Kolsky 2010). Fredrick Lugard wrote that, although there was a gradual shift toward rationalization and systematization of practices and attempts at efficiency, it was accompanied by the flexibility of bureaucratic procedures that were suited to the conditions on the ground (Lugard 1922: 94).

Nevertheless, flexibility did not mean administration was not based on rules and a hierarchy of writing, documents, and files. Raman shows how the "document raj," in which the early colonial state established its paper mastery, gave rise to a racialized, hierarchical bureaucracy of "trustworthy Europeans" and "mendacious Natives" (Raman 2012: 26). This particular model of racial bureaucracy is a mixed type, one that Sudipta Kaviraj defined as the colonial rationality that has "feet of vernacular clay," where the state separates the vast lower bureaucracy from a narrow band of European officers (Kaviraj 1984: 227). This complex bureaucracy was in part a result of the administrative jurisdiction of the provincial governments in India being incommensurable with the internal governance of the Princely States, as well as a legacy of the patchwork of criminal, military, and administrative jurisdiction developed during the reign of the East India Company.

The driving force of the constitutional changes implemented by the colonial state was the challenge to the legitimacy of its rule because of its racialized structure and breach of universal equality. The Government of India Act in 1919 made India a diarchy, which divided the executive branch of each provincial government into authoritarian and publicly elected sections. The first section was composed of executive councillors, appointed, as before, by the crown. The second section was composed of ministers chosen by the governor from the elected members of the provincial legislature. These latter ministers were Indians. Diarchy was a hybrid system of indirect rule that legitimated its racial hierarchies with the gradual training of local officials about India's self-rule (Sen 2013).

The challenge to the myth of universality underpinned the political context in which Cromer exposed his model of bureaucracy. Cromer, alongside Lord Milner, who ruled the Transvaal, and Lord Curzon, Viceroy of India, believed that imperial governance was what made Britain a great nation (Owen 2004: 378). Yet under the British liberal government, at the turn of the century, bureaucratic heavy-handedness came under attack – from Milner's rule of the Transvaal to Curzon's reign in India. Cromer wrote a systematization of imperial bureaucracy in response to the liberal critique in London about the despotic measures rampant in the colonies. In the hybrid model described in "On the Government of Subject Races," Cromer presented race as a central category that necessitated an alternative to universalist order.

Curzon justified the "difference between Dominions possessing responsible government and an administration like that of India"; the civilizing mission remained, and it was an "elementary fact that the rule of India is still, and must for as long as we can foresee, remain in British hands." While there was a "necessity of a progressive increase in the employment of Indians in the administration of their country," Curzon argued there was also a requirement for "a strong British personnel in the higher ranks of the Administration" (Curzon 1909: 39). Furnivall, a colonial official in Burma and critical scholar of the British Empire, wrote on the relationship between colonial administration and social order that: "common to all colonial practice is that the responsibility for maintaining order is assumed by the colonial powers; and organic autonomous society maintains order with more or less success in virtue of its inherent vitality, but its dependencies are kept alive, as it were, by artificial respiration, the pressure exercised mechanically from outside of the above" (Furnivall 1939).

In the repeated explanations of the shattered myth of universality, racial hierarchy was both an underlying political belief and an organizing principle of administrative action. When Lord Curzon jettisoned the term "self-government," he wrote of oriental "inferiority" from a comparative perspective:

It is a pity that the word self-government has such different meanings. To some (for instance myself) it means the Indians acquiring by stages an ever-increasing influence in the administration, until they become the predominant factor . . . . but all this under the guidance of Great Britain. To others [. . .] the British mission is not to govern but to go, and self-government means that the Indians will govern themselves . . . much as the Russians, who are true Orientals, are doing at this moment, and no doubt with similar results. There is great danger in the use of phrases that admit of such contradictory interpretations. (Curzon 1909)

Furnivall was clear, despite his humor, about the predicament of universality in colonial administration:[14]

The prime care of any colonial power must be to maintain order, for order is essential to such advantages as it anticipates from imposing its rule of dependency. In maintaining order, the colonial power must choose between the western principle of law and the tropical system of relying on personal authority, between direct and indirect rule . . . the colonial power must choose between the western principle of freedom and the tropical system of compulsion. Colonial practice divides along these two main lines. (Furnivall 1939: 8)

This vision of bureaucracy outlined by Cromer in his writings materialized on the ground, focused on population management through restrictions of mobility. As Timothy Mitchell describes (1991: 97), the British established in Egypt a system of domination that, Cromer admitted, was tantamount to the introduction of legal exceptions. The early administration relied upon the so-called Brigandage Commissions, and was composed of secret police, local informants, mass imprisonment, and forces that conducted abrupt military raids and systematic use of torture (see Baring 1908: 289). These practices remained more prevalent in settler colonies. A decade later, colonial officials replaced these commissions with a more disciplined and consolidated bureaucratic system that included selective use of the law, which was a multitude of decrees and an abruptly changing set of regulations that enabled restrictions on the mobility of the population (Mitchell 1991b; see also Shenhav & Berda 2009). The police and hired watchmen enforced these measures (Mitchell 1991: 96).

These methods of domination were not only to maintain colonial rule through a security apparatus but were also designed and applied to capitalist production in Egypt. Mitchell (2002) describes the process used to prevent labor desertion from lands in which colonial crops were grown. To coerce villagers to cultivate export crops and deliver them to government warehouses, the British applied methods such as taxation, penalties, and dispossession of land. When villagers resisted this crop monopoly by deserting their militarily guarded territories and moving to agricultural lands beyond government control, a permit regime was introduced to prevent any departure from the locality of one's village (Mitchell 2002: 60–61). The land decrees constituted attempts to compel the natives to remain on their lands and to confirm the seizure of lands from those who fled from them. Restrictions on mobility of laborers, or forced displacement, were part of the relations of master and slave throughout the empire, a sphere of imperial law that the hybrid bureaucracy enforced through policing and punishment (Hay & Craven 2005: 4–5).

Cromer also introduced land reform for the Bedouins, to control their movement. Bedouins who were willing to surrender to the authority of the military officer assigned to their locality were offered small plots of land. Mitchell (2002: 62) describes the decree that organized registration and subsequent surveillance:

They were to give the officer a list of the heads of the sections of each tribe, with the number of persons and a description of each individual enumerated tribe-by-tribe, section-by-section, name by name. The officer would then issue a permit with the name, physical description and tribe of every individual under his authority. A person, who wished to move from one tribal section to another, or to another part of the country, required this permit to travel.

During revolts, the reasons for administering permit systems and suspect lists shifted from the economic justification of preventing desertion to prescribed control over those who posed a security threat. Villagers were required to round up "depraved and malicious persons and suspicious characters" (Mitchell 2002: 97) in their localities, and the colonial officials ordered them to be sent to labor. If, after an assigned period, the suspicious characters were found in the districts, the headmen were punished. The bureaucracy also roped into service with the police local thugs and gangs who handed out a system of "tickets" to workers in their villages before they traveled to their work sites, "but only to those men whom the local police deemed not to be troublemakers" (Mitchell 2002: 97).

This form of hybrid domination that incorporated both violent despotism and expansive legal elaboration was not exclusive to Egypt. Cromer referred to an explicit model that should travel as "an ideal" from India to Egypt (Baring 1908). One of its central features was personalism – that administrative outcomes were the product of the identity of the colonial official and the colonial subject – while maintaining the impersonal distance that Michael Herzfeld calls the bureaucrat's "rejection of common humanity and the denial of selfhood" (1992: 1).

HOW THE BRITISH EMPIRE DIFFUSED THE HYBRID FORM OF BUREAUCRACY

There were three main ways that the hybrid form of bureaucracy diffused in the horizontal circuits between British colonies, as administrators throughout the empire quickly adopted the theories, practices, policies, and political culture of the bureaucratic model developed in India. Beyond the circuits of knowledge that developed when imperial officials and technical staff moved from post to post, or the technologies that developed in the colonies – from forensics (Blum 2017) to counterinsurgency technologies (Khalili 2015) – one method of diffusion of legal weaponry was through the India Office and the Colonial Office. A central node of British imperial administration that straddled the constant, mostly performative negotiation on the explicitness of the violence of colonial laws, the Colonial Office distributed policies and printed forms, codes of conduct, and circulars. As it aspired to export an ethos of "British Policing," which they perceived as an essential component of liberalization (Sinclair & Williams 2007: 222), the Colonial Office attempted (and failed) to standardize legislation of special measures during protests and uprisings.[15] As we shall see in Chapter 3, in times of crisis, such as the Cyprus Revolt of 1931 when the Colonial Governor's house was burned and the Arab Revolt in Mandate Palestine (1936–39), the Colonial Office sent bureaucrats who had gained their expertise in India, mainly Bengal, to aid the local colonial governments.[16] The templates and toolkits of colonial governance during emergencies were developed and were adapted by colonial officials, commanders, and magistrates through decrees and orders that circulated in times of crisis.

Information about administration flowed unevenly from one colony to another, as the Colonial Office at once offered ad hoc solutions and made efforts to standardize laws, decrees, and responses to crises, both locally and across the empire. Standardization was an impossible task in a bureaucratic model that cherished wide discretion and flexibility, and whose officials resisted the very idea that their local expertise could be expropriated, without relocating them personally to do the job. In their writings, the British imperial bureaucrats consistently distinguished themselves from other European empires, emphasizing their independence, discretion, and self-reliance. Yet the decentralization illuminates a paradox of organizational diffusion recognized in neo-institutional theory (DiMaggio & Powell 1983). Despite resistance to centralization, resulting in the failed attempt of the central office to standardize its administrative practices, bureaucrats in different locations agreed and made similar administrative choices and decisions, particularly about classification and categories of what they perceived as "dangerous populations," as we shall see in Chapter 3.

A second method of diffusion that imperial officials used was to "copy and paste" generic administrative templates and forms to the local context. For example, local bureaucrats adapted the Indian bureaucratic forms for naturalization applications and residency permits for use in Mandate Palestine and Cyprus.[17] During the Arab Revolt, in 1936 the government of Palestine modeled its local standing orders on decrees promulgated in Bengal in the 1930s. When they enacted martial law, Mandate officials followed emergency measures used in India.[18] Moving colonial officials from post to post, particularly in times of crisis, was a third method of diffusion. Imperial historians identified these so-called professional delegations as an inventive way to spread bureaucratic methods from India to other British colonies (Sinclair 2006).

Although the principles of hybrid bureaucracy did not provide a stable and distinct model, Cromer and his compatriots devised a particular form of administration, in which race was a category of action that produced differentiated rules for populations. Perpetual emergency enabled an expanding sphere of executive power in which officials employed wide discretion and administrative flexibility.

ORGANIZING PRINCIPLES OF HYBRID BUREAUCRACY

Five organizing principles arise from the writings of the British imperial bureaucrats, which are separated here for analytical purposes, although they overlap and produce each other in administrative action and writing: racial hierarchy, personalism, secrecy, wide discretion and administrative flexibility, and systematically producing exceptions.

Racial Hierarchy

The bureaucratic sovereign uses racial distinctions in laws that subsequently form institutions, regulations, routines, and procedures that promote or maintain segregation between Europeans and local natives. This early distinction between Europeans and natives formulated a system of classification of population based on race, very broadly bound, and officials employed practices and routines that corresponded to the racial category. The difference became apparent regarding enforcing and implementing formal laws, as well as establishing separate organizational structures, practices, and routines within the same government, at times creating overlapping institutions to deal with similar populations. In Chapter 2, I explore how the bureaucratic ordering of the population shapes the administration and its practices of independent India, Israel, and Cyprus.

Cromer justified racial bureaucracy by arguing that the rule of law is "foreign to the subject races" and that its inflexibility endangers "dynamic operation" (1908b: 263). For him, European liberal bureaucracy did not accord with the "Oriental habits of thought" (1908a: 13). Because of the natives' lack of "political maturity," he wrote: "Before Orientals can attain anything approaching to the British ideal of self-government, they will have to undergo very numerous transmigrations of political thought" (Baring 1908a: 14).

Cromer was first sent to Egypt from India to exercise indirect authority by advising the local khedive. To him, coercive methods of domination were legitimate, since "the inhabitants of the countries under British rule are not of Anglo-Saxon origin" (Baring 1908a: 1). Their origin, he argued, informed their intellectual capacity. The governing practices developed in India were to empower the bureaucrats for the monumental task of building the capacity of the "inferior" Egyptians:

the civilized Englishmen to extend to [the native Egyptians] the hand of fellowship and encouragement, and to raise them, morally and materially, from the abject state in which he finds them . . . He looks towards India, and he says to himself with all the confidence of the imperial race – I can perform this task. (Baring 1908b: 130)

Ironically, administrative exceptions to regulations or customary practices and the lack of transparent procedures further justified to Cromer that the racial ordering of bureaucratic routines was necessary. Cromer distinguished between the ways the legal orders delineated their limits of operation: "the [Egyptian] legal order is based on particularistic, deviant, eccentric, arbitrary and exceptional actions" (Esmeir 2012: 205). Despite the fact that Cromer's model did not conform to what the European legal order represented as a system of generalizable, universal, bounded state-centric actions, Esmeir shows how for Cromer the rule of law in Egypt was conducted according to a defined set of prescriptions rather than the will of an individual (Esmeir 2012: 209). Not unlike the linear and simplistic interpretations of Weber's forms of legitimate domination,[19] Cromer juxtaposed the "oriental" messy, patrimonial bureaucracy with a rational-legal order that advanced general procedures, unmarred by the racial hierarchy.

Lord Edward Cecil, who served under Cromer, lamented the vexing interactions with Egyptian subordinates, as "native officials are far too fond of referring to bureaucrats as a 'growling mob of officials'" (Cecil 1921: 54). Moreover, Carthill, like Cromer, defined the subjects of bureaucracy as "subject races" (1924: 151), who were "not yet ready for Western conceptions of justice and freedom." Liberal legal rule in India was impossible, thought Carthill (1924: 245): "We desire that British control ... even be increased, because we are aware that the masses of the population are still very far from being true liberals" (1924: 245). He observed that the "subject races would deflect questions to superior authority, partly because they are timid, and partly because they have no sense of proportionate importance" (Cecil 1921: 54). He attributed these tendencies to both the underdeveloped nature of the natives and their tradition of ineffective bureaucracy and explained that local Egyptians would not have "minded a few capricious acts of tyranny" (Carthill 1924: 26). Carthill argued that the "transfer to Indian hands of a large proportion of posts of control would certainly lower the standards of administration" (Fuller 1913: 380).

Carthill expressed apprehension about the ability of "Indian Orientals" to serve as district officers:

For the oriental, as soon as he ceases to be a barbarian (and often before he ceases to be so), [he] becomes essentially a bureaucrat and a paper-chewer. He is accustomed . . . to look for a "superior command." As soon as he finds it, he is happy. Its existence frees him from that odious thing, responsibility. (Carthill 1924: 145)

Personalism

The most important manifestation of personalism is its associated administrative uncertainty: The calculability of results of administrative action in hybrid bureaucracy has little to do with laws, administrative regulations, or projected outcomes. Rather, the identities of the officials or the subjects shaped the outcomes of administrative decisions.

In his ideal type, Weber emphasized, "the typical person in authority, the 'superior,' is himself subject to an impersonal order" (1978: 217). Hybrid bureaucracy produced bureaucratic distance, in which bureaucrats developed moral aloofness toward their "subject races." This indifference is not at all exclusive to colonial bureaucracy, but aloofness was normatively prescribed and legitimized by racial ideologies. Hyperimpersonality was considered a remarkable trait of British colonial administrators by Curzon (1909).

Cromer argued that imperial bureaucrats were not mad or vicious rulers, but administrative "systematizers." They were to act "by the light of western knowledge," but they also considered the colonial locality and performed in the "best interest" of the natives (Baring 1908a: 6). The enlightened idea of rationality was inscribed in rule-based government: "The principles of government . . . guide our relations with whatsoever races are brought under our control and must be politically and economically sound and morally defensible" (Baring 1908a: 2).

Hannah Arendt pointed to Cromer's "indifference, aloofness, and [his] genuine lack of interest in [his] subjects"

Aloofness became the new attitude of all members of the British services; it was a more dangerous form of governing than despotism and arbitrariness, because it did not even tolerate that last link between the despot and his subjects, which is formed by bribery and gifts. (Arendt 1951: 92)

Responding to the imperial bureaucrats' assertions that they had replaced the despotic authority of the Mughal and Ottoman empires with enlightened rational bureaucracy (Curzon 1909; Baring 1908a), Arendt wrote on the effects of racial hierarchies in bureaucracy:

The very integrity of the British administration made despotic government more inhuman and inaccessible to its subjects than Asiatic rulers and reckless conquerors had ever been. Integrity and aloofness were symbols for an absolute division of interests, to the point where they are not even permitted to conflict. In comparison, exploitation, oppression, or corruption look like safeguards of human dignity, because exploiter and exploited, oppressor and oppressed, corruptor and corrupted still live in the same world, still share the same goals, fight each other for the possession of the same things. (Arendt 1951: 92)

The culture of instrumental rationality was embedded in imperial bureaucracy. Cromer argued that "personal influence" devoid of written legal treaties was crucial for "effective supervision" (Arendt 1951: 93). Personalism replaced the formalized and visible decision-making process, so colonial officials could change regulations on the spot, avoiding a cumbersome and limiting interaction with the metropole (Cecil 1921: 87). Cromer lamented that he had "to work through British agents over whom [he] possessed no control, save that based on personal authority and moral suasion" (Baring 1908b: 325). Indeed, he privileged personal influence over formal policy.

Impersonality itself was racialized. Colonial officials complained that Indian administrators, unlike their British counterparts, lacked the "virtue of impartiality" (Spangenberg 1976: 5), yet Lugard described British bureaucrats as exerting close personal influence and pressure (Lugard 1922: 97). The 1930 Simon Commission, which investigated British officials in India, discovered that British bureaucracy developed "highly personalized techniques, based on the special local knowledge of the officials and the 'trust' of the mass of the population" (Spangenberg 1976: 6).

Colonial officials made decisions based on the identities of both the official and the subject. This decision-making was not only on the basis of classifying subjects according to race, religion, or caste but also on the relationship of the subject to the state – usually classified on a continuum of loyalty and threat (i.e., loyal citizen, cooperative subject, suspect, or security threat) – this classification was based on degrees of threat or suspicion. In turn, suspicion shrouded the classifications of the population themselves in a veil of secrecy.

Secrecy

Colonial administration based many of its decisions upon unpublished rules and internal directives. On the one hand, colonial bureaucrats, police, security forces, and magistrates seemed to create a magical effect, a reenchantment of power through bureaucracy, beyond the direct or inhibited threat of violence (Das 2006: 162) that was omnipresent and ubiquitous, multiplying, intervening, and regulating life wherever they saw fit. On the other hand, authority was elusive (Stoler 2002), and the source of an administrative decision was hard to trace, particularly when one wanted to know how to make an appeal or locate an official upon whom to make demands. This principle, coupled with flexibility, turned the colonial bureaucracy into a "phantom sovereign." Though secrecy, intelligence, and clandestine operations represent inherent functions of any executive branch of the state, in the colonial bureaucracy, secrecy was not confined to issues of national security, the military, or managing crises. Secrecy functioned as an organizing principle. There were direct consequences from the frequent use of unpublished rules, obfuscated procedures, and opaque administrative processes that complemented the flexibility and personalism of official decisions.

Secrecy was critical not because of a threat to the authority and legitimacy of the administration from its subjects, but rather as a shield from parliamentary oversight, government directives, or liberal criticism of the hybrid bureaucracy's methods. Cromer shunned written documents "in order to be free to obey only the law of expansion, without obligation to a man-made treaty" (Arendt 1951: 96). Secrecy, in turn, was an integral component of administrative flexibility.

Wide Discretion and Administrative Flexibility

The British administrative repertoire was decentralized, and its ideology defined continental state-centralized bureaucracy as "disease" (Subramaniam 2009: 61). Explaining the importance of flexibility in hybrid bureaucracy, Cromer referred directly to the Indian model that inspired him. He criticized the "Continental [i.e., French] school of bureaucracy" as overly formal and too centralized (Baring 1908a: 15). He condemned "the tendency of every French central authority ... to allow no discretionary power whatever to its subordinate," which he argued resulted in a reciprocal tendency of the subordinate "to lean in everything on superior authority" (Baring 1908a: 15). Subject populations were unable to conform to a "ready-made system" (Baring 1908b: 238) or to "more rational administrative systems" (Baring 1908b: 311). This view explains how he perceived the existing native administrative structures as being integrated with rather than separated from the colonial state. Cromer compared the French and English systems of rule in Egypt to advance the virtue of administrative flexibility and wide discretion:

Look, again, at the theoretical perfection of French administrative systems, at their elaborate detail, and at the provision, which is apparently made to meet every possible contingency, which may arise. Compare these features with the Englishman's practical systems, which lay down rules as to a few main points, and leave a mass of detail to individual discretion. (Baring 1908b: 237–238)

Administrative discretion represented a key concern for Weber in this model of bureaucracy. He rejected the inherent suspicion of state civil servants and the view that "general norms [were] held to play primarily a negative role, as barriers to the officials positive and 'creative' activity, which should never be regulated" because individual freedoms and personal circumstances were (and remain) of the utmost importance in an administrative decision. In his model of bureaucracy, "this freely creative administration would not constitute a realm of free, arbitrary action and discretion, of personally motivated favorites and valuation such as we shall find to be the case among pre-bureaucratic forms" (Weber 1978: 979). In contrast, he asserted that the official must serve the strictly rational and objective idea of *raison d'état*:[20] "To have any kind of equality before the law, it is imperative to have formal and rational objectivity of administration rather than the grace of the old patrimonial, pre-bureaucratic domination" (1978: 980). The concept of a rational *raison d'état* assumed a central role in Weber's description of the boundaries of operation within administrative discretion, which generally adhere to universalistic principles. Juxtaposed with patrimonial bureaucracy, Weber's conception of *raison d'état* provided a potential for stability in administrative outcomes. However, the racialized and decentralized imperial bureaucracy did not revert to the patrimonial discretion but to a racialized *raison d'état*. Administrative flexibility and wide discretion were necessary to navigate the administrative patchwork and contingencies created by practices that varied according to the administered population (see also Joyce & Mukerji 2017).

One feature of the decentralized British imperial bureaucracy was the small component of civil servants from the metropole who performed a diverse range of administrative tasks (Cell 2002). Cromer idealized them as young, ambitious, well trained, and highly reliable, willing to renounce the human aspiration of notoriety, and replacing credit with the anonymous power afforded by secrecy, informality, and lack of accountability. Cromer epitomizes this concept of veiled power, as he prided himself on "remain[ing] more or less hidden [and] pull[ing] the strings" (quoted in Arendt 1951: 94). Cromer constructed an archetype of invisible management, "having surrounded himself during his tenure in Egypt with bureaucrats willing to subordinate the natural human desire for recognition to the bureaucratic need for invisibility" (Bivona 1998: 27–28).

Cromer thought that flexible decision-making and wide discretion were particularly necessary in India because of its distance from the metropole and the incidence of "unforeseen" events that rendered its administrative frontier in a state of flux and the government of India as "half-sovereign" (Johnston 1973: 217). Similarly, for Carthill, accountability to parliament and the threat of reprimand harmed the autonomy and effectiveness of the colonial bureaucracy:

It is invariably the case that the local agent, knowing that he, if he acts on his own initiative, may be censured and exposed to the humiliation of having his policy reversed, prefers, before doing anything, to get preliminary sanction. In this case, you have the man on the spot who is legally responsible but impotent, and the official at home who is all-powerful but in no way responsible. This cannot but result in the general enfeebling of the executive. (Carthill 1924: 135–136)

Cromer prided himself on his perceived independence and autonomy from London, From which he had "never asked for any such instructions" (Baring 1908b: 323). His fundamental principle was to handle "purely local matters on the spot, with as little reference as possible to London" (Baring 1908b: 327), yet it seems plausible that the motivation to outline his model was precisely the severe criticisms and frequent inquiries from London.

Systemically Producing Exceptions

Creating exceptions to the law is a feature of bureaucracy that is different from the condition of perpetual emergency in the colonial state. The condition of emergency provided the wide executive power to rule by decree, and it facilitated the other elements of flexibility, secrecy, and personalism. The systemic production of exceptions provided flexibility, marshaled new categories and classifications, and included the practice of creating judicial forums and commissions that could permeate social life at every level (Esmeir 2012: 242–244). Alongside martial law and the promulgation of general security laws, specific decrees and decisions could be enacted for specific populations or for specific times of crisis.

According to imperial officials, periodic emergencies warranted bureaucratic flexibility and action based on unpublished rules. When crises occurred, bureaucrats introduced emergency measures that further expanded executive discretion, yet they did so through decrees, semilegal rules, and regulations. For Cromer, political emergencies required bureaucratic flexibility and common sense – and they could not be curtailed by orders from London. Moreover, the Egyptian "[did] not recognize emergencies, and he spurn[ed] common sense" (Baring 1908b: 240). As Carthill noted, in between London and the local native stood the imperial bureaucrat that needed "emergency" for his legitimate action:

Repression is justifiable when, and only when, it is necessary. If the emergency does not exist, repression is inadmissible. When it does exist, and repression is decided on, repression should be carried out coldly, calmly and ruthlessly until the emergency is passed. (Carthill 1924: 257)

In this tautological and teleological reasoning, Carthill emphasized that emergencies warranted capricious castigation, which was legitimate since the "Oriental understands no other form of government" (1924: 43). Emergency measures were both routine and justified by racial hierarchy, which became increasingly difficult to maintain administratively and necessitated "more emergency."

Underlying the justification of exceptions was the constant struggle of colonial modernity, the failed project attempting to reconcile conquest and the rule of law, as well as the endless attempts to perform adherence to the rule of law, through the transparent, limited, and general rules. The permanent failure of the exception included possessing power for limitless violence and positioning the "politics of preemptive counterinsurgency as defensive holy war by presciently racializing its theological enemy" (Feldman & Medovoi 2016: 3). In Chapter 3 I expand upon the inner workings and effects of this organizing principle in the administrative toolkit of emergency that would shape the transition of subject populations in the new states into citizens and suspects.

EFFECTIVE INEFFICIENCY AND THE MANAGEMENT OF SUBJECT POPULATIONS

Colonial officials justified, when challenged, the flexibility of administrative decision-making with two related reasons: the state of emergency and the administrative need to react quickly to ever-changing, hostile environments. These justifications for wide discretion applied to not only territories viewed as "fortress colonies,"[21] governed by the British for the "security of the British Empire," but also those places whose the primary purpose was to allow them to extract resources and access commercial markets. Some populations turned hostile to British rule when its orders for "peace and good government" either were carried out with extreme violence or favored a rival population (Mitchell 2002).

At the same time as they campaigned for autonomy, secrecy, and discretion, the imperial officials also viewed the bureaucratic apparatus as inefficient. Local officials sought to magnify and extend their offices and control. Local bureaucrats were preoccupied with written documents and printed materials that had little bearing on administrative efficiency. Lugard admitted, in tandem with the writings of Milner, that the decentralized bureaucracy in India curtailed efficiency (Lugard 1922: 96). Preoccupation with document-making procedures and the ordering of paper trails did not negate the aforementioned invisibility of the colonial official and its lack of written rules. These two seemingly contradictory aspects of bureaucracy did in fact coexist. Spangenberg argues that administrative efficiency in India was a myth generated by British bureaucrats to justify their monopoly of higher positions: "The 'efficiency' of British officials becomes a racist desideratum for the exclusion of Indians, who are branded inefficient and incompetent" (Spangenberg 1976: 347).

As I discussed at the beginning of the chapter, Weber conceptualized rational-legal bureaucracies as instruments to secure rationality, predictability, precision, speed, ambiguity, knowledge of files, continuity, direction, unity, strict subordination, and reduction of friction to "raise efficiency to its optimal level" (Weber 1978). According to this ideal type, the prevalence of uncertainty created irregularities and inconsistencies, complicated planning while maintaining causal linkages between means and ends.

Administrative flexibility and a lack of jurisdictional boundaries resulted in conflicting decisions, uncertainty, and confusion for governed subjects and for the various agents and officials operating in the departments and ministries of the colonial bureaucracy. If one viewed Weber's model as a template, one would expect that flexibility of discretion and deviation from the model of rational-legal bureaucracy founded upon a fixed division of labor and a hierarchy of offices defined by clear rules, transparency, and visibility would lead to inefficiency and friction, confusing both the subjects and the officials themselves. Rather than create chaos and disorder, confusion and ambiguity led to a complete dependency of the subject upon the bureaucracy. Uncertainty and ambiguity became a formidable tool of discipline and control. (These were not only a feature of British rule; see Haque 2007.)[22]

Cromer valued administrative flexibility, and deplored codification. He marveled at the possibility of invisible management along with flexibility and fluidity of administrative decision-making, and believed it was the only possible way to rule the colonies. The *raison d'état* of the colonial state departs from Weber's state project to the project of racial domination and its maintenance. In the hybrid model, the bureaucratic sovereign was not bound by the principle of separation of powers, because any legislative body was part of the executive branch of the colonial government. Authority and administrative power were not centralized, nor were they necessarily hierarchical. Officials had wide discretion in decision-making, not only within the legal domain but also in deciding which laws were applicable, or whether situations warranted exceptions to the law. Therefore, decisions were neither predictable nor stable; laws could be annulled or suspended with decrees, and changes in personnel would immediately affect the outcomes of administrative decisions.

Cromer and his compatriots valued administrative flexibility and legal exceptions because flexible decision-making created uncertainty, which made the subjects highly dependent on colonial officials. The concept of effective inefficiency captures the way that inefficiency can serve the overarching goals of a regime. Although modern rational bureaucracy aspires to efficiency, it can benefit from ambiguity, friction, and power struggles as a means to control the population, through procedural violence. Therefore, the more confused the subject is during their futile attempts to decipher the bureaucratic entanglement concerning decisions or the possibility for appeal, the more dependent they are on the system. This dependency disciplines the subject, and fear and uncertainty stymie their actions and enable surveillance and monitoring (Berda 2017: 108–109).

Effective inefficiency was useful to manage populations defined in liminal legal and administrative categories as "legally inferior," while achieving projects of extraction and creating a new political order of space, time, and personhood (Mitchell 2002). In this new political order created by Cromer and his compatriots, it was not their exclusion from but their inclusion in the law that was a colonizing force over colonial subjects which engendered its own form of violence (Esmeir 2012: 9).

HYBRID BUREAUCRACY AND THE MODERN STATE

The effects of explicit racial hierarchies, the absence of sovereignty, and perpetual states of emergency forged a hybrid bureaucracy in the British colonies. Nasser Hussain saw the fragility of the rule of law in the colonies, due to the perpetual state of emergency, not as exclusive to the colonies but as a condition of modernity. The explicit invocation of emergency based on pronounced racial difference made the colonies an extreme case of the fragmented nature of liberal rule of law (Hussain 2003; De 2012: 73). The organizing principles of hybrid bureaucracy are a conceptual tool to deviate from Weber's rational-legal model of bureaucracy as it is imagined in modern liberal states, and trace administrative practices through a lens that acknowledges the political conditions of colonial rule embodied in the routines of administration. However, a closer look at the complexity of Weber's forms of legal domination – and the way that colonialism informed the possibility for imperium to exist within rational-legal bureaucracy – calls into question the historical separations scholars make between imperial forms of administration and state bureaucracy in the modern liberal state. The justification of British imperial bureaucracy as based on a universal rule of law, despite prevalent and explicit racial hierarchies, shifted how the administration worked because of its constant proliferation of population classifications and differentiation of practices based on identity. Racial hierarchy and the inherent inequalities it produced were more prominent than the gaps in sovereignty or authority that distinguish between imperial forms and modern states.

If we are to take seriously the administrative legacies of British imperial rule, following Mahoney and Thelen (Mahoney 2003; Mahoney & Thelen 2010), then we need to view colonial bureaucracy as a set of historical institutions and networks that frame the present, or, from a different perspective, as a historical assemblage of organizations, material practices, and personnel that continues to share the authority and legitimacy of the modern state (Joyce & Mukerji 2017). Although it is not a framework for direct causal evidence of path-dependent legacies, a synthetic model of hybrid bureaucracy is useful to trace trajectories of colonial bureaucracy as a living set of scripts and templates of state administrations that in turn define core political concepts such as citizenship and security through classifications, forms, and possibilities for mobility.

CONCLUSION

The organizing principles of hybrid bureaucracy presented in this chapter, which arise from the self-narration of and correspondence between a network of colonial bureaucrats, are far from a formal model of colonial bureaucracy. However, following Hannah Arendt's intuition that Lord Cromer's writings amount to a "theory of bureaucracy", this chapter challenges the prevailing view that colonial bureaucrats governed based on ad hoc, random, and improvised administrative solutions, and did not operate based on theories of administration.

Cromer was a central figure in a network of British bureaucrats that developed a set of organizing principles particular to British colonial bureaucracy, which was based on racial hierarchy and maintaining a perpetual state of emergency, through fluid laws "to keep peace and good order" that expanded executive powers and the bureaucratic authority to make law. These organizing principles – including racial hierarchy, personalism, wide discretion and administrative flexibility, secrecy, and the constant creation of exceptions – diffused between the colonies through the personal influence of administrators that moved from colony to colony and their negotiations with the Colonial and India Offices, and the circulation of regulations, forms, solutions, and responses to perpetual crisis. The hybrid bureaucracy shaped the repertoire of practices to map and classify populations on a graded axis of suspicion that upended all other categories, matching differentiated practices of mobility and dependence on the administrative structure.

PART II

THE AXIS OF SUSPICION: CLASSIFICATIONS OF IDENTITY AND MOBILITY IN CRISES

INTRODUCTION

Population management, and particularly practices geared toward making populations legible to bureaucratic administration and amenable to techniques of state officials (Scott 1998: 82) require processes of simplification, individualization, standardization, and homogenization. These processes of population management are inherent to any modern nation-state, but for the hybrid bureaucracy that developed in the British colonies in the late nineteenth and twentieth centuries, attempts at population classification were the centerpiece of colonial ordering and maintenance of rule. At first, ethnologies and ethnographies were the colonial forms of knowledge that were used to separate between good, revenue-generating subjects and undesirables, the poor, bandits, and thugees[1] (Singha 2000). The colonial state's hybrid bureaucracy introduced a nomenclature of racial hierarchies into the administrative structure, transforming Weber's imaginary universalistic prerequisite of "without scorn and bias" (Weber 1978: 87) into a complex system that matched sets of rules to specific populations. The principle of racial hierarchy meant that even when government bodies operated based on a single law, different populations were governed through different bureaucratic practices in the same territory, so administration was more concerned with regulating and monitoring population movement rather than controlling territory. Population management practices diffused throughout the empire when colonial officials transferred from colony to colony, when delegations of officials were sent to train at other colonial locations, and when the colonial administration adopted laws and regulations that were in turn revised at the local level of a particular colony and returned to legal advisers in the Colonial Office for scrutiny. This was particularly the case during moments of crises when the colonial administrations needed both methods and expertise to address population control during inter-communal conflicts. The less-known crises were not those of insurgency but the administrative crises of governing populations, as intercommunal conflicts turned into national ones in the twentieth century.

Gradually, free movement itself was perceived as a threat to the colonial administrations' attempt at organizing and ordering the daily life of the state, a threat that reached its peak between the two world wars. Although Michel Foucault omitted the anxieties of racial hierarchy from his definition of governmentality as "power that defines its population as its target, political economy as its major form of knowledge and apparatus of security as its technical element," the classification and movement of the population were the central concern of colonial bureaucrats, for both capitalist extraction and securing authority of the colonial state (Mongia 2018).

Keeping "Peace and Good Order": Monitoring Mobility through Emergency Laws

The security apparatus transitioned from a "technical element" and merged into the very way that colonial bureaucrats defined the population and its relationship to the state (Legg 2008; Berda 2013), through an array of emergency laws enacted to help police and administrators "keep the peace and good order" (Tomlins 2006; Valverde 2006; Raman 2018: 123). Because colonial bureaucrats needed to effectively implement this vast array of emergency laws, home departments and district commissioners categorized populations according to a scale of suspicion or undesirability, so that clerks and police would know which populations were targets of administrative measures or monitoring. In turn, local bureaucrats and police informed classifications of suspicion, through lists and reports, and the routine classifications they made regarding applications for mobility permits and licenses. Colonial officials making these classifications were not, as sometimes depicted, all-powerful, violent, and manipulative (Graeber 2015) – or running a messy system of racialized tropes orchestrated by local elites (Fuller & Harriss 2000) – but worked through administrative negotiation between bureaucrats and themselves (Mathur 2016) and with different population groups. Personalism, an organizing principle of hybrid bureaucracy, meant that the category of the applicant and the category of the civil servant, within their departments, affected the results of the request for a license, permit, or post.

Two Axes of Population Classification

In India, Cyprus, and Palestine, bureaucrats attempted, through the forms and templates they employed, to understand and control both imagined and material aspects of identity through the classification of populations. I argue that there were two axes of classification in British colonial rule: categorization of populations according to demographic traits and classification according to the security threat that a population posed to the state. Suspicion upended other types of classification, shifting constantly according to changing political or economic needs in each location, or in the wake of an agenda of the home department or official. Practices of classification circulated in the horizontal circuits of the British Empire as each colony developed specialized administrative expertise shared and innovated upon in other colonies.

In the second axis of classification, the colonial state classified people according to their relationship to the government: loyal citizens, collaborators, and cooperators, and those of doubtful loyalty, suspects, and enemies. These were not only used in times of crisis or counterinsurgency but were central in the administration of the everyday. Clerks recorded the different categories of suspicion in the rubric marked "recommendation" on official forms. Sometimes, these categories were explicitly stamped in the box for "evidence of good character" that existed on the forms people used to apply for posts as civil servants or to request special status as British nationals or British-protected persons.[2] For example, in India these categories were also included as placeholders for describing "antecedents," a staple of every application for residency, naturalization, or nationality.[3] They were noted in the endorsement letters for people applying for passports, travel permits from state to state, and on applications for permit to travel to sensitive areas such as Kashmir, which had its own set of published rules for visitors.[4] Classifications of suspicion as well as an updated list of suspects were also included in the fortnightly reports that district commissioners generated from the Ministry of Interior.

Classification according to suspicion infused the creation of census categories and administrative forms. While statistical surveys, reports, and censuses did not create a uniform template of rule, they enabled the hybrid bureaucracy to operate a selective and differentiated project of governance (Raman 2012: 230). Population classification entailed three processes, which took place simultaneously: individualization, in which the individual is a distinct object of surveillance and control; standardization, in which populations are grouped into manageable categories even if they are distinct communities; and homogenization, in which groups are lumped together according to involuntary traits and lines of distinction (Loveman 2014: 28). Census procedures, representation in the civil service, and limited participation of colonial subjects in the work of rule of India, Cyprus, and Mandate Palestine were sites of negotiation with subject populations which were suspicious of the colonial administrators and of each other. Groups negotiated with the administration over classification, as a form of acquiescence or resistance to colonial rule, as well as the shaping of national projects and, later, partition. (In Palestine, see Sinanoglou 2016; for Cyprus, see Rappas 2008.)

The Horizontal Circuits of Diffusion: Classification by Suspicion

The particular legacies of classification in India, Cyprus, and Israel/ Palestine developed through what Laleh Khalili (2015) has called the "horizontal circuits of empire" through inventories of knowledge, expertise of civil servants, laws drafted by the Colonial Office, and negotiations with local leadership (see also Stoler et al. 2007: 9). Processes of classification reflected the different anxieties and anticipation of hostilities in each colony (Stoler 2002), and did not form a uniform template of rule that was applied wholesale at the moment of conquest. Yet through processes that can be defined as "diffusion" or "circulation," they were deployed as part of an organizational toolkit that transferred between India, Cyprus, and Palestine, as well as other colonies.

Research on circulation between colonies has been a response to scholarship that privileged accounts of diffusion from metropole to colony, rather than addressing the impact colonial rule in each colony had on the metropole and on other colonies (Cooper & Stoler 1997; Go 2018). Hussin (2014) argues that circulation anchors diffusion of law (and, by extension, bureaucratic practices) to particular movements of people, rather than the adaptation of wholesale models. Beyond the mobility of laws and practices, circulation acknowledges the temporality of legal and administrative diffusion during particular moments of crisis (Mawani 2014). These advances in the circulation of law and practices between colonies resonate with the early sociological institutional theory of diffusion, in which Strang and Meyer (1993) suggested that the conditions for diffusion are cultural linkages between categories or social actors. These links are part of the cognitive map of actors or organizations (Strang & Meyer 1993: 491). Common categories produce similar institutional structures through a process of institutional isomorphism (DiMaggio & Powell 1983). This homogenization is influenced by the standardization of dominant organizations (such as the Colonial Office), or by imitation in times of crisis (such as uprisings). Practices diffuse rapidly if there is a general theory or model about the cause and effect of practices, and furthermore when there is a distinct population or category of potential practitioners, called adopters (Strang & Meyer 1993: 498).

These theories have been mostly applied to trace the diffusion of policies and practices from a metropole to peripheries (Go 2018). However, a relational account of the way bureaucratic toolkits of classification diffused between the three colonies in times of administrative crises fits well with this set of assumptions. Such an account emanates from the archive where a competitive politics of comparison accelerated circuits of knowledge production and imperial exchange, between the colonies and between other empires (Stoler 2010a: 39). The diffusion of bureaucratic practices traveled with theories that officials created about similarities and differences of populations, what types of policies would be effective or legitimate, and a great deal about making exceptions, which was an organizing feature of hybrid bureaucracy. Practices of population classification did not only diffuse through colonial officials who exchanged expertise and adapted paper formats and enumeration techniques, like the census commissioner in Palestine who sought the help of former commissioners in India to enumerate the Bedouin. They also diffused through the comparisons that local leaderships made between themselves and colonized groups in other territories when negotiating with the colonial administrations, particularly as partition was advanced as a solution.

Officials in the central offices often aggregated information from district commissioners, creating a theory about populations that would then be transferred to the Colonial Office, such as which tribes should be designated as criminal tribes[5] (see also Major 1999; Brown 2001), or which population groups were considered as "dangerous populations" or bad characters (e.g., Bryant 2003). These theories usually justified measures for restricting movement or confining entry into certain areas. However, official theories represented only one type of diffusion because, as each location developed its own practices of population management, it also shifted perceptions of the kinds of practices and forms that were needed, the regulations required to implement those practices, and the methods to make them legitimate.

Adaptation and innovation of the colonial toolkit of classification were informed through officials' interaction with the community and negotiations between departments. On the one hand, implementation of practices from the Colonial and Foreign Offices were negotiated with local governors, but domestic politics in Britain also greatly influenced such policies. On the other hand, the colonies themselves were cosmopolitan, and while some officials were acutely aware of the global impact of their decisions, others were oblivious to it and surprised by its circulation. In times of crisis, as officials sought answers and solutions, while they did not appreciate prescriptive solutions from the Colonial Office, they gladly received a script for a set of practices or a template for an administrative form.

Part II follows the development of the axis of suspicion that linked identity to loyalty in Mandate Palestine, India, and Cyprus by tracing how officials classified their populations from loyal subjects to suspicious subjects to threats to the state. This classification was driven by an expanding repertoire of emergency powers, as well as the escalating intercommunal conflicts around classification, statistics, and census enumeration, as partition neared. It focuses on the origins of the colonial bureaucratic repertoire inherited by the independent states.

Chapter 2 begins with how population movement itself became a threat to British colonial administration in the aftermath of Ottoman rule in Cyprus and Palestine, and the Mughal Empire in India. It then traces the development of the colonial census as a toolkit between the three colonies, demonstrating how the battles over census categories in the colonial state were to affect administrative forms and classifications in the wake of partition. Chapter 3 focuses on the development of an administrative toolkit for monitoring mobility, based on emergency laws developed in India after the First World War, and the way that toolkit diffused, innovated upon, and transformed during times of crisis, as the colonial governments attempted to quash anticolonial and intercommunal uprisings in Palestine and Cyprus.

Forms of Suspicion: Mobility As Threat, Census As Battleground

TRANSITION TO THE BRITISH COLONIAL "STATE"

British official accounts of the transition from the Muslim empires that proceeded them, the Mughals in India and the Ottomans in Palestine and Cyprus, indicate a sharp shift in organization and administration, presenting themselves as savior bureaucrats that have come to order the shambles of unruly and backward administration. In Cyprus, British arrival marked the end of the rule through the millet system, in which communities communicated with the imperial state through designated leaders, and the anticipated abolition of official hierarchies and their replacement with a minimal form of equality before the law, which was to enable public participation in negotiations with, or resistance to, the new colonial power (Bryant 2004). It also marked the fall of Turkish Cypriots from ruling community to numerical minority when in 1878 Cyprus passed into British rule, which used it as an army base. In 1915, during the First World War, Britain had offered the island to Greece, but Greece rejected it (Varnava 2017: 3), a move that fueled the Greek Orthodox majority claim to *enosis* (unification with Greece).

In Palestine, British military rule in 1917 was supplanted by a civil administration similar to the crown colony in Cyprus. British arrival marked the singling out of the Jewish minority as the community that would bring progress to Palestine, perceived as a "backwater of the ottoman empire" (Norris 2013). Championing economic self-sufficiency, the Jewish minority were considered European proxies of colonizers, whom the British could identify with to some extent (Yacobi 2015: 3–5). The Balfour

Declaration had been incorporated into the Mandate, so the civil administration's mission was to promote Palestine as a national home for the Jews.
The legal text of the Mandate would later become a major political obstacle
for British rule in Palestine. It divested the British of the legal power to enact
the one policy that could appease the Arab population, for whom Jewish
inclusion was proving to be a gradual exclusion: stopping Jewish immigration and acquisition of land.

In India, the transition from the Mughal Empire that ruled over a non-
Muslim majority to the British Raj was mediated by a patchwork rule of
the East India Company until the mid-nineteenth century. The Company
state was a militarized entity preoccupied with legal justification for its
actions and obsessed with the statistical knowledge and intelligence
reports that formed the basis of its rule (Raman 2018; Saumarez Smith
1985). The colonial states' preoccupation with classification and development was exemplified in anxieties about populations that moved around
too much to be effectively monitored and ordered.

Chapter 2 compares two elements of colonial population management
through the axis of suspicion across the three colonies: monitoring of
mobility and battles over population classifications and census forms.
But first, a very brief history of Mughal and Ottoman legacies of population management is in order.

Mobility As Threat: Monitoring Movement As the Crux of British Colonial Administration

It was not only British colonial administrators that believed groups who
moved frequently across territories were a threat. The engagement with
the harnessing of mobile communities, whether they were native or indigenous or not, conceived of as tribal or nomadic, was central to imperial
civilizing projects, from the Romans and Chinese who labeled their tribal
and nomadic adversaries as "barbarians" to the Ottoman rulers who
incorporated tribal interests into efforts to expand and consolidate imperial state power (Kasaba 2011: 8), despite their perceptions of tribals in
Palestine as underdeveloped (Amara 2018: 920).

The difference with modern colonial empires was that modern European
empires saw nomad populations as a threat to their conceptual legal order
(Shamir 1996). Moving populations defied administrative control, creating
anxiety about lawlessness at the margins of the state, as Das and Poole write
(2004), or at the imperial frontier (Kolsky 2015). The margins and frontiers
were not designated territories; they were created by failed attempts to

regulate the mobility of populations. British imperial bureaucrats, echoing the social scientists of their time, made a point of showing they harbored the view that previous rulers – the Mughal Empire in India and the Ottoman Empire in Cyprus and Palestine – seemed to "permit mendicant and pilgrim throngs, pastoralist and hunting bands, and other itinerant communities . . . without sufficient scrutiny" (Singha 2000: 151). When some of the British colonial projects to settle these communities failed to destroy traditions of mobility, their members were regarded as suspicious (Kothiyal 2016: 213). Tolerance of vagrant communities such as Bedouin, ascetics, and gypsies (Lucassen & Willems 2003) allegedly reversed the stabilizing effects the administrators expected from the caste system in India and the religious divides of the millets in Cyprus and Palestine. However, when we view British colonial bureaucracy as a hybrid bureaucracy, based on racial hierarchy, administrative flexibility, secrecy, and personalism, rather than a model of rational-legal bureaucracy, the declarations of imperial officials regarding their modern difference from the previous despotic empires seem less convincing, and the legacies of population management in the premodern empires more significant.

The Mughal and Ottoman empires had elaborate systems of population management and classification as well, but their partially patrimonial bureaucracies categorized relationships to the state and their regulation differently (Subrahmanyam 2006). British colonial modernizing efforts relied on the more flexible administrative and legal infrastructures (Barkey 2008) the Ottomans had applied to govern the mobility of populations, also in Palestine and Cyprus, more persistently through identity documents from the end of the nineteenth century (Kasaba 2011; Gutman 2016). Much of the Mughal network of surveillance and reporting survived the transition to East India Company rule. Similarly, Ottoman census practices that denied rights to populations because of their mobility, particularly the Bedouin (Frantzman et al. 2014), were incorporated by British officials into the imperial census. These legacies were justified by colonial officials as continuity with previous categories, while at the same time boasting new scientific methods of measurement and enumeration, which shadowed the role of practices they had inherited from the Ottomans in Cyprus and Palestine. Decisions to keep or discard the administrative templates of classification and suspicion as they took over Palestine in 1917 and Cyprus in 1878 were critical, considering some of the performative orientalist gestures of disdain toward the perceived backwardness and unscientific methods they inherited from Ottoman methods of rule over subject populations (Deringil 2003).

LEGACIES OF SUSPICION FROM THE MUGHAL AND OTTOMAN EMPIRES

In the seventeenth-century Mughal Empire, loyalty was a great source of power, established through a vast network of informants. A constant scrutiny of loyalty and suspicion, classifications, and categories of worth based on loyalty were ensconced in the information flows. Mughal imperial structure built political power on a centralized bureaucratic apparatus that included revenue collection, record-keeping, and local administration under the patrimonial, loyalty-based *mansabdari* system (Gilmartin 2017). Networks of scribes included official and clandestine reporters and advisers (Fisher 1993).

In the territories that came under its military power after 1757, the English East India Company combined some of the scribes, the *Akbar nawis*, with its own network of British agents: Residents (Fisher 1998). Residents reported on virtually everything: disposition, genius, talents, character, connections, views, interests, revenues, military strength, and even domestic histories. Each Residency had an "Intelligence Office" to coordinate, translate, and interpret the information these agents and other informants gathered, and to assist the Residents in drawing up regular analytic reports for the Company (Bayly 1999). The reports that Residents sent to the East India Company later evolved into a format of fortnightly reports of the home department of the government of India, which included a suspect list at the end.

In the Ottoman Empire, any Muslims who held national allegiances or identification with lands, languages, or people outside the empire were suspicious, yet diversity of loyalties was a prominent feature of administrative organization of the millet system (Gingeras 2016: 94). The millet system, a loose set of central-local administrative arrangements, was a script for multireligious rule that was not equal across communities (Barkey 2008). Intermediaries with a real stake in maintaining the status quo administered various religious communities, which were organized into autonomous, self-regulatory units that regulated loyalties to the state, within the communities (Barkey 2005) while creating a legibility of the population for the state through community institutions of registries.[6]

The Ottoman census classifications first lumped populations into religious categories, then into millets, and finally into categories of mobility. The census takers in 1831 tried to determine the exact number of Muslim and non-Muslim males registered in three age categories: below sixteen, between sixteen and forty, and above forty. The middle group were listed in separate conscription registers that were turned over to the army. Christian and Jewish males were not yet subject to military service, but they were required to pay the head tax and therefore were enumerated and divided into the traditional three categories of wealth according to ability to pay. Those unable to pay because of destitution, old age, or infirmity were listed separately; non-Muslims were recorded according to millet, with a separate register for foreigners, who were termed "Franks" (Behar 1998).

Census enumerators counted nomadic tribes separately based on estimates supplied by their chiefs. Bedouin tribes knew that the Ottoman state considered them to be a suspicious population, and the Ottoman state knew that the census "terrified the population" at the edges of the empire. Nevertheless, Ottoman administrators stressed the need to establish administrative and political divisions to deploy executive power and control the population (Deringil 2003: 327).

In India, the upsurge of colonial administrative efforts to categorize the population began after the 1857 rebellion, when the East India Company established a specialized department charged with registering, indexing, and archiving individual biographies of colonial subjects (Singha 2003: 88). By the end of the nineteenth century, the British had built up ethnologies to distinguish between those who provided good raw material as productive, revenue-generating subjects, and those whose peripatetic way of life made it difficult to tax, surveil, and police them.

As the Indian economy integrated into the global market for labor and commodities, new institutional contexts emerged in which colonial subjects had to verify their identity. Modernization was changing the role of the district colonial official who "knew the people" (Singha 2000: 156–157), so local knowledge and individual experience would not suffice. Surveyors, emigration agents, the sanitary inspector, the official vaccinator, and the postmaster were all roped into the project of collecting census data. By the twentieth century, every official in the colonial state was, in some way, part of the process of collecting, processing, interpreting, or implementing data about the population through lists, reports, and tables that found their way to the desks of the district commissioners. The most central and prominent element of population management was, obviously, the imperial census.

CENSUS AS STATE TOOLKIT, CENSUS AS COMMUNAL BATTLEGROUND

The transition from Mughal and Ottoman rule to British rule marked the transition of Muslims to the category of demographic minority in India and Cyprus (Devji 2007: 126; Bryant and Hatay 2020) and transposed the

Jewish community from a minute religious minority without a homeland to a population working to establish a national home with the support of the world's strongest imperial power. The census turned into a demographic battleground between communities, with the rise of organizations and institutions that turned religious minorities into political minorities.

Contemporary debates in sociology of the state focusing on the role of statistics are between those who employ the cultural and cognitive views of the state, which emphasize official statistics as a vector of state power that constructs population categories and, through them, constructs race and ethnicity (Loveman 2014; Hacking 2007), and those who challenge the view, claiming that social categories in the census are also the product of societal pressures and negotiations (Emigh et al. 2015; Mora 2014). This critique has been deployed regarding societies in the West but is particularly salient to the colonial census, which became a central inter-communal battleground within the context of partition.

The consensus on the role of the census is that it is the primary source of information for any state, and systems of official statistics are fundamental to the constitution of state administration (Leibler & Breslau 2005). The growth of statistical capabilities is dependent on government departments and organizations, and, in turn, statistics serve as the quantifiable infrastructure of policy (Desrosières 1998).

The British colonial census was a vehicle of administrative knowledge to control populations, but also a grand biotechnical project to perform modernity, a way in which bureaucrats and experts justified their mission of keeping the peace, promoting social order, and ushering in economic development through data. The imperial census has been studied as an artifact and a fetish of the officials, with its systemic quantification of ethnoracial identities (Anderson 2006: 163). Census commissioners and superintendents were often "official anthropologists," notorious for their racial beliefs, and were enthusiastic about turning ethnologies into statistical tabulation. At times, their technical innovations for enumeration and delineating new groups also helped ignite communitarian and nationalist identities that eventually undermined colonial rule (Appadurai 1993: 315).

This section compares how hybrid bureaucracy in different states deployed the census as a toolkit of government, in which categories of religion language and region gradually solidified into ethnonational identities. Through attempts at standardization, homogenization, and separation, communities were constituted as essentially different, which justified selective pairing of administrative practice to population. These processes also constituted communities as majorities and minorities, so the census became not only a site for negotiation between subjects and officials but an arena for rivalry between communities (Kaviraj, in Chakrabarty 1995: 3378). Suspicion or embrace of enumeration techniques depended on one's proximity to negotiation over resources, amid fears of control. As important as the census was in shaping the growing suspicion between communities and toward the colonial government, enumeration did not supersede the role of daily practice and social life in the creation of identities (Guha 2003: 151–152). Communities negotiated categories of religion, region, and ethnicity, categories that they adapted, innovated, annulled, and readopted, as they diffused through government departments between provinces.

Colonial census commissioners sought to convey the ethnological complexities of the societies they ruled in statistical terms, yet they persistently made "religion the central factor superseding all forms of social relationships" (Jalal 2002: 40), in a communalist perception of representation (Devji 1992). Although the imperial governments sought and systematically failed to produce comprehensive statistical surveys of the empire, each colony classified the population according to its own set of criteria and purposes (Christopher 2005).

The bureaucratic toolkit of classification changed in each colony along with local politics, as the meanings of "race," "language," and "religion" were interpreted by the bureaucracy, eager to demonstrate that enumerative practices were justified by "science and modern administration." In Cyprus, religious and linguistic classification gradually merged into ethnonational categories, creating a binary of representation between Greek Orthodox Cypriots and Turkish Muslims, and basically leaving all other minorities out. In India, the colonial census was a political battleground where suspicion of Muslim communities entrapped in the category of "minority" drove a challenge to religious and linguistic classifications, the fluid category of "Hindu," and the very integrity of enumeration. After partition, the refugee census included sets of questions about not only demographic characteristics but also loyalty to the state. In Palestine, the shift away from classifications according to religion, from Muslim, Christian, and Jewish to Arab vs. Jew, created a categorical separation that would grow into differentiated practices of policing, land ownership, development, and access to information.

Even though racial hierarchy was the most prominent organizing principle of hybrid bureaucracy in the writings of colonial bureaucrats about their perceptions of colonial subjects, there were no clear administrative definitions of race.[7] For example, in India, the census commissioner in Calcutta used "race," "nation," and "caste" almost interchangeably: "It is no exaggeration of language to describe the population of Calcutta and suburbs as an agglomeration of races, for no less than 397 separate nationalities, races and castes are returned" (India 1913: 41). When driven to justify the term "race," the census commissioner in Malaya in 1932 explained how political allegiance and social affinities were intertwined:

The term "race" is used ... in a particular sense, for lack of a more appropriate term, to cover a complex set of ideas of which race, in the strict scientific sense, is only a small element. The term race is used for census purposes ... a judicious blend, for practical ends, of the ideas of geographic and ethnographic origin, political allegiance, and racial and social affinities. (Vlieland 1932; see also Hirschman 1987)

In an examination of the census as a bureaucratic toolkit in Cyprus, India, and Palestine, the term "race" was mostly used to differentiate between rival communities. The next sections follow the attempts of census commissioners to promote generalized processes of standardization, homogenization, and separation as they grappled with the particularities of conflicts. As we shall see, in Cyprus, an island of minorities, the colonial census forms themselves created a binary identity, Greek Cypriots and Turkish Cypriots, that translated into separate voting registries and sequences of identity cards, which instituted a binary administrative separation between communities.

Lumping Populations Together: Census Forms and the Making of Binary Identities in Cyprus

In Cyprus, Ottoman rule, which preceded the British, governed through the "millet" system (Barkey & Gavrilis 2016), which empowered non-Muslim local religious communities to operate as semiautonomous civil units, as the empire permitted these religious communities to exercise autonomous legal, fiscal, and educational functions.[8] When the British arrived in 1878, the formal recognition and "modernization" of the millets by the British effectively institutionalized the separation between religious groups that would gradually turn into ethnic classifications (Peristianis 2008: 108; but see also Aymes 2013). The millet system was similarly innovated upon in Palestine, where the Mandate government extended its scope to include Muslims as a millet and invented various communal institutions that were to function, but mostly failed, as the basic structures of communal participation (Robson 2011: 44).

British modernization and the scientific census represented a horrific demise for Turkish Cypriots. They were the "leftover community" from the previous empire; "they had lost their status as ruling millet [in the Ottoman system], and reduced to a numerical minority in a system in which all were supposed to be equal under the law."[9] Despite the ambivalence of officials regarding the question of whether religion or language constituted the key racial indicator, colonial administrators gradually coupled religious identity with linguistic identity to form clear ethnic divisions.

Cyprus was the first colony in which communal representation was first formalized in a legislative council (Peristianis 2008), a decision taken after intense debate among senior officials of the Foreign and Colonial Offices. In response to concerns that a communal approach to representation might divide the two ethnic groups, this approach prevailed because "history, custom and language" had already done that (Hall 1937: 245), and therefore representation needed to reflect the ethnoreligious divide.

The census categories were not only the product of British administrative work; they reflected the process by which Turkish Cypriot leadership attempted to create a body of institutions that could make them into a sovereign community, a demographic minority with legitimate claims to state-like institutions. However, in the binary demographic battle over categories, minorities like Maronites and Armenians were classified as "other" and simply fell out of the administrative landscape of the island because there was no official category to describe them, and no such thing as indigenous Cypriot identity existed (Varnava 2010).

From census to census, the categories of religion and mother tongue had solidified into an ethnonational identity.[10] In 1881, census schedules (questionnaire forms) divided the population based on religion and mother tongue into categories for Greek Orthodox, Muslim, or Other and Greek or Turkish, respectively. In the census of 1931, Muslims who spoke Greek and Greek Orthodox Christians who spoke Turkish were noted, but in the next census they were no longer recorded. By the 1946 census, mother tongue and other cultural markers for ethnicity determined whether a person was either Greek or Turkish.[11]

The census reflected the political changes that had occurred in the long decade of the 1930s. In 1931, political riots in Cyprus revealed the fault

lines between Greek and Turkish Cypriots, culminating in the burning of
Government House, and igniting Turkish Cypriots' deep fear of subjugation. The anticolonial violence was a reaction to high-handed colonial
rule, exploitation, and taxation, against the backdrop of an economic
crisis, and to Greek Cypriot demands for autonomous government
through *enosis* (unification with Greece). The revolt began in the cities,
but spread quickly to the countryside, spreading with it popular awareness of the growing ethnic division that, significantly, did not spark
intercommunal violence (Kitromilides 2019: 112). The British administration's inability to cope with the violence turned into a harsh rule of
emergency that would shape the legal repertoire of the colonial administration in the 1930s, which abolished representation in the legislative
council, suspended municipal elections, and prohibited demonstrations.
This period was notoriously named "Palmerokratia" as a metonym for
the most authoritarian period of British rule in Cyprus, because of the
systemic repression of national sentiments through bureaucratic measures
(Rappas 2008). Repression through emergency went hand in hand with
a plan by Governor Herbert Palmer to instill "public spirit" in the minds
of the Cypriots to secure their obedience.[12]

In the 1940's David Athelstane Percival, the superintendent of the census
of 1946, championed its scientific use as a full survey of a population that
had been "accustomed" to enumeration since 1878, professionally administered, with an experimental design, which he hoped would be used
comparatively by other enumeration projects in the Middle East. Race
was only loosely used to designate distinction. Pointing to the distinction
of two "racio-religious" communities, he explains that demographic differences are much less due to "effects of race and religion" than educational
and economic circumstances (Percival 1949).

Shortly after the census of 1946, Turkish Cypriot leaders proposed
"*taksim*" (partition) in response to the Greek Cypriot movement for
enosis. Bryant and Hatay write that close contact between the Turkish
Cypriot leadership and their counterparts in Pakistan led them to
model their own future on the division of the subcontinent. In the
1950s, this solution took the form of demands for "double union"
that would unite the newly created parts with the "motherlands" of
Greece and Turkey. These demands for self-determination were
imagined roughly on the map (Figure 1), but took hold in the census
enumeration, conducted by village leadership under the payroll of
district commissioners, for reasons of administrative thrift in 1950.
The census was no longer a grand project of development and scientific

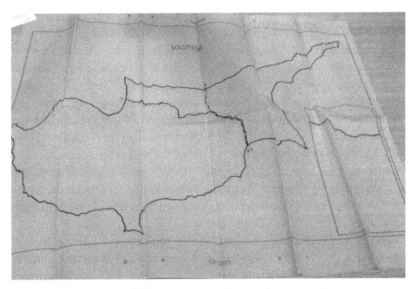

FIGURE 1 Proposed British partition plan during the Cyprus Emergency 1956 (Source: TNA CO/926/546, p. 107)

pride, but a burden, conducted in response to a request by the United Nations.

The pivotal category of distinction was no longer language or religion; it was ethnicity. Instead of language and religion, the plan was to classify people as "Greek," "Turk," and "Other." At this point, the colonial government thought this type of classification was effective and inexpensive "since Mukhtars under supervision of the district staff, coordinated by the statistical officer, can affect such enumeration at negligible cost."[13] It was easier to lump the population into three groups, according to the two languages, and employ a residual category of "other" for all other minorities, which remained to some extent, invisible to the administration.

The census was not taken again in Cyprus until after independence, but the administrative categories dividing Cypriots into Greeks, Turks, and other minorities, had far-reaching implications for the way the two communities, and minorities who were lumped into the category "other," experienced daily life and the growing political enmity between the communities.

Despite the transition in the census into two ethnonational communities, British colonial administrators continued to refer to the division between Greek and Turkish Cypriots as a division between races. Such divisions appeared on both maps and internal reports of the Interior

Ministry, as shown in Figure 2, in which the title of the map includes the word "race" and the categories are Greek, Turk, and Other.

Shortly after its establishment in 1956, the registration department – in charge of instituting a system of registration of residents of the island – compiled separate electoral rolls for the Turkish and Cypriot communities, which played a major role in elections in Cyprus. By 1960, the registration department oversaw the distribution of identity cards to the population, and appointed district inspectors to act as registration officers. Identity cards were issued in numerical sequence, and a person's identity number was never changed.[14] Identification numbers were divided according to ethnicity, a practice that also occurred in Israel, where minorities had a separate series of numbers on their identity cards (Tawil-Souri 2011).

The first census in independent Cyprus took place on December 11, 1960.[15] The Interior Ministry continued to use the classification by race as an adversarial relationship, a language instituted by colonial governments: "In the census of 1960, the population of Cyprus was 577,615 out of whom 448,000 were Greeks, 104, 350 were Turks and 24,408 of other races. Thus the percentage was 81.1% Greeks against 18.9% Turks."[16] Minorities were lumped in with Greek Cypriots "against" Turkish Cypriots, turning Cypriot identity into a hyphenated one because, as Costas Constantinou writes, "in post-colonial Cyprus, being simply and singly Cypriot is a constitutional impossibility" (Constantinou 2008). The constitution defined citizens of Cyprus as being either of "Greek origin and spoke Greek, or shared the Greek cultural traditions or belonged to the Greek Orthodox Church" or of "Turkish origin and spoke Turkish, or shared the Turkish cultural traditions or who were of the Muslim faith." Citizens outside of these two defined communities had to elect membership into either ethnic group. When the Republic of Cyprus gained independence, its power-sharing constitution granted 30 percent of civil service posts to Turkish Cypriots; Turkish Cypriots held fifteen out of fifty seats in parliament and their own communal chamber.

When, in 1963, the president proposed constitutional changes, Turkish Cypriots walked out of parliament in protest. Violence erupted and the Turkish minority retreated to armed enclaves. Greek Cypriot legislators unilaterally abolished the bicommunal nature of the state. The constitution was suspended and, a state within a state, the institutions of the Turkish Cypriot community operated in enclaves. The Cyprus government, which was now a Greek Cypriot government that

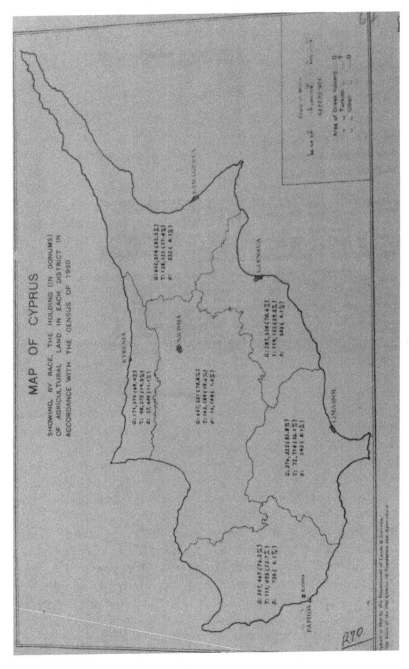

FIGURE 2 Land ownership map by "race" Cyprus census 1960 (Source: CSA/MI/82/196)

75

operated without the partner community required by the constitution, had no access to demographic data about the Turkish Cypriot community. It also lacked data regarding land in the Nicosia district, since such records were housed in the government building in Konak Square, which had become the Turkish Cypriot enclave in Nicosia.[17] From 1963 onwards, the census collected demographic data that was primarily about Greek Cypriots and other minorities, as the administration had limited abilities to engage in population management. From 1963 to 1968 Turkish Cypriots lived under siege, in the enclaves. Although they formed government institutions, they did not collect systematic demographic data.

The role of census categories in Cyprus shifted and changed in tandem with both the intensification of the intercommunal conflict and the British attempts to manage and control it through bureaucratic means. The conflation of categories of religion and language, and its sloppy grouping into "race," was a signature British imperial formation, in which manipulation of population classifications built upon indigenous ones in ways that inflected local politics about which the British administrators initially were only dimly aware and indirectly concerned. Nevertheless this meant that census categories and techniques of enumeration, and the forms and categories of the census, participated in the formation of the binary, mutually exclusive identities in Cyprus. Lumping together the categories of religion and language as the primary markers of division, the loose language of "racial" divide, used to describe every type of difference, on the one hand, and the adversarial language of "ratio" between populations, to delineate allocation of resources and posts in reports and maps, on the other, were to shape and reify nationalist discourses, while using emergency laws to repress them. In other words, the census forms and rough maps of partition contributed to nationalist divisions, while suppressing self-determination by bureaucratic means.

Distinctly different from in Cyprus, which was strategically significant but perceived as a backwater of the Empire, in India the production of census data on a national scale was celebrated as the epitome of scientific achievement and administrative devotion, in which ethnography was forged into statistics for administrative benefit. D. A. Percival's grandfather Athelstane Baines, who was the national census commissioner of 1891, wrote the early census definitions of "Hindu" and "Muhammadan" that became crucial for the political battles of the 1930s and 1940s, when the focus moved from caste to religious and then national identities. After

partition was introduced, enumeration was both resisted by subject populations and embraced by local elites that engaged in the demographic
battles.

Separating Populations: Census As the Battleground of Partition in India

In India, population statistics on religion and language were particularly
critical because communities demanded entitlements from the colonial
government based on regional population numbers. Despite debates
about whether the census created or reified categories of identity, there
is little doubt that as a process of objectification and commensuration to
contract administrative knowledge (Cohn 1989) enumeration was
a major site for manipulation and negotiation between communities and
colonial bureaucrats. It was where scientific techniques and administrative definitions not only served administrators to designate categories of
loyalty and suspicion but also created suspicion in rival groups of each
other and of colonial bureaucrats.

From the mid-nineteenth century, Muslim, or "Mohammedan," was
a fairly stable category, while the plethora of religions and faiths practiced
by non-Muslims were lazily lumped into the category of "Hindu," based
on a directive of the census commissioner in 1881 "that every native of
India must be presumed to be Hindu unless he belongs to some other
recognized faith."[18] Lumping various religious groups under the category
Hindu was the product of data collection, interpretation, and application
of categories that viewed Hinduism as the default religion (Haan 2005). In
1911, the census commissioner distinguished between religion and territorial belonging: "Hindi means any native of India, and Hindu means
a non-Muhammadan native of India."[19] He also was aware that the
religious fault line that guided the classification of Hindus and non-
Hindus was upended by social classifications, mainly along caste lines
(Bhagat 2006).

However, as partition neared, religious classifications in the census had
flared up as sites of contention. One of these sites was the battle over the
category of Adivasis[20] (i.e., "tribals" or "original inhabitants"). This
battle was one small episode in the way colonial policies shaped the
relations between those categorized as tribes and others, through categories of suspicion and regulation of mobility (Sundar 1997), in which the
fluctuating definitions of "original inhabitants"[21] were harnessed to the
battle of headcounts. The 1931 census considered Adivasis – who held

a distinctive set of faiths and religious and cultural practices – to be Hindus; but by 1941, the census rules had changed. Adivasis were no longer classified as Hindus, but as tribals. The reclassification of Adivasis was the result of a successful negotiation on the part of the Muslim League with the census commissioner.

In tandem with the negotiations, the Muslim League had launched a massive protest campaign across India against the government of India, the census commissioner, and the census superintendents of Bengal, Assam, Bihar, Central Provinces, and Bombay, requesting that they rectify their classification of "Santhals" and other "tribals" as "Hindus."[22] Otherwise, the League had warned, Muslims and other minorities would have no choice but to challenge the entire census, and would have to demand a new census "by a cent-by-cent paid staff, under gazette officer appointed with fair representation for all communities in the census agency." The League achieved its demand to establish a separate category for tribals. To create the distinction of "tribals" as a separate category from Hindus, the commissioner issued new instructions to the census enumerators in Bengal in 1941 that focused on classifying rituals and religious practices:

If he says, he observes Bakrid – write Mohammedan, if he says he observes Diwali write Hindu, if he says, he observes Christmas write Christian. If none of the above festivals are observed put an X. In the case of aboriginals that are baffled by the question, ask if they observe the festivals that their ancestors observed. If the answer is yes, do not write any further but write the name of the tribe.[23]

The campaign to separate tribals had been successful, where numbers would later affect the partition maps. According to the 1941 census, the entire undivided Bengal Presidency had 61 million people. In the census, 54 percent were classified as Muslim, 42 percent were classified as Hindu, and 3 percent were classified as tribal.

The contention escalated further during this campaign, as Hindu parties and organizations complained to the viceroy of their suspicion that the rising number of Muslims was due to irregularities carried out by Muslim census enumerators (see also Maheshwari 1996), especially regarding the mandatory census questions on caste and whether people wrote in Hindi or Urdu script. The response to the trumpeted suspicions, of M. W. M. Yeatts, notoriously named "the Iron-willed census commissioner," was radical (Rath 2011). Yeatts not only refrained from tabulating the returns on written language but also made the extraordinary recommendation to the government that it drop any inclusion of language and script altogether, "until the population of India is able to respond to a factual inquiry on them."[24] Disgruntled by the lack of public legitimacy for statistics on language, Yeatts failed to understand that public resistance to manipulation of the written language was not only fueled by communitarian demographic politics but was a precursor of a type of participation in census politics that would later engender popular investment in independent India's democratic politics of universal franchise (Shani 2017: 20).

The prospect of partition exacerbated the demographic battles because population numbers became evidence for future territorial claims, or so they were perceived (Jones 2014). But despite his awareness of the political power of the census, Yeatts thought that public involvement had been surprisingly passive and was worried about participation in enumeration processes.[25] In 1940s India, as partition became a real possibility, the politics of numbers flared up, and battles over census categories, particularly the imagined binary of Hindu/Muslim, had significant effects on participation and enumeration in the census itself. Both community leaders and colonial officials conflated representation as "standing on behalf of" with representativeness as "coming from a particular community" (Sundar 2000; Appadurai 1993).

But perhaps the most dramatic decisions Yeatts made in 1941 were to introduce individual returns (instead of enumerating households) and discontinue the enumeration of caste in the census. Yeatts justified shifting away from costly All-India tabulations of caste that he thought had catered to scientific interests throughout the British Empire. Instead, he proposed using categories for nationality and religion, which were more useful to the government; knowledge about the caste system should be "left to anthropologists."[26] Finally, the 1941 census produced very little data, which led to further anxieties in the Home Office and preoccupation with classification as partition neared.

Subjects to Suspects? Loyalty and Suspicion in India's Refugee Census of 1948

Yeatts remained census commissioner when the first independent India Census Act was promulgated in September 1948 and died by the end of the year. For Yeatts, a bureaucratic entrepreneur, the census was a major national project that grew the state's infrastructure and the loyalty of its civil servants: "the Indian census is a tour de force carried out by enlisting the full weight of the provincial and state administrations ... every district collector should feel himself part of the organization which produces this fundamental data."[27]

For the national census, celebrated as the first administrative event when the population turned from subjects into citizens, nationality became the primary category, instead of religion, race, caste, or community, which had been the primary classifications of the colonial government. Since 1872, the rubric "race, tribe, or caste" had been the central category for gathering information. In the 1948 census enumeration, Yeatts introduced a two-tiered question about nationality and community belonging: "What is your nationality? If an Indian national, state your community or tribe."[28] Yeatts justified the consolidation of categories as thrift, but it reflected an attempt to politically shift away from the principle of racial hierarchy that fueled the proliferation of categories during colonial rule toward lumping together broader categories of the population.

The first census included a count of those who had become refugees and displaced persons because of partition violence.[29] The refugee census was a critical component for not only establishing rehabilitation efforts for the displaced population but also shaping the civil service in Bengal and Punjab through the appointment of refugee civil servants. In the refugee census, the axis of suspicion was explicit, no longer a set of classifications hidden in one's antecedents or endorsements. Instead, a list of questions attempted to gauge one's religious practices, language, and affinities of belonging, including past and recent mobilities, that indicated loyalty. (See also Roy 2012: 13.)

The official schedule of the refugee census defined a refugee both spatially and temporally. The census determined their status based on the time and location of their entry into India (although the borders of independent India were still in flux), which had to be after March 1, 1947, and their declared reasons for leaving their residence, which had to be either "civil disturbances" or other consequences of the "setting up of the two dominions of India and Pakistan." Although the government published the refugee census only in 1951, classification as a refugee in 1949 had immediate implications for access to relief, rehabilitation resources, and government positions that were determined according to identity (Kaur 2007).

The questions on the refugee census schedule revealed the logic through which the administration attempted to classify the displaced population: one set of questions collected information on their demographic characteristics, and a second on their degree of loyalty to independent India. The census included questions about religion and regional belonging in Pakistan, and it collected information about the value of any immovable property the family had owned in either Pakistan or the Indian union prior to partition. Questions regarding the outcomes of displacement were on contemporary location, employment, and rehabilitation benefits accessed.[30]

Very different from the binary identity in Cyprus of religious and linguistic ethnonational identities forged into Turkish Cypriot "minority" and Greek Cypriot majority, religious categories in India were upended by classifications of loyalty and suspicion in the regions destined for partition. Because religious categories were fluid, as populations shared regional languages and other social markers, the axis of suspicion was highly significant in delineating identity.

But perhaps there was no place where the suspicion of enumeration and the significance of performing impartiality and administrative expertise by the bureaucratic officials were more dominant than in Mandate Palestine. There, the census was viewed as an essential tool for the economic development of the native Arab population and the promise of the British colonial government to develop a Jewish national home.

Separating Populations from Religious to National Categories in Palestine: Jew vs. Arab

The end of Ottoman rule in Palestine did not change the status of the Arab population from ruling community to numerical minority as it did in Cyprus. When the British declared military rule of Palestine in 1917, Jews and Christians were each 1:7 in terms of the ratio to Muslims.

Census categories in Mandate Palestine reflected the rapid change both in political conditions and in British population management policy that occurred in the two decades from the Balfour Declaration stating Britain's commitment to building a "Jewish National Home" in Palestine in 1917 against vocal opposition from the Arab population. The declaration revolutionized the politics of the Middle East in its recognition of the Zionist project and provided a "protective umbrella" that enabled the Zionist movement to proceed toward its goal of establishing a Jewish state in Palestine (Shlaim 2005: 251). The Balfour Declaration was the baseplate for a system of dual colonialism (Shamir 2000; Said 1992: 57) that ensconced Jewish settler colonialism within the British hybrid bureaucracy directed, through differentiated and uneven practices, toward the entire subject population.

At the outset of their rule in Palestine, British officials initially chose religion as the key ethnic division between populations,[31] materially dividing Jerusalem into four equal quarters, which was not the way communities in Palestine experienced their relationships with each other, or with the state (Tamari 2000; Campos 2010; Jacobson 2011). In their efforts to maintain the "millets" as stabilizing institutions of rule (Robson 2011: 44), the administration practically constructed an imaginary Muslim millet that they perceived as a semiautonomous community. Rather than determining national identity, the British introduced census categories that produced the frame for nationhood itself (Wallach 2011). By conflating Jewish nationality with religion, and officially legitimizing settler colonialism in the Balfour Declaration (Banko 2016: 57), a parallel administrative Arab identity emerged, which, by 1931, was incorporated into the census.[32]

In 1931, the questionnaires schedule included a new column to record citizenship in addition to the traditional questions of religion and sect. After recording one's citizenship, the enumerators were to add the self-described categories "Jew" or "Arab."[33] The census officials acknowledged that national identity had become a subjective question of belonging, different from religion.[34]

Banko shows how the process for acquiring Palestinian citizenship affected enumeration (2012). In 1925, an order in council offered more favorable means for the acquisition of Palestinian citizenship to Jewish immigrants than to Arabs from the former provinces of the Ottoman Empire, Egypt, and North Africa (Banko 2016: 24–25). Rules for enumerators provided the guidelines for determining someone's category of citizenship. Turkish subjects prior to 1925 who had not assumed another nationality were considered Palestinian. Non-Turkish subjects born in Palestine before 1925 were classified as whatever citizenship they held, "e.g., Palestinian, French, German, etc., etc."[35] If the person was not born in Palestine, enumerators were to enter present citizenship, "e.g., Palestinian, or British, or Polish, or Trans-Jordanian, or Egyptian or Syrian, etc. etc." "Papers" was a category for those who had pending applications for Palestinian citizenship. If the person did not hold citizenship, the enumerator was to enter "none." The final instruction for completing the citizenship column was to record their subjective national identity. The instruction was: "in all cases when any person claims to be 'Arab' or 'Jew,' enter after citizenship 'Arab' or 'Jew,' respectively, e.g., Palestinian, Arab; or Palestinian, Jew." (See also Campos 2014: 586.)

The binary categories of Arab and Jew represented a shift away from the system that categorized people by their religion. Because of the principle of racial hierarchy that matched people's identities to administrative practices, the disparities between being classified as Jewish "provisional" citizens or Arab natives affected people's freedom of movement and their ability to obtain passports and receive diplomatic protection (Banko: 2016). The categorical separation between Jew and Arab in Palestine was the result of the Palestinian–Zionist conflict (Seikaly 2015: 26; Campos 2010), and the differentiated treatment by the British because of the Balfour Declaration and the inherent inequality in British policy marshaled by it (see also Loevy 2021).

The census of 1931 was a highly contested project in the eyes of both the Palestinian communities in Palestine and the Zionist leadership of the Jewish community – the Yishuv. For the Mandate government of Palestine, the census enumeration was an exercise to maintain the authority of British rule and to manage the recalcitrant parties that did not appreciate the necessity of statistical information for the state's progress. In the eyes of Yishuv leaders, enumeration constituted a threat to their claims to a future homeland, despite the rapid growth of what Norris called the "Zionist industrial complex" on the scaffolding of the Mandate administration during this era (2013).

The Census As "Existential Threat" in Mandate Palestine

In September 1931, a call to all Jews to boycott the census enacted by the Mandate government deeply perturbed the Colonial Office. A small pamphlet called for an immediate response from the Zionist leadership against the census ordinance, claiming the census was an existential threat to the Zionist project:

[The census] was part of the scientific program, beginning with Sir John Hope Simpson's inquiry[36] purporting to liquidate "scientifically" the Balfour Declaration and oppress the Jewish community in Palestine. The census will be taken with a view to proving that the Jewish community in Palestine is a "negligible minority."[37]

Whether it was a performative tool for negotiation with the British colonial government or an expression of real fears in the Jewish community, Zionist representatives expressed deep concern about potential census inaccuracies and political tampering by Arabs in the census, "the results of which will be a weapon in the hand of any liquidator of Zionism. Our only response should be to take no part in it."[38]

Eric Mills, the Census Superintendent of the government of Palestine, was painfully aware that the Jewish and Arab communities would perceive his decisions to be political choices either for or against them. As he requested staff and materials, he attempted to record his impartiality and underscore his attention to communal representation: "From the point of view of census administration, it is immaterial to me whether the staff is composed of British, Jewish or Arab persons; but it is probably desirable, from a more general standpoint, to have a staff which shows some sense of balance between Arab and Jew."[39]

The issue of representative "balance" between Arabs and Jews in the colonial administration was a great preoccupation of the Mandate government (Wasserstein 1977: 173); so much so, the royal commission for Palestine later described it as running "a government by arithmetic."[40] Mills's decision to have equal representation in the census team interfered with what he perceived as professional standards, for he clearly held the Jewish statisticians in higher regard: he claimed the only qualified statisticians in the Mandate government were Jews, as neither Arabs nor British staff had such skills. Mills recommended recruiting an Egyptian official, along with two Jews and two Arabs, including David Gurevitz, head of the statistics department in the Jewish Agency; Reuben Katzenelson, head of the statistics department of the Hadassah medical organization;[41] Moussa Nassir, a civil servant in the southern district he described as having "some mathematical training and an accurate mind"; and accountant Fuad Saba,[42] who was to do some of the statistical work of the Arab Executive Committee.[43]

To avoid accusations of political bias, Mills established two advisory subcommittees for the census, one Jewish and the other Arab.[44] The Jewish committee members all had statistical training and battled Mills on his own terms. The Arab committee members belonged to the Arab Executive Committee; Auni Bey Abdul Hadi, Jamal Husseini, and advocate Moghannam E. Moghannam were highly respected and politically savvy, yet they had no statistical training. From the protocols of the negotiations over the census questionnaire, while the Jewish population was a small minority in 1931, the Jewish Advisory Committee had won the battle over the census. The Jewish Agency's central concern was that questions about landlessness and unemployment be avoided in order to protect the land acquisition methods of the Jewish National Fund that were considered politically controversial, not only by the Arab leadership but by some officials in the colonial government as well (Forman & Kedar 2003; Stein 1984). The Mandate government employed a new method of land settlement that registered and redivided village lands in a form of joint tenure – "Musha," inherited from Ottoman law (Atran 1989; Nadan 2018). As a result of this process, Zionist brokers bought cheap land in joint form from absentee owners and granted temporary leases on the land to the Palestinian villagers. After they registered and divided the land, its value skyrocketed. The Arab absentee owners who had sold the properties had to legally displace the villagers once the registration process was underway (see Shafir 1996). Census questions on landlessness and unemployment threatened to expose the scope and extent of the land acquisition process and could have effectively jeopardized the entire settler colonial project.

In the meetings of the advisory committees, the census tables and the questionnaires themselves played a formidable role in the conflict; every form and each category became an arena for political negotiation. The form was more than just a tool of the British administration for classification; it was a means by which they asserted their authority and unsuccessfully attempted to demonstrate their scientific impartiality. Although it was less visible than the maps of partition, the census form encapsulated the demographic fears of the Jews that they would be counted as an insignificant minority in Palestine, and the suspicions of the Arabs regarding usurpation of their lands. The census form and its changes over time became an actor in the demographic battle between communities (Riles 2005: 985), and the meetings a site to contest the legitimacy and authority of the colonial government.

On June 23, 1931, Mills welcomed the Jewish Advisory Committee, expressing his regret that it was not possible to have one joint advisory committee for both Jews and Arabs. The Jewish committee was concerned about the accuracy of the census, considering that so many Jews and Arabs resided in Palestine illegally owing to the severe mobility restrictions on entering Palestine. Despite assurances that the government would not use enumeration as evidence in criminal or civil proceedings, the council worried that Jews who had entered Palestine illegally and had secured identity documents would refrain from participating in the census questionnaires for fear of prosecution or deportation. Beyond the concern that Jews who had entered Palestine illegally would be absent from enumeration, the committee voiced racialized beliefs that Arabs were illiterate, and that Arab enumerators would make mistakes that would go unchecked and unsupervised.

To assuage their fears, Mills deployed his imperial experience of conducting censuses in other colonies to assure the committee of the scientific validity of the enumeration. For example, addressing the committee's concern about the enumeration of the Bedouin population, Mills explained that a Bedouin enumerator would employ a method used in India of nonsynchronous tracts for enumerating tribal populations.[45] Mills reported that, in his unofficial meeting with the Arab advisory committee, they recommended including questions about unemployment, land shortage, and race, and "felt strongly" about the latter.[46] Yitzhak Ben Zvi, who would become Israel's second president, expressed the wishes of the Jewish National Committee to aid the enumeration, warning that: "The census may be a complete failure if the public should suspect it to have any political motive."[47] However, he flatly refused to include the questions regarding unemployment or land tenure that the Arab committee thought were critical, claiming that a demographic census was the wrong method for questions about landlessness. They also wanted to maintain the distinctions between populations based on religion – Jewish, Muslim, and Christian – rather than nationality, ethnicity, or country of origin.

As he attempted to dispel fears, Mills explained that, although the questionnaire was different than in other European countries, it had been successful in India: "the Indian census in India, with one-fifth of the world's population, with almost every possible variation for economic structure, is a better model for Palestine."[48] However, as we shall see in the next section, the census was only one battleground of population classification for the Zionist project that depended on expanding settlement and population.

Population Statistics and the Making of the "Jewish National Home"

Quantitative statistical research was a strategic component of the Yishuv's project of building settlements in Palestine. David Gurevitz, who trained at Stanford University and headed the statistics department of the Jewish Agency from 1924 until his death in 1947, was considered the Jewish Yishuv's primary expert regarding demographic studies, the census, and its effects upon the achievement of a state for the Jews in Palestine.

The Yishuv leadership was extremely unhappy with the new categorization by nationality, in which the colonial government lumped Muslims and Christians into the single category of "Arab," because they wanted religion to remain the primary political category.[49] Categorization by religion would enable them to make an important distinction between Muslim Arabs and Christian Arabs, one that the Jewish establishment hoped to leverage politically in their national struggle. Christian Arabs were overrepresented in the colonial administration in proportion to the community, and they were perceived by both the British and the Yishuv as possessing better technical skills and speaking more western languages, and in general were higher on the scale of the bureaucracy's racial hierarchy. Although Christians comprised only one-tenth of the Arab population of Palestine, the number of Christian Arabs and Muslim Arabs in the civil service was almost equal.[50] This situation created enmity between Muslim and Christian Arabs that enabled the Jewish establishment to form ad hoc political and economic alliances with Christian Arabs.

When an influx of Jews fled Nazi Germany and Poland for Palestine in the 1930s, the Arab population regarded it as a political and economic threat, and the Mandate government reduced immigration quotas on Jewish immigration and tightened enforcement of entry into Palestine. During this time, the Jewish Agency began independently collecting its own population statistics. The Jewish Agency generated statistical reports using religion as a category, while government statistics shifted to a national distinction: Jews vs. Arabs.

A decade later, Gurevitz harbored a growing concern about the discrepancies in the numbers of Jews as recorded in three statistical sources: the 1931 census of the Mandate government, Department of Migration population reports, and Jewish Agency data. He attributed the differences to the administrative categorization of the Jewish population – people the Mandate government classified as illegal immigrants,[51] and viewed as being ineligible for naturalization.[52] Population classifications critically affected the representation of each community's allocation of civil servants. While the identity of the civil servants and the deployment of the axis of suspicion would change in passed onto the national administrations following independence, the politics of classification during the mandate would shape the way bureaucrats perceived the boundaries of citizenship, national loyalty, and their own political affiliations.

CONCLUSION

The processes of the bureaucratic negotiations around freedom of movement and census classifications and procedures described in this chapter were shaped by the particular shifting racial hierarchies in each colony, but ordered through similar perceptions of bureaucrats in their

88 *Forms of Suspicion*

negotiations with national elites, as anticolonial struggles turned into intercommunal ones.

In Cyprus, the homogenization of communities, through the conflation of categories of religion and language into the significant markers of division, erased minorities and promoted a binary nationalist discourse, while attempting to repress its political manifestation. The use of "race" as a general code for differentiation and the persistent measure of a binary population ratio to loosely justify uneven and unsystematic allocations of resources and posts meant that to be counted one had to be Turkish Cypriot or Greek Cypriot. When the ideas of partition and *enosis* reached their peak, the hyphenated identity was far from an imagining of belonging to the "motherlands"; population ratios were prevalent in every official report. As we shall see in Chapter 4, the ratio as a key for representation of government positions would become the administrative justification to declare the political impasse in 1963 that brought about the legal implosion of the republic.

In India, suspicion went from an implicit and elusive mode of classification of subjects by the bureaucracy to the suspicion of enumeration itself, and a full-fledged intercommunal battle to separate populations as partition became a salient possibility. Very different from Cyprus, where the lumping together of populations steadily created a binary identity, classifications of identity were more fluid and solidified around the campaigns of partition. The work of separating populations, rather than lumping them together, led to questions about daily rituals and religious practice, and the simultaneous abandonment of language and script as markers of identity. In the refugee census of independent India, classification according to suspicion became explicit through new questions of political affiliation, belonging, and mobility.

In Palestine, the census and other population statistics were the centerpiece of the demographic battle that began with the Balfour Declaration and the imperial legitimacy it afforded the Zionist settlement project in Palestine. The census was a battleground of contention and suspicion, where the goals of the British colonial government clashed with the Zionist settlement project. The achievement of a demographic majority, the main goal of the Zionist movement, was not realized during the Mandate period, but the process of immigration and settlement, and Palestinian resistance to them, had shaped the battles over the census. In the 1931 census schedule, the subjective identification by nationality was a precursor to the transition from classifications by religion to classifications by nationality that occurred in the mid-1930s, right before the Arab Revolt that eventually led to the recommendation of partition.

The formal classifications of the census, which were pivotal for quotas of the limited representation in legislative councils or self-rule institutions, the distribution of land, licenses, and government positions, were intertwined with implicit classifications of suspicion. Between the two world wars, the use of a grid of emergency laws, the classification of "dangerous populations," and increased monitoring and restrictions of mobility through routinization of emergency measures expanded the scope and importance of a central organizing principle of hybrid bureaucracy: rule through the systemic creation of exceptions. Population classification according to suspicion and the census categories were crucial building blocks of the bureaucratic toolkit of emergency that diffused between the colonies.

3

The Bureaucratic Toolkit of Emergency

INTRODUCTION: THE ORIGINS OF THE PERMIT REGIMES

After independence and partition, in 1947 in India and 1948 in Israel, bureaucratic officials relied on colonial emergency laws as the building blocks to structure administrative practices in the new states. The reliance on colonial emergency laws was not only a question of legal continuity or state succession.[1] One of the organizing principles of hybrid bureaucracy was the constant creation of exceptions to rules. Emergency laws codified and expanded the power of colonial officials to create these exceptions that in turn became new internal regulations, practices, and documents. The vast repertoire of organizational tools of emergency, inherited from British rule, expanded bureaucratic discretion and allowed officials to match practices to different types of persons based on their identities and political affiliations. Colonial emergency laws were used widely to curb immigration and monitor borders, control commodities, deploy subsidies, and force the manufacturing of supplies. Most important for our story of how bureaucratic legacies shaped political status is how the nascent state bureaucracies also used emergency laws to establish mobility regimes that monitored and prevented the return of refugees exiled by partition violence in India and the Nakba in Israel/Palestine. In India, bureaucrats used colonial emergency laws in tandem with the republic's constitution. Israel never had a written constitution, and emergency laws were central to the state's operation (Gavison 2003). However, in 1960, the new Republic of Cyprus denounced the colonial emergency laws upon its independence, relinquishing the bureaucratic power to a representative constitution that guaranteed representation as the political basis of the republic. While in Israel and India emergency laws were central to bureaucratic power and action in the early decades of the state, used as a baseplate to govern civilian populations, the absence of the bureaucratic toolkit of emergency in Cyprus shaped an entirely different outcome in its time of crisis in 1963, when its power-sharing constitution would be suspended.

This chapter traces how colonial administrations used emergency laws to enact legal-spatial measures that expanded the scope of bureaucratic power in colonial states in the twentieth century, developing into a repertoire of administrative tools to prevent and control mobility. The term "toolkit" is used by sociologists to describe how people draw upon elements from their culture to inform and justify their behavior and decision-making and their strategies of action (Swidler 1986: 273). The bureaucratic toolkit of emergency did not only define what colonial administrators could do but also formed a set of scripts, templates, and classifications to manage populations in times of crisis. These tools ranged from the confinement of bodies, through preventative and administrative detention without trial, to the containment in an area through curfews and closures; the monitoring of movement through blacklists to the declaration of whole towns and territories as "disturbed areas" and danger zones that could be accessed only with a specific individual permit from a district commissioner to denying natives of the colony the right to enter or exit. Instead of separating between criminal law, martial law, and the administration of the everyday state, an organizational vantage point reveals how the bureaucratic toolkit of emergency became the scaffolding of the state apparatus, managed through the ministries of home affairs.

Rather than compare similarities and differences in the way colonial bureaucrats used emergency laws in the political context of each colony, this chapter tracks the development of the bureaucratic toolkit of emergency to control the movement of populations and designated territories in India. It then highlights examples of the diffusion of the bureaucratic toolkit of emergency to Palestine and Cyprus during critical junctures of crisis, when colonial bureaucrats were most preoccupied with managing the movement of populations as the core method of maintaining control throughout the intercommunal conflict and anticolonial resistance.

DEVELOPMENT OF THE BUREAUCRATIC TOOLKIT OF EMERGENCY

At the outbreak of the First World War, when Britain enacted the Defence of the Realm Act across its empire, a series of emergency laws were gradually incorporated into the hybrid bureaucracy. First, the colonial government departments developed practices of surveillance and classification by the axis of suspicion by implementing emergency laws. Second, these practices of suspicion formed a repertoire of spatial-legal practices that originated in India's anticolonial struggle and diffused throughout the British Empire, especially in the interwar period. These practices, which I call the bureaucratic toolkit of emergency, served as a baseplate for the permit regimes that monitored movement in India and Israel, to surveil remainder populations that aimed to return following partition and the Nakba.

Rule by emergency had two principal institutional effects: rule through decrees and the continual manufacturing of administrative exceptions to previous laws (Shenhav & Berda 2009). Emergency laws extensively empowered colonial officials to enact decrees for the sake of "peace and good government," expanding policing powers further (Neocleous 2007, 2011; Tomlins 2006). However, to use emergency laws as effective executive tools, administrators had to classify and categorize the dangerous populations that such laws would target. Obstruction of movement and surveillance of entire populations were as costly as they were unnecessary. Emergency laws thus targeted particular communities that were fluidly classified as "dangerous populations" (Kemp 2004). Identifying "dangerous populations" was a complex matter mostly left to the decision of local administrators. Consequently, the administrative toolkit of emergency bestowed on its colonial officers a broad executive discretion to restrict and define entire regions as "danger zones." The suspicion of the security threat that a community posed to the state was conflated with racial, regional, or other characteristics, producing laws that referred to "criminal tribes" (Mahmud 1998; Major 1999), "goondas" (Nandi 2010), frontier populations (Hopkins 2015), "fanatics" (Kolsky 2015), and other populations defined as hostile and dangerous, classified according to their political leanings, principal occupations, or geographic concentrations, that also enabled the confiscation of the lands of civilian populations labeled as "hostiles" (Sundar 2011).

The development of demographic classifications was a crucial component of rule by racial hierarchy that was intertwined with an axis of suspicion, in which the state classified people according to their relationship to the government, on a scale of loyalty, suspicion, or threat. Classification based on suspicion upended other administrative categories and was a ubiquitous experience that affected interactions with organizations and departments of the colonial state (Mitchell 1991b). These bureaucratic practices transformed the binary opposition between friend and foe into an ever-expanding index of suspicion that not only conflated security threat with political threat (Berda 2013) but provided the potential for manipulation of "intractably divisive primordial loyalties" for the surveillance and monitoring of entire communities, regardless of their political involvement (Stoler 2016: 63).

From the sixteenth century, the Virginia Charter in British colonial America had already deployed sophisticated population management practices, for economic extraction, that mostly harbored an aspect of security (Hay & Craven 2005; Tomlins 2010: 77). Martial law and emergency laws were features of colonial rule beginning with the early colonization by the East India Company. The first statutory legislation of emergency powers in India that relegated authority to the governor general to enact decrees was promulgated in 1861, after the Great Rebellion against the East India Company, in the Code of Criminal Procedure and the Indian Councils Act (Kolsky 2005). Raman shows that the spatial trajectories of martial law developed in relation to a particular threat to the company's monopoly. She demonstrates how, in the early nineteenth century, the splicing of criminal and military jurisdictions turned entire regions into areas where the rule of law was neither in suspension nor firmly in place. The fluidity between criminal law and military law allowed officials to designate different types of laws, courts, and commissions according to levels and types of suspicion (Raman 2018: 137).

The consolidation of the bureaucratic toolkit of emergency in the last decades of British rule turned it into the core apparatus of the state, but rule by emergency was nothing new. One of the most powerful tools of hybrid bureaucracy was the way it constantly created exceptions to rules and expanded bureaucratic discretion. However, despite the lack of representation or separation of powers in the colonial state – what Arendt called "bureaucracy instead of Government" – colonial administrations were preoccupied with juridical normativity. This preoccupation with legality and legitimacy meant that officials used an array of emergency laws that were promulgated and employed as useful tools to clerks, magistrates, police officers, and commissioners to control and crush opposition, monitor population movement, and prevent disturbances to the regime or to economic extraction.[2] Nasser Hussain (2003) shows how emergency laws were a central feature of the colonial state, necessary to uphold its racial hierarchies, which in turn justified the use of emergency measures. The creation of exceptions was not only relegated to instances of crushing insurgency and political opposition; it was a bureaucratic method that enabled expanded discretion, wide flexibility, and the fluid use of laws, decrees, and regulations to govern the civilian population.

The imperial bureaucratic toolkit of emergency was an expanding set of legal-spatial practices for managing populations, developed as an alternative to direct state violence against "hostile populations" (Scott 2009).[3] The classifications of suspicion translated into people's possibility for movement because most of the constraints were directly linked to slowing, monitoring, and stopping mobility.

Fueled by the belief that any form of political activism toward liberation from British colonial rule was a threat to "peace and good government" (Tomlins 2006: 249), colonial governments developed a set of bureaucratic practices of population control and surveillance through emergency laws.

The structure of the rest of the chapter is as follows. First, I explain theoretically how emergency laws changed bureaucratic action and introduce the repertoire of administrative practices of classification and surveillance in British colonial India and the techniques for managing populations that developed there. Second, I elaborate on the range of spatial-legal practices developed in India – namely, border control, travel and exit permits, blacklists, and suspect lists – which laid out the institutional groundwork for permit regimes established to monitor minorities during the first years of independence. Third, I briefly explore how officials and departments facilitated the circulation of these administrative repertoires, particularly in times of crisis, from India to Mandate Palestine and Cyprus by means of four methods, focusing on the innovation and adaptation of practices for managing populations in the last decade of colonial rule. The bureaucratic toolkit of emergency, a practical repertoire of laws, practices, and bureaucratic theories about population classification, scarcity of resources, and political risk, developed and changed as it moved from one crisis in a colony to another and back. The toolkit of emergency shaped population management practices in the final years of British rule, as well as the heavy-handed rule against new minorities in the aftermath of independence.

Population management was consolidated through a plethora of emergency laws. These emergency laws enabled the bureaucracy to decide on possibilities of movement for populations and the individual political and civil rights of colonial subjects. Emergency laws proliferated in the horizontal circuits of the British Empire, its fulcrum located in Bengal, and later Palestine (Silvestri 2019: 279). Inventories of knowledge and legal weaponry (Esmeir 2015), which harbored shifting imaginaries of racial ordering and schemas of "suspicious" populations, were imported from India and Ireland, directly or via correspondence with the Colonial Office, and were innovated upon in Palestine, in the 1930s during Arab Revolt and again in 1945 during the counterinsurgency of Jewish militias, and in Cyprus, where emergency was declared in 1955.

In the last decades before their independence, the administrative spatial-legal repertoire of technologies for monitoring populations became a bureaucratic toolkit of emergency that circulated between India, Palestine, and Cyprus. The toolkit investigated in this chapter included blacklists and suspect lists, monitoring movement of populations across frontiers, exit permits, the designation of "dangerously disturbed areas," the Armed Forces Special Powers Act, and preventative detention and registration of foreigners.

The Registration of Foreigners Act was an early template of the permit regimes. The Registration of Foreigners Act of 1939, established during the Second World War, required police officers and district magistrates to survey the movement of foreigners on a daily basis. The Defence of India Rules of 1939 enacted a permit regime on the frontier with Burma to monitor foreigners and undesirables, instead of a passport system. Officials at the ministry of external affairs attempted not only to tighten identity verification along international borders but also to monitor movement between provinces, shifting the spatial scale of surveillance: "With the object of obtaining a verification of an applicant's antecedents from the authority best qualified to give it, I am to request that ... reference to the Government of the Province may invariably be made before such facilities are granted in another Province or state."[4] The Registration of Foreigners Act introduced an interprovince registration system that would later become a template for monitoring Indians who had turned into foreigners after partition.

BUREAUCRACY AND PERPETUAL EMERGENCY

The hybrid bureaucracy developed under the three scope conditions of the colonial state – racial hierarchy, fractured sovereignty, and perpetual emergency – that shaped its institutions and organizational practices. The disparate administrative mechanisms developed for "subjects," who were European citizens, and "subject races," who were not, were the foundation of the colonial political order (Hussain 2019: 113). Colonial emergency laws have been studied as a set of political tools to quash opposition, and as methods of counterinsurgency against anticolonial struggle. Criminalization of dissent and censorship practices to quash political organizing and decapitate leadership have been distinguished from martial law and other practices to manage civilian populations and labor in the everyday state. Following Nasser Hussain's (2003) early work on the permanent emergency, necessity, and the rule of the law in the British Empire, scholars of colonial rule have perceived the use of emergency laws in the colonies as a "state of exception," based on Carl Schmitt's notorious definition of sovereignty as the executive power to decide on a "state of exception" that suspends the rule of law, in which the primary political distinction is between friend and foes. Those declared as foes are abandoned by law (Agamben 1995: 28, 109). Hussain later presented a different view: that the suspension of law brought about "hyperlegalization" and the proliferation of more emergency laws, racialized classification, and commissions (2007; see also Ballas 2020). Historians such as Lauren Benton have perceived modern liberal legal, judicial, and administrative systems that structured rule in the colonies as fundamentally different from analogous systems of rule in the metropole because of fractured sovereignty and the persistent lack of separation of powers or representation, and the use of "exceptional" and "extraordinary law" (Benton 2009: 197) that stripped subjects of their rights and abandoned them from the rule of law.

However, from an administrative viewpoint, rather than exclude colonial subjects from the rule of law or relegate the state's violence toward them into a "zone of lawlessness" (Hansen & Stepputat 2006), their bureaucratic inclusion in the patchwork of laws, decrees, and ad hoc arrangements was a colonizing force that engendered procedural violence through a grid of emergency laws that ruled their lives, through the restriction and monitoring of mobility. As Esmeir (2012) has argued, the continued state of crisis of the colonial state did not divorce it from the ideal of the rule of law, and its universal humanity and even legitimacy. The hybrid bureaucracy gained legitimacy through the proliferation of rules and the ability to maneuver between jurisdictions of criminal and military law enabled a "rule by law" rather than the rule of law (Neumann 1942: 470).[5] The exceptions of modern colonial law, and the way it roped in colonial subjects through massive sets of rules and regulations, reified it as a universal juridical order and control through inclusion (Esmeir 2012: 242–243; Ballas 2021).

Hybrid bureaucracy used "emergency" as an elastic legal category that allowed colonial administrators to stretch the scope of their executive authority and administrative discretion. While Benton has claimed that imperial administrators had no official handbook and they treated European legal traditions as a "useful collection from which they might draw selectively in crafting colonial legal systems" (Benton 2002: 261), emergency laws provided bureaucrats with a template for administration, easily adaptable because of their universal wording and the possibility to control both the movement of people and the designation of territory. This expansion was messy and uneven, and covered everything from political disturbances such as riots and insurgencies to enacting permit regimes to monitor the movement of suspect populations, procuring manufacturing supplies for extraction projects, or preventing workers from leaving their plots of land as a way to protest taxation.[6]

Decrees were tools of administrative adaptation, but they were rarely innovative. Most decrees were exact replicas of other previous decrees. Exceptions made other exceptions legitimate, and officials constantly compared types and degrees of emergencies to justify the need for another exception.

In India, following the 1857 uprising and the consolidation of British control, the Indian Councils Act of 1861 authorized the governor general to legislate outside the ordinary law-making process in emergency situations by issuing ordinances to ensure "the peace and good government" of India, on the grounds of security, economic instability, or the hostility of the subjugated population. This was a manifestation of a well-established British governance ideology of population management through police powers (Tomlins 2008; Neocleous 2007). Two subsequent framework statutes, the Government of India Acts of 1919 and 1935, which were the legal foundation for what would become India's constitution (De 2018: 7), granted clerks and magistrates emergency ordinance-making authority. Through a process of "civilizing" and legitimizing martial law as police power, emergency powers were incorporated into the peacetime administrative system, effectively routinizing emergency as both a form of governance and a tool of law enforcement (Kalhan et al. 2006).

BUREAUCRACY AND ROUTINIZATION OF EMERGENCY

For the sake of the political legitimacy of the colonial project, bureaucratic power could not be entirely discretionary or arbitrary. The colonial state's excessive violence had to be institutionally legitimate.[7] In the twentieth-century interwar period, the process of formalizing emergency laws to expand administrative power was an ongoing and persistent negotiation between the officials in the India and the Colonial Office and local bureaucrats in other colonies. The attorney general at the time wrote that there "was no such thing in English Law as a regime of martial law which could be established by the mere fact of its proclamation."[8] Despite the consistent resistance of bureaucrats on the ground to parliamentary oversight and to directives from the Colonial Office, the plethora of emergency laws gradually became institutionalized and incorporated into practices and routines of decision-making and administrative regulations. For the officials on the ground, the time-tested companion to martial law was using emergency laws to promote policing powers that defined the spaces of government and restrictions on movement (Valverde 2006).

In a cyclical pattern, more emergency laws, decrees, and orders proliferated during times of crisis and war and were then incorporated into "peacetime laws" (Kalhan et al. 2006: 112). This method, which I call the "routinization of emergency," persisted after independence. Not all emergency regulations were routinized. Of all emergency practices of security and the quashing of political opposition, or of economic emergency measures (Reynolds 2012), those that remained after major crises were orders that differentiated between jurisdictions, restricted movement, designated areas as dangerous or disturbed, and created more opportunities for surveillance, to satisfy the growing demand for documentation that established one's identity in order to move.

EXPANDING THE BUREAUCRATIC TOOLKIT OF EMERGENCY

In India, the bureaucratic capabilities for monitoring movement developed and expanded in the interwar period, as the preoccupation with security threats during the First World War exacerbated anxieties about growing anticolonial resistance. Officials incorporated powers they received in the emergency laws from the general Defence of the Realm Act,[9] first promulgated in London at the brink of World War I and extended to the colonies. As a departure from the legal and scholarly separation between criminal law and martial law that distinguishes between laws to confine individuals and laws to control movement across territories, this section demonstrates how, from an organizational point of view, the use of criminal laws for the detention of individuals; military laws to designate regions as disturbed or dangerous; and to institute curfews, closures, and monitoring movement of civilians-formed a repertoire of spatial-legal tools, on a growing scale of severity, which I call the bureaucratic toolkit of emergency. In turn, this toolkit would circulate to Palestine and Cyprus, among other colonies, and would shape the bureaucratic scripts of monitoring populations in the new states.

Emergency laws were used unevenly by the bureaucracy that incorporated the Defence of India Act and Rules, the Detention and Restriction of Movement Act, the Armed Forces Special Powers Act, Public Safety Acts, and Disturbed Areas Acts. In the 1930s, emergency defense regulations[10] granted extensive powers to conduct (without a warrant) arrests, searches,[11] seizures, and deportations; and to enact retroactive legislation and preemptive punishment, such as administrative detention without trial.[12] These regulations enabled administrators to suspend basic rights, such as habeas corpus and the right to due process, to confiscate private property, and to enact sentences for deportation or even the death penalty for political insurgents. Their regulations authorized the restriction of individual movement[13] by forming checkpoints and roadblocks, declaring an area to be either a "closed zone" or a dangerously disturbed area, and preventing the movement of civilians. These provided the hybrid bureaucracy with a consolidated set of tools, which had already existed but were now more organized, more accessible, more standardized and adaptable.

The bureaucratic toolkit of emergency included blacklists, detention and registration of foreigners, closed military zones, the designation of "disturbed areas," exit permits, confinement to the colony, preventative detention, and military rule. These tools were on an escalating scale of severity, from the confinement of the body in detention, to confinement to a particular territory, to monitoring and surveillance and the prevention of free movement.

The identification of threats, from either individuals, groups, or regions, was the first step in the effective deployment of emergency laws to prevent or monitor the movement of individuals or monitor the boundaries of particular territories. The fluid axis of suspicion for classifying the population according to loyalty or threat was formalized in the interwar period into a particular form of data, blacklists, that were to become a central tool of the bureaucracy's population management project.

Tools for Monitoring Individuals: Blacklists

Lists of people or communities deemed undesirable or dubious circulated from the mid-nineteenth century. Their systematization and expansion into blacklists began with the deployment of new emergency powers. The British Home Office suspect list began in World War I as a list of criminal offenders that had escaped the law. It quickly expanded to include impostors, spies, and other enemies of the realm. While at first the list was focused on the movement of foreigners, gradually such lists enabled the administration of emergency measures to turn the executive powers given in the emergency laws into effective administrative tools of population control. The clerks and officers adapted and produced categories of suspicion, which were fluid, changing over time, and always subject to the discretion of civil servants, intelligence workers, police officers, and border security guards.

Although blacklists were primarily used for surveillance of movement, they were also used for deterrence, as punishment, and to recruit collaborators. Blacklists were born out of messy collaborations and negotiations among rival officials and organizations that competed to define security priorities and delineate definitions of loyalty.

During the Second World War, as borders were established and surveillance tightened in India, the suspect list gained prominence and was incorporated into the administrative practices of identification, sent by the Home Ministry to all provincial governments and district commissioners. In India, creating and maintaining blacklists were a prerequisite for the permit systems that colonial administrations established to prevent or slow down population movement. The process of obtaining a permit was also an administrative opportunity to gather intelligence. Methodologies for the compilation of blacklists varied across India, but like most administrative tools to monitor foreigners drew much administrative attention and debate at maritime border entry points such as Calcutta.

In 1942, the Calcutta Security Control Officers described the frustrating practice of checking foreigners' entries, with no less than four separate suspect lists: the war security blacklist; the Home Office suspect list; the Intelligence Bureau's list of suspect seamen; and a miscellaneous blacklist. As one colonial officer reported, "Every ship submitted a crew list and each crew list means approximately 1.5 hours of work for each officer. The list is then further checked against the record of security office's own information and means a further 1.5 hours of work each for two officers."[14] Upon entry, colonial officers updated and then dispatched the lists to immigration officers.

The suspect list was an artery of information; not only did it enable immigration officers to prevent suspects from moving freely, leading to detention or confinement to a particular territory, but it was also a method of surveillance and intelligence gathering. The instructions for the use of the index suspect list[15] emphasized its utility for monitoring movement: "In all cases where a passenger arrives whose name is in the index, a report should be sent to the chief inspector. Reports made by telegram or telephone should be followed by a written report."

However, the structure of the blacklist lent itself to intelligence gathering, in the absence of a rubric to record suspects' locations. The form consisted of the following categories: name; date of birth; nationality; and description of occupation and/or political tendencies. This last column reveals the peculiar logic of the blacklist. The boundaries defining suspicious populations were constantly in flux, and, as a result, either a person's occupation or their political tendencies could render them suspect: fascist, prostitute, ship's cook, merchant agent, soldier, lawyer, journalist, motor mechanic, tailor, assistant, salesman, communist.[16] While the classifications that landed one on the suspect list were fluid and unpredictable, the degrees of suspicion were static for natives as well as foreigners. They ranged from "loyal subjects" to those of "dubious loyalty," to "suspicious persons," and finally, "enemies of the realm."

Suspect lists were both technological devices and sites for collaboration and negotiation between the Home Department, the criminal investigations department, and district commissioners. Used across India, the suspect lists required a great deal of effort to manage their dispatch, storage, and communication.[17] The British colonial administration incorporated blacklists into various permit regimes that monitored population movements in times of communal unrest or popular uprising. Although colonial administrators enacted permit regimes during emergencies, they gradually became an inseparable part of the day-to-day administrative routines during peacetime. A good example of the routinization of a permit regime was the opening of the frontier with Burma in 1944. The government of India decided to use Articles 24 and 25 of the Defence of India Rules (DIR) to enact a permit system that would prevent anyone from entering India without a permit. A. W. Lovatt, the undersecretary for the political external branch of the Home Department, justified the use of the DIR in peacetime:

The government of Assam already possesses the powers under rules 24 and 25 of the Defence of India regulations to control traffic across the frontier, although those powers were originally delegated for use in the event of hostile activity in India. We may agree to their using these powers during the continuance of military administration in Burma.[18]

The Home Department routinized emergency so rules that had been enacted to regulate traffic in a time of war were used in a civilian border control system. This was a curious move, considering that the Indian Passport Act and Rules of 1921,[19] although cumbersome, provided ample authority and sufficient procedures for border surveillance through verification of documents, and had already been used, generally to keep out "undesirables" (Sherman 2011). However, using the DIR meant granting full discretion to security forces regarding the fate of those considered suspicious upon entry, including the ability to detain or restrict their movement within their village.

Blacklists monitored individuals across India, functioning as growing archives of the types of person that were deemed suspicious and merited surveillance. During the Second World War, another tool for monitoring populations who were designated as "dangerous" or suspicious was the classification of security detainees.

Classifying Groups: "Suspicious" Civilians and Security Detainees

On the northeastern frontier of India during World War II, particularly in Assam, all persons entering India from enemy-occupied territory, such as Japanese Occupied Burma, needed to pass through interrogation centers, after which they were transferred into a holding camp for "reconditioning" and "rehabilitation."[20] At the interrogation centers, border police and interrogators classified civilians into "Blacks," "Whites," and "Greys," according to their assigned level of suspicion, which was a matter of official discretion. As one secretary explained, "An exact definition of the tests on which this classification is made is impossible to give, circumstances of each case need to be considered regarding what is known of the enemy's activity."[21] The classification categories were loosely based on the following formulation: Blacks were actively cooperating with the enemy and were a high risk for spying; Greys were types of people that worried the authorities enough to restrict their movement; and Whites did not pose any security risks. Officers of the interrogation center detained Blacks and treated them as dangerous security prisoners whom they closely guarded.[22] They released "Greys" but confined them to their villages for a month, and they released "Whites."[23]

The colonial officials sent the list of "Greys" to their respective provincial governments so that they could enforce the restriction orders, based on the detention and restriction rules. Restriction orders from the central government confined persons to their villages or districts for a period of up to six months "with a view to preventing [the person] from acting in a manner prejudicial to the defence of British India."[24] These restrictive orders were part of the process of repatriation of security detainees. Thus, for example, in the case of Purkha Ram from Jodhpur, "restrictive orders ... should be passed on him confining him to a given area and insuring he has not freedom of movement or association. However, he may be allowed sufficient freedom of movement within the state to enable him to earn a livelihood and yet enable the police to keep him under surveillance."[25]

The procedure for classifying "Blacks" who were of Indian domicile, right before their general release at the end of the Second World War, demonstrates how classification according to suspicion became a shared language and means of communication between the police, military, and provincial and central governments, all of which had very different administrative agendas. "A copy of the interrogation report under which a man is recommended for classification as 'black' was forwarded by the Eastern command to the C.I.D of the province to which the man concerned is being released."[26] The shared meanings of classification by suspicion enabled a more standardized view of what kinds of people, actions, and movements constituted security threats.

The bureaucracy's management of security prisoners was critical to the politics and tactics of counterinsurgency employed by the British, particularly when intercommunal conflicts splintered anticolonial and national liberation movements. Therefore, the colonial administration's classification of former security detainees and suspects was especially important when there was a political decision to release prisoners or attenuate enforcement against members of a particular national movement.[27]

After the Second World War, political prisoners were grouped into two main categories: those who had been convicted of offenses of a political nature and were either serving a prison sentence or awaiting execution of a death sentence, and those who were detained without trial. Those who were detained without trial were classified into four categories: members of the Indian Congress Party (Category I – also referred to as Gandhiites); those considered to be dangerous "detenus" (Categories II and III – terrorists, saboteurs, and other politico-criminals); and goondas,[28] who were criminal security prisoners (Category IV).[29]

Standardizing the security classification of all prisoners across the provinces grew into a major problem. The messiness and unevenness of classification was a point of contention in the Home Department, whose staff faced considerable pressure from the central legislative assembly to fix discrepancies in the classification and treatment of prisoners. Home Department officials attempted, relatively unsuccessfully, to standardize the reporting and classification of security prisoners for all provinces:

A very real degree of uniformity has been secured. This is ... Illustrated by the fact that the assembly has rather swung away from the general question of treatment of security prisoners to the specific case of alleged hardship, maltreatment ... classification and non-classification, carried on for congress security prisoners as well, [in Bengal and Orissa] that had not yet classified their security prisoners.[30]

Standardization was a crucial policy issue because how prisoners were classified determined the conditions for their release based on political developments. Members of the Indian National Congress convicted of nonviolent offenses were assigned a separate category. However, Home Department officials were anxious about categorizing prisoners according to the degree of violence of their actions: "all persons serving sentences for crimes committed in the course of the congress rebellion had committed serious offences and it is quite safe to say that the activities for which they are in jail go right outside non-violent political activity." One Home Department official commented that despite the "difficulty of defining political crimes" and "deciding what 'crimes of violence' are, it is necessary that the provincial governments do so."[31]

After independence, when the Indian National Congress turned into the leading political power, despite the difficulty of defining the legitimate boundaries of what exactly made political activity a security threat, the political affiliation of political prisoners became the Home Department's primary category of classification. Although Congress activists were no longer detained, the tools of administrative detention – that is, classifying opposition leaders as security prisoners and issuing restriction orders that prevented entry or exit from provinces that were opposition strongholds – continued against others.

Mechanics of Foreigner Registration: Monitoring Circus Performers and Enemy Aliens

The bureaucratic templates for monitoring movement in the Home Department grew with efforts to control the movement of foreigners into India. The mechanics of registering foreigners in India at the peak of the Second World War are particularly worthy of attention because these were the templates and scripts of bureaucratic practice that appear, almost in their exact form, in the post-independence/partition permit regimes.

By 1940, as the scope of monitoring populations burgeoned into a major preoccupation, the Home Department split into two branches – political internal and political external,[32] the latter charged with monitoring the movement of foreigners and maintaining the Home Office's suspect index, which we encountered in the earlier section on blacklists. A year later, the political external branch divided yet again, which created a political external (war) branch that was responsible for monitoring enemy foreigners.[33]

Populations that moved around often were a major source of anxiety for the Home Department's Intelligence Bureau. Although these practices predate the Second World War, as security tightened during the war, the department made repeated attempts to standardize practices of surveillance across India.[34]

For two years, the Home Department held an ongoing discussion and negotiation on procedures for the administration of surveillance of foreigners.[35] The massive correspondence on this issue reflected the different views held by provincial government officials, who based their opinions on "disturbances" they experienced on the borders that they monitored, the types of foreigners "their" borders attracted, and how much they perceived the tightening border as a "problematic one."

The Foreigner Registration Rules required foreigners to register where they lived and notify the authorities every time that they were more than five miles away from their registered residence. Two examples of foreigner registration, circus performers and enemy aliens, demonstrate how the bureaucratic routines to monitor foreigners turned movement itself into a suspicious activity for certain groups. As movement was registered, recorded, and reported, it became an event worthy of administrative scrutiny and suspicion. Each of these events invited an opportunity for bureaucratic discretion and intervention, even in the most mundane activities.

Circus and amusement performers were especially problematic because of their peripatetic livelihoods. They moved constantly and needed an exemption from the burden of registering every day with a different official. Correspondence on the issue of peripatetic foreigners reveals the logic of the colonial foreigner rules, a logic that had an important effect on the formation of the permit regimes a decade later. The issue of circus performers goes to the heart of population management – it was not that acrobats were particular security threats to the Raj but that their movement was administratively difficult to monitor and record. Unpredictable mobility made them a threat that demanded attention.

Besides circus performers, "enemy foreigners" were another major problem. Section 32 of the Foreigners Act of 1940 required that an enemy foreigner obtain a travel permit to visit another district. The internal administrative rule was that the registration official in the district to which the foreigner desired to travel had to consult with the provincial government where the foreigner was a registered resident, before granting a permit for a journey. When a foreigner halted for more than twenty-four hours, they had to report their arrival to the police; these check-ins had to occur within twenty-four hours of arriving at the new location, and the foreigner was required to use a specific form to submit their identification information. The local police would then post the form to the office where the foreigner was registered permanently.

The general goal underlying the foreigner rules was to tie the foreigner to a particular place in India. Every foreigner had to have a registered address, and there had to be an officer personally responsible for watching each foreigner. Ideally, this officer worked within the district in which the foreigner was registered.[36]

In Assam, which was considered a problematic borderland in the northeast, the procedure for issuing travel permits for enemy aliens was adapted from "the provisional instructions for the control of foreigners in war."[37] If foreigners wanted to change residence, they had to request a permit from the civil authority in the district to which they wanted to move. If it was in another province, they had to obtain written permission from the Deputy Inspector General of Police. If an enemy foreigner was more than five miles from their registered address for more than twenty-four hours, they had to report daily to the civil authority. Rather than being defined by where the foreigner actually lived, residency was determined based on documents they were able to procure as evidence for their residency, similar to what modern states demand as evidence of "life center" from those wishing to establish residency or citizenship.

The travel permit was not only filed in the issuing office and carried by the applicant. Once issued, officers had to send "a duplicate of every travel permit ... to the registration officer of the district of the foreigner's destination."[38] The chief secretary cautioned the registration officers, "an enemy foreigner travelling without a valid permit, or varying his itinerary or not reporting daily in the absence of more than 24 duration (unless he has been definitely exempted from such reporting) is liable to severe penalties." Therefore, in order to obtain a permit, a foreigner had to obtain consent from three officials: one in the district of their residence, another in the district of their previous residence (to check for antecedents), and a third from in the district to which they desired to travel. Obtaining a travel permit as a foreigner was no easy task.

Classifying Territory: Closed Military Zones and "Dangerously Disturbed Areas"

The repertoire of legal tools for monitoring populations ranged from confining persons to the colony itself or to a particular district or village, to declaring a dangerous space, and even to requiring permission for everyday movement from district commissioners or security forces on a regular basis across a designated area.

Based on the Defence of India Act, the Detention and Registration Order of 1919 provided officials with powers to confine and restrict the movement of suspicious persons or communities to an area. The Bengal Special Powers Amendment Ordinance 1946[39] gave local police inspectors the power to declare curfews and to require that people travel with a valid permit. Breach of curfew became a new criminal offense under these laws, and persons who violated curfews were subject to up to six months in prison.[40] The Madras Disturbed Areas (Special Powers of Armed Forces) Ordinance 1947 granted the head constable authority to fire upon those who contravened orders such as curfews.[41]

The Punjab Public Safety Act of 1947 provided "for special measures to ensure public safety and maintenance of public order."[42] Its third section established a regime under which the magistrate could confine suspicious people to any geographical area, and such persons had to obtain a permit from the magistrate to enter or to exit a territory, which could be as large as a district (because people could not be deported from their own province). Declaring an area as disturbed or dangerously disturbed also had consequences for the impunity of armed forces in their action against civilians.

The technologies of rule for monitoring populations were on an escalating scale of severity and scope. On one end of the scale were practices that restricted an entire population from moving freely in a large space, such as exit permits. On the other end of the scale were measures that prevented particular people from moving at all. Preventative detention was a measure reserved for persons whom the state considered a potential security threat or political threat because they stirred political opposition. Yet these measures were considered part of a bureaucratic repertoire in which confinement to the colony, or demanding an exit permit, was an alternative to mass detentions.

Exit Permits and Confinement to the Colony

John Torpey (2000: 12) argues that the invention of the passport as a technology for monitoring population movement began with the exit permits that states established to prevent young men from defecting during wartime. He posits that identity documents were initially part of an agenda of state penetration, whose purpose was to contain people within the national territory so they could be drafted. This history of the exit permit becomes a little different, however, if one shifts the gaze from France and Germany to British colonies.

Exit permits were a method to monitor persons leaving the colony, particularly those who were on suspect lists, at times justified as an alternative for mass administrative detention. The requirement for exit permits in the British Empire began with the Defence of the Realm Act (1914) and diffused to India, where all persons regardless of nationality were required to request permits to exit. These permits were conditioned on obtaining a "no objection" certificate from the military authorities or police.[43] The demand for these certificates created opportunities for monitoring the population, updating registries, and gathering information. In India, the sole purpose of exit permits was for surveillance rather than for expanding the administrative capacity of the state. The colonial governments in both Palestine and Cyprus used exit permits during times of popular uprising, at first to monitor the exit of suspicious persons and closer to partition as a general requirement for the entire population.

Preventative Detention

Preventative detention is rarely viewed as a bureaucratic tool to prevent mobility. In her study of spaces of confinement in contemporary counterinsurgencies, Laleh Khalili (2012) argues that preventative detention is part of a repertoire to prevent freedom of movement. From a bureaucratic perspective, preventative detention is the most severe restriction on mobility. The modern form of preventative detention in India emerged between the two world wars in the Defence of India Act of 1915 and the Emergency Powers (Defence) Act of 1939. These laws expired at the end of the wars, to be replaced by acts such as the notorious Rowlett Act[44] and the Bengal Criminal Law Amendment

Ordinance.[45] These acts permitted the government to detain any person thought to be a threat to public order, national security, or the maintenance of essential supplies. The Rowlett Act was a focal point of Mahatma Gandhi's noncooperation campaign against the British Raj in 1922, when popular opposition to preventative detention was intense and fierce. The government allowed the act to lapse, but continued to detain persons through executive decrees, which Prime Minister Ramsay MacDonald notoriously characterized as "government by ordinance."[46] It was really a regime of civil martial law.

In 1935, the Government of India Act changed the administrative structure of the government, redistributing legislative authority between the federation and the provinces and promoting an "Indianization" of the administration. As the Indian National Congress (INC) Party leadership entered the provincial governments, they strove to repeal the emergency powers that the British established before 1935. An election manifesto from 1936 promised the INC "will take all possible steps to end the various regulations, ordinances and acts which oppress the Indian people and smother their will to freedom."[47] However, by 1937 they began to use the emergency powers themselves. The provincial governments enabled preventative detention in the Public Safety Acts.[48] The efficiency and convenience of using the British tools against militant political opponents and splinter groups of the national struggle perpetuated the legal framework, garnering the support of Congress Party members, who had previously opposed the DIR vocally.

Besides preventative detention, the primary administrative legacy from the colonial government was the spillover of emergency powers from wartime to peacetime; the DIR were incorporated into Public Safety Acts, and Home Department officials advised provincial governments to use the exact same detention orders against persons who were "potential threats to the state," but to issue the order with the phrase "the public safety" substituted for "the defence of British India."[49]

That said, officials were constantly debating and negotiating, and disagreeing about the use of emergency measures and the constant stream of exceptions created in the hybrid bureaucracy. The legislative department, which opposed granting military commanders the authority to declare martial law, criticized provincial governments when they enacted martial law ordinances.[50] Some Home Department officials believed that emergency measures carried out by the administration should be formally incorporated into the law. They claimed that if there were a few emergency powers, "it might be justifiable to retain as part of the law of the land ... to deal with serious internal trouble, if it arose ... in the form of another massive civil disobedience movement."[51]

Between 1946 and 1950, during the transition to independence, almost all provincial governments enacted Public Safety Acts to replace rules that had lapsed at the end of the war. They included the authority to detain persons because of their political action against the state, including aiding workers' strikes:

The provincial government if convinced that any person acting or likely to act in a manner prejudicial to public safety, order or tranquility, or is fomenting or inciting strikes with the intent to cause or prolong unrest among any group or groups of employees may ... make an order ... that he be detained.[52]

After independence, India's provisional parliament enacted the Preventive Detention Act (PDA) in 1950. The PDA was highly contested and challenged as unconstitutional.[53] An opposition leader demanded from the council of state:

Will government state why even on the advent of national government at the centre and congress ministries in most of the provinces, ordinances have been issued authorizing detention without trial, arbitrary imposition of collective fines, executive control of public meetings, serious curtailments of civil rights of the people and the continuance of the defence of India rules in some form or another?[54]

Yet, the Indian Supreme Court ruled that it fulfilled the constitutional prerequisites to curb civil rights for the sake of national security.[55]

Armed Forces Special Powers Act

The Armed Forces Special Powers Act (AFSPA) is the most controversial and contested legislation in India (Akoijam & Tarunkumar 2005; Singh 2007). Originally known as the Armed Forces (Special Powers) Ordinance,[56] this regulation was established during the Second World War to protect the eastern borders of British India from the invasion of Japanese forces.[57] It was a departure from the Internal Security Instructions of 1937, which provided that "Indian States Forces units shall never be employed for internal security purposes outside the state to which they belong except in extreme emergency."[58] However, the colonial government used the ordinance throughout India in its attempt to quash the civil disobedience campaigns of Gandhi's Quit India movement.

After the war, the AFSPA was extended to certain parts of India and incorporated into local orders.[59] In 1946, the Home Department was concerned by "shoot on sight" orders issued in Bombay against rioting civilians. The department determined that the AFSPA did not grant immunity to those soldiers who had not issued warnings to disperse an assembly,[60] and they therefore suggested the order be worded according to the AFSPA model:

Members of the public will be liable to be shot by troops or police operating in any area affected by such crimes if they failed to halt when challenged by a sentry or do anything to endanger property, which it is the duty of such troops to protect.[61]

Through the impunity that it granted the armed forces in relation to actions against civilians, including arrests without warrants, damage to property, and even the killing of detainees, this act codified a categorical distinction between ordinary citizens and those who allegedly engaged in violence. The latter were construed as a "dangerous population" and stripped of their rights as citizens (Samaddar 2006: 30). This categorical divide was entrenched through the spatial zoning of so-called disturbed areas by security forces using the act.

During the process of partition, the central government declared that Bengal, Assam, East Punjab, and the United Provinces were "disturbed areas" in which the civil authorities would require the support of military forces to administer civilian life, and where the security forces were granted special powers (Lokaneeta 2021) and immunity against litigation for violations of civil rights. The reasons for and boundaries of a "disturbed area" were flexible, with the latter sometimes encompassing an entire state (Baruah 2014: 190). The impunity granted by the AFSPA resonated with article 34 of India's constitution, which "provides for indemnity to public servants and others for any action taken by them for the maintenance or restoration of order in any area where martial law was in force."[62]

After independence, the provisions were incorporated into the Assam Maintenance of Public Order Act of 1947[63] to confer extraordinary powers on armed forces to control the insurgency of the population in Nagaland and Manipur, which had become a "constitutional problem" for the central government (Akoijam & Tarunkumar 2005). Between 1947 and 1953, "disturbed area" acts that were like the AFSPA incorporated measures from the colonial ordinance regulating the movement of individuals, associations, and political activities. These "disturbed area" acts empowered officers to shoot and kill, conduct searches, arrest people without warrant, and impose collective fines. The article that protected officers from any legal proceedings against them[64] was the core of the still current AFSPA of 1958, promulgated as a temporary measure but consistently used in India's northeastern provinces and in Jammu and Kashmir.

DIFFUSION OF THE ADMINISTRATIVE TOOLKIT OF EMERGENCY

The administrative toolkit of emergency, the bureaucratic repertoire for managing the daily lives and mobility of "dangerous populations," is best described as an "imperial formation" of practices and categories, which was produced and diffused in the British Empire's moments of crisis, an active contingent process of its making (Stoler, McGranahan, & Perdue 2007: 8). The diffusion of practices, expertise, and templates of action was a central feature of imperial rule, based on sophisticated state infrastructures of surveillance and intelligence (Bayly 1999; Silvestri 2019). These infrastructures did not always provide sound information, nor did they make the population "legible" to colonial governments in crisis, at times feeding the British administrators' fear and insecurity (Condos 2017) or even contributing to organizational forms of anticolonial resistance (Mitchell 1991b: xi). However, these infrastructures of intelligence and surveillance, which expanded in the interwar period, enabled the diffusion of practices between colonies because of the potent exchange of information between connected actors (Axelrod 1997). The diffusion of administrative practices within what Laleh Khalili calls the "horizontal circuits" of the British Empire is no surprise[65] because the likelihood of diffusion of policies, information, artifacts, and personnel mostly between the colonies (and not necessarily through London as a central hub), rises through social structures of affiliation and shared attributes (Strang 1991). Legal historians have established how the interlegality of British colonial law was a labyrinth from which colonially manufactured laws were easily exported from one juridical territory to another (Baxi 2003) through institutional connections and networks of personal affiliation (Laidlaw 2013).

One of the most powerful vehicles of the diffusion of the bureaucratic toolkit of emergency was the set of colonial emergency laws. The diffusion of bureaucratic classification according to the axis of suspicion and the use of powerful legal-spatial tools occurred as administrators learned from each other through analogies of crisis, as emergency powers were expanded (Simmons & Elkins 2004). Legitimate practices flow and diffuse more readily than illegitimate practices (Davis & Greve 1997; Lee &

Strang 2006), so the expansion of emergency laws provided legitimacy to bureaucratic use of spatial control and violent enforcement, even when colonial administrators perceived the difference between the political situations in their particular locale from that in other colonies, as well as the objective material constraints that limited possibilities for the deployment of differentiated bureaucratic tools of repression. These material constraints influenced the focus on mobility restrictions and the construction of the grid of mobility based on suspicion (see Zuckerman 2012).

The bureaucratic toolkit of emergency that developed in India in the interwar period was not a single or unidirectional source of diffusion. Practices developed in Ireland, especially of policing and interrogation, were also highly influential in shaping the repertoires colonial officials used for repression throughout the 1920s and 1930s (Khalili 2010; Sinclair 2017). Each colony adapted and innovated these practices to suit the local conditions of popular uprisings or militant campaigns. As we shall see in Chapter 5, when these colonial states became independent, they used the colonial administrative template for managing populations against their own minority groups.

This section outlines four methods of diffusion of the bureaucratic toolkit of emergency developed in India in the interwar period that diffused through the circulation of the emergency laws themselves. Although it was not legislated, the repertoire of practices that administrators had developed, from blacklists and the classification of various political detainees to closed zones, quarantines, and permit regimes, was transferred through the emergency laws (see Figure 3).

FOUR METHODS OF INSTITUTIONAL DIFFUSION

British hybrid bureaucracy grew through its diffusion, as colonial bureaucrats articulated and justified their actions, as we saw in Chapter 1. The diffusion of the legal toolkit of emergency occurred through the proliferation of theories and methods for distinguishing "dangerous populations," as the axis of suspicion upended population classification, linking political risk to security risk. Strang and Meyer (1993) offer an institutional theory to explain the diffusion of practices in a global context. They suggest that the conditions for diffusion are the cultural linkages between categories or social actors. These links are part of the cognitive map of actors or organizations (Strang & Meyer 1993: 491). Common categories produce similar institutional structures through a process of institutional isomorphism (DiMaggio & Powell 1983). This

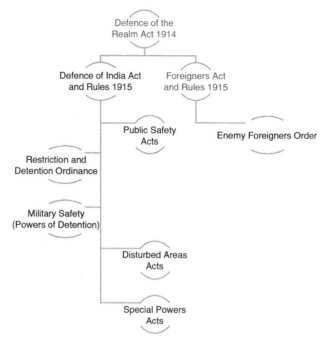

FIGURE 3   The legal toolkit for managing populations, India 1914–1945

homogenization is influenced by the standardization of dominant organizations (like the Colonial Office) or by imitation in times of crisis (such as uprisings). Practices diffuse rapidly if there is a general theory or model about their cause and effect, particularly when there is a distinct population or category of potential practitioners, called adopters (Strang & Meyer 1993: 498). Actors relate to institutional rules as a repertoire or toolkit of alternative models or schemas (Clemens & Cook 1999; Minkoff 1994; Swidler 1986). The presence of alternatives facilitates innovation through recombination. Haveman and Rao (1997: 1620) demonstrate that in an environment of multiple competing institutional mandates, hybrid forms can emerge that combine the various properties of competing models. The toolkit of emergency was a practical repertoire of laws, practices, and bureaucratic theories about population classification, scarcity of resources, and political risk which developed and changed as it moved from one crisis in a colony to another and back.

New institutionalist accounts of the diffusion of law and administrative repertoires have been critiqued for being both unidirectional and focused on the diffusion of models, rather than on practices (Hussin 2014; see also

Go 2013). However, the diffusion of population management practices in the colonies fits well with the set of assumptions presented above, particularly when we take into account that the practices were also the product of the resistance or compliance of local political elites, anticolonial and national liberation movements, as well as the political debate in Britain.

The Colonial Office, the dominant organization in the administration of the colonies, initiated laws, commented on implementation practices, and attempted (with limited success) to standardize practices across the empire. Practices diffused in times of crisis through mimicry, at times the literal "copying and pasting" of forms, templates, and regulations. Diffusion occurred efficiently when there was a formal model to pass along to training delegations that traveled in order to learn from experts in other colonial governments, for example in the case of census enumeration in India or methods for controlling immigration in Mandate Palestine. Imperial historians have focused on the movement of officials, particularly those harboring expertise in the quashing of political opposition and insurgencies, as a major method of diffusion (Hay & Craven 2005; Sinclair 2006; Anderson 1993). Celebrity officials served as the technical experts for quashing revolt and managing dangerous populations, consulted during times of crisis. A notorious example was Charles Tegart, who was recruited to Palestine during the Arab Revolt, based on his expertise in India. Tegart was the founder of the special branch of police in Calcutta, known for his ruthless skill in the torture of detainees from among the Calcutta revolutionaries, but also for his ability to decipher the "inscrutable natives," to determine their motivations and, most importantly, their loyalties (Silverstri 2019: 201).

Officials and departments facilitated the circulation of their administrative repertoires by means of the following four methods:

1. Colonial Office: The Colonial Office was the central command of the colonial administration. It promulgated laws, distributed policies, and printed up forms, codes of conduct, and circulars. Information flowed from one colony to another as colonial governments attempted to standardize laws and practices. An example of this standardization was the Colonial Office response to the request of the Governor of Cyprus to deny entry to natives who were subjects of the colony and whom the government considered to be threats to the state. The Colonial Office policy had been to deport persons who were security threats, but not to deny them entry. Instead, they suggested a solution later implemented in other

colonies: Allow suspicious persons to enter but require that they possess short-term permits for residency and employment that they must renew frequently, and that allow for surveillance.

2. Copying and Pasting: Indian bureaucratic forms served as templates for similar documents in Mandate Palestine, such as naturalization applications and residency permits.[66] During the Arab Revolt in 1936, the government of Palestine used laws promulgated in Bengal in the 1930s as templates for local standing orders. A pamphlet of laws from India was used as an example of emergency measures in response to the disturbances of 1936, and for the enactment of martial law.[67]

3. Professional Delegations: Delegations and missions for the purpose of adopting methods in other colonies increased during the 1930s (Frenkel & Shenhav 2006). The Department of Immigration in the Palestine Government was a resource for administrators to learn "methods of control of foreign visitors and residents."[68] Not only the fulcrum for counterinsurgency practices (Khalili 2015), the high volume and sophisticated mechanisms for filtering requests for immigration to Palestine turned the Department of Immigration into a de facto training center for officials from other colonial jurisdictions who were interested in learning about population management across borders. At the same time, India was the training ground for many colonial administrators who began their careers in India and continued to other territories in the empire.

4. Diffusion of Practices by Colonial Officials: While this is the most researched aspect of the circulation of policies and practices in the empire, most of these histories rely on the biographies of colonial officials and their writings. Studies of colonial officials tend to focus on policy and devote less attention to the techniques and details of administration. High-ranking officials – the usual subjects of study – did not often record information about specific practices.[69] Previous studies have traced the diffusion of practices of emergency to Palestine and Cyprus to policing techniques that originated in Ireland. Khalili (2010) and Sinclair (2006) have shown that the experience learned from counterinsurgency practices in Palestine shaped a generation of imperial police officers and soldiers who would become senior officials in post–Second World War colonial insurgencies (Khalili 2010: 415). The origins of colonial policing are traced to the disbanded forces in Ireland and their influence on policing in Cyprus (Sinclair & Williams 2007).

DIFFUSION OF THE BUREAUCRATIC TOOLKIT OF EMERGENCY TO MANDATE PALESTINE AND CYPRUS

The vehicle for the diffusion of the bureaucratic toolkit of emergency to Palestine and Cyprus was the similarly worded emergency laws that were incorporated and amended in times of crisis and perceived threat to British rule. The regulations were the method of transmission of the set of technologies, classifications, forms, and methods of documentation that had been adapted and incorporated into the hybrid bureaucracy. At the end of the First World War, in tandem with reforms to advance Indian self-rule, colonial administrators in India feared losing the executive powers they had employed during the war, and justified the extension of the wartime Defence of India Act by the necessity of granting colonial administrators extensive powers to combat militant anticolonial activities. However, the extension of wartime measures enabled the proliferation of provincial laws and ordinance throughout the 1920s that provided administrators with the legal-spatial tools they employed widely against the civilian population (Ghosh 2017: 59). The bureaucratic toolkit of emergency developed in India during the decade in which British rule expanded in Palestine from military rule to mandate in 1922 and assumed full control of Cyprus as a Crown Colony in 1925. While the High Commissioner of Palestine and Governor of Cyprus had authority to enact ordinance "for the peace, order and good government" of the colony from the outset of their rule, the expansion of emergency powers and the incorporation of the bureaucratic toolkit of emergency into the administration occurred several years later, following the Jewish–Palestinian disturbances of 1929 in Palestine and the Greek Cypriot riots in Nicosia demanding *enosis* (unification with Greece). While in India the proliferation of emergency laws and legal-spatial tools for the control of the population were coupled with political reforms to advance Indian self-rule, in Palestine a legislative council was never established, and in Cyprus the legislative council was abolished with the expansion of emergency powers.

The Bureaucratic Toolkit of Emergency in Palestine

The colonial administration of the British Mandate in Palestine was preoccupied with controlling the movement of populations from its inception, not least because its attempts to monitor Jewish migration and settlement in Palestine – the most controversial political issues at the time – demanded a sophisticated system of statistics, regulations, and documents (Zureik 2001). Classification based on the axis of suspicion, blacklists, collective fines, demolitions, and authorities to declare areas as "disturbed and dangerous" were established as early as 1921.

The emergency laws enacted in 1931, after the violent events of 1929, were the scaffolding of the British response to the 1936 outbreak of Arab rebellion against the British colonial regime, which was perceived as collaborating with Jewish immigration and economic development (Norris 2013). In the early stages of the revolt, as the Mandate government searched for practical ways to crush the uprising, they turned to the emergency laws in India and specifically to a "collection of enactments which give special powers to deal with terrorists and other subversive activities," published as a pamphlet by the Home Department of India in 1934.[70] In 1936, the High Commissioner, following the formula used in India and Burma for applying defense regulations,[71] declared martial law by decree.[72] The Order in Council of 1931 permitting the use of emergency powers and martial law remained unpublished until 1936, thus earning its controversial status as a secret law.[73] One of the organizing principles of hybrid bureaucracy was administrative flexibility, which included operating under the authority of secret laws.

The colonial government compiled blacklists similar to those used in India but less elaborate in terms of the details and characteristics, focusing on the level of threat to colonial rule. They also compiled separate suspect lists, one for Arabs and one for Jews. The Jewish suspect list did not include occupation, since it was less relevant for immigrants, but focused instead on both country of origin and political affiliations with communist organizations.

Classification by degrees of suspicion in Palestine was simpler than the classification matrix in India, not least because from 1935 onwards the Mandate government divided the population of Palestine categorically into Jews or Arabs. Still, the array of spatial-legal means was as rich as the repertoire in India, partly owing to the importance of land mapping and jurisdiction in the ongoing struggle between Jewish settlers and Arabs, and partly owing to the British preoccupation with preventing illegal Jewish immigration.

Between 1936 and 1939, Palestine's Arab population was under severe military occupation, as the Mandate government carried out collective punishment for villages and towns in which rebels were located (Hughes 2009). The Central Intelligence Department (CID), working as the investigative body for the police and the British military, compiled suspect lists enumerating over 2,000 individual suspects who were categorized according to their familial affiliation, political ties, and geographic location. Officers checked the suspect list during each raid and search of villages, and they used an Arab informant (hooded to prevent identification by villagers) to identify the faces behind the names on the list.[74] Similar to the designation of Blacks, Whites, and Greys in northeast India, informers in armored cars would identify suspects of different levels of threat as oranges, lemons, or grapefruits (Hughes 2019: 216).

In 1936, Mandatory permit regimes for travel were introduced in certain areas and towns,[75] and a voluntary system of ID cards served to slow down and monitor movement between 1936 and 1938, expanded to a nationwide permit system for the Palestinian population (Hughes 2019: 226). Exit permits were another technology for monitoring the movement of suspicious persons during the uprisings. During the Arab Revolt, the government of Palestine introduced a system of exit permits, which required that every person attempting to leave Palestine obtain permission from the director of the Department of Immigration. (British subjects, foreigners, and Jews who were not communists were exempt from this requirement.) An assistant secretary explained that requiring everyone to possess a permit was more effective at stopping departures than preventatively detaining people on the suspect list.[76]

Preventative detention in interrogation centers, confinement to one's village, and the demand for daily registration at a police station were all part of the bureaucratic toolkit of emergency. Hughes estimates there were a staggering number of detained Palestinians – over 500,000 during the years of the Great Revolt (2019: 247).

In 1945, Jewish militias launched a joint armed struggle against the Mandate government's restrictions on Jewish immigration and land settlement. Senior officials in the Jewish Agency, previously viewed as allies by the Mandate government, took an active part. In response, the Mandate government drew on the emergency toolkit it had developed from the laws inherited from Bengal and Ireland during the Arab Revolt to establish the Defence (Emergency) Regulations, 1945, which enabled expulsions and the demolition of family homes of suspects, as well as the death penalty for political militants. After a spate of attacks on bridges, prisons, and railway tracks, the "special suspect list" of Jews expanded to 3,500 names.[77] In June 1946, during Operation Agatha, British police arrested over 2,000 people named on the Jewish blacklist.[78]

The levels of violence and repression used by the British against Jews, however, were attenuated in scale and scope: the Mandate government was reluctant to use its tools of counterinsurgency and massive collective punishment in Jewish settlements in the same way it did in Palestinian towns and villages.[79] This difference in approach was rooted in the earlier alignment between the Jewish Yishuv and British officials who viewed the Jewish settlers as a proxy for European colonizers (Yacobi 2015: 3–5) because they were European-born and, unlike the Palestinian natives, they were not presumed to support terrorism collectively. Jews on the blacklist were thus evaluated based on their political and organizational affiliations. The most significant difference between the response to the Jewish and Arab revolts was the scale and severity of permit regimes (see also Ben-Natan 2021).

During the last years of the Mandate, Britain's heavy-handed rule by decree was at the forefront of the critique advanced by the Jewish Yishuv to delegitimize the British presence and demand independence. Following independence, Israel's decision not to incorporate the Defence (Emergency) Regulations, 1945 as formal legislation was central to the nascent state's campaign for political legitimacy as a democratic state. It reserved the use of the Defence (Emergency) Regulations for those who were deemed "violent" opposition, thus distinguishing between the political community of citizens and those who engaged, or were likely to engage, in acts of political violence, who would be governed by their provisions. The bureaucratic toolkit of emergency, from blacklists to the designation of disturbed areas to the institutionalization of a permit regime for the Palestinians that remained after their exile during the Nakba, was the baseplate for the military government that would rule from 1949 to 1966, which we will encounter in Chapter 5.

The Bureaucratic Toolkit of Emergency in Cyprus

The bureaucratic toolkit of emergency was incorporated into the administration of colonial Cyprus during two major periods of crisis. In the 1930s, the toolkit served for the repression of political activity and the "reeducation" of Cypriot subjects that were perceived as incapable of self-rule. In 1931, Greek Cypriots protested for *enosis*, revolted against British colonial rule, and burned the house of Governor Ronald Storrs. In response, the governor's emergency powers were extended, and the Colonial Office seized the opportunity to abolish the representative legislative council (Markides & Georghallides 1995: 67). Between 1931 and the beginning of World War II, the bureaucratic toolkit of emergency was implemented in a period that was called Palmerokratia (Palmerocracy) after Governor Herbert Richmond Palmer – the most repressive era of British rule (Rappas 2008: 365), in which representative institutions were abolished, including villages and municipality councils, assemblies. Political organization was prohibited in criminal law amendments, and administrators were preoccupied with the classification of identities based on the axis of suspicion, as they equated political threats with criminal and security threats,[80] aiming to quash the particularly threatening "species" that instigated unrest: communists and the Greek Orthodox Church.

After the Second World War, colonial administrators in Cyprus faced a new political reality as they sought to retain in peacetime, the vast powers of population classification and surveillance that had been used liberally during wartime. Emergency measures had become a politically sensitive matter and it was not as simple an affair as copying and pasting from the counterinsurgency laws in Bengal. The political sensitivity was due to the international attention the intercommunal conflict in Cyprus received from the United Nations and the European Commission for Human Rights, as Britain had signed on to the Human Rights Convention and extended it to the colonies.[81]

The colonial administration in Cyprus experienced a higher level of supervision and intervention from the Colonial Office. The Colonial Office scrutinized the diffusion of emergency practices to Cyprus, curbing the attempts of the governor and attorney general to expand emergency powers. The method of widening executive discretion to the bureaucracy through emergency practices was to incorporate "enabling powers" into local laws:

Most of the defense regulations contain enabling powers, which are exercisable under some order or other instrument ... what I shall do will be to incorporate the text of the regulations in local law enabling the authority concerned to issue the necessary orders.[82]

Despite the efforts of the Colonial Office to block emergency practices that were used in other colonies, local administrators deployed blacklists, entry and exit permits, and other innovative solutions to monitor and restrict mobility. One of the extreme measures the governor wished to employ – in addition to deportation – was to deny entry to natives of the colony if they were on the suspect list, or if they had committed criminal offenses. The problem with this proposed policy was that British subjects who were natives of the colony could not be prevented from entering. "Cyprus is not a fortress colony like Gibraltar, where such powers can be defended,"[83] Colonial Office administrators wrote in an angry letter to the governor. They thought the lack of metropolitan scrutiny of the local administration of the island had resulted in exceptional measures. In response, officials in the Colonial Office offered an alternative – a temporary permit restricting the length of stay. One wrote:

> Some comparable arrangements under which British subjects could enter without restriction but could not remain in the colony for more than a stated period without special permission. The easiest way of exercising the sort of control seems to me clearly to be by limiting the length of time visitors can stay rather than by specifying the purpose for which they can stay.[84]

This suggestion provided numerous opportunities for monitoring the activities of those on the suspect list when they asked for permission to remain in Cyprus.

From 1955 until the end of colonial rule of the island, the Greek Cypriot organization Ethniki Organosis Kyprion Agoniston (EOKA) launched a fierce armed struggle against the colonial government and against any Turkish or Greek Cypriots whom these militants believed were collaborators with the colonial regime. Contrary to the administrative response in Palestine, where a permit regime restricting travel was established months after the revolt, the bureaucratic response with mobility restrictions against the civilian population was quite slow.

In 1955, the government had enacted the Emergency Powers (Restrictions on Departure from the Colony) Order, 1956,[85] a regulation that required all persons (except British officers) to apply for an exit permit to leave the country (in addition to having a passport). Permits were issued for a single journey on a specified date of departure and return. In 1956, as a gesture to "restore harmony to the island," the regulations were repealed and only those people who the government suspected of having political or military involvement with EOKA were required to have exit permits.[86]

Also in 1956, the Cyprus government enacted a new set of emergency regulations declaring "Danger Areas," preventing civilian movement on certain roads, and enabling commissioners to ban the movement of vehicles and pedestrians on sight.[87] That same year, the Emergency Regulation (Registration of Households) was promulgated to give officials the authority to search villages and find persons on the suspect lists. "Our intention is to apply it immediately as a pilot scheme for troublesome villages,"[88] the governor wrote to district commissioners of police. Enacted in 1956, the Public Officers Protection Regulations were similar to the AFSPA, preventing any civilian access to courts seeking redress for an action committed not only by security forces but by any government official, without the prior consent of the attorney general.

However, by January 1958, the government of Cyprus had launched a massive identification and surveillance system of all persons attempting to enter or leave the island by air or sea.[89] The system included thorough measures for screening all passengers entering or exiting the colony, a practice that was unheard of at the time.

The Cyprus Emergency began a decade after the pre-partition crisis in India and Mandate Palestine. Yet the arsenal of practices for classification and surveillance of civilian populations by legal-spatial means was very similar. In Chapter 5 I show how this colonial toolkit of emergency measures, used to manage subject populations, was used by the successor independent states against those that had become minorities following partition, independence, and the Nakba.

CONCLUSION

Perpetual emergency was a characteristic of governance of colonial bureaucracy, justified to maintain racial hierarchy and differentiation of status, decoupling universally worded laws from the racialized administrative practices. Yet, because of the concern with juridical normativity and the preoccupation with legality and legitimacy, officials constantly sought to use an array of emergency laws, promulgated and employed as useful tools to clerks, magistrates, police officers, and commissioners to control and crush opposition, monitor population movement, and prevent disturbances to the regime or to economic extraction. The use of emergency laws proliferated in tandem with a decline in the legitimacy of colonial rule.

This chapter has followed the development of what I call the bureaucratic toolkit of emergency in India in the interwar period. From an organizational point of view, this involved the use of criminal laws for the detention of individuals, administrative classifications to delineate suspicious groups, and military laws to designate regions as disturbed or dangerous, to institute curfews and closures, and monitor the movement of civilians classified according to the axis of suspicion. These formed a repertoire of spatial-legal tools, used by bureaucrats on individuals, groups, and spaces, established during periods of crisis but gradually turning some of the forms, lists, maps, and population classifications into a conceptual grid for routine population management during times of relative peace.

The bureaucratic toolkit of emergency included blacklists, detention and registration of foreigners, closed military zones, the designation of "disturbed areas," exit permits, confinement to the colony, preventative detention, and military rule. These tools were on an escalating scale of severity, from the confinement of the body in detention to confinement to a particular territory, to monitoring and surveillance and the prevention of free movement. The technologies of rule for monitoring populations were on an escalating scale of severity and scope. On one end of the scale were practices that restricted an entire population from moving freely in a large space, such as exit permits. On the other end of the scale were measures that prevented particular people from moving at all. Preventative detention was a measure reserved for persons who the state considered a potential security threat or political threat because they stirred political opposition. Yet these measures were considered part of one bureaucratic repertoire in which confinement to the colony, or demanding an exit permit, was perceived by the bureaucracy as an alternative to mass detentions.

The Registration of Foreigners Rules were a template for permit regimes, as they required foreigners to register where they lived and notify the authorities every time that they were more than five miles away from their registered residence. Two examples of foreigner registration, circus performers and enemy aliens, demonstrated how the bureaucratic routines to monitor foreigners turned movement itself into a suspicious activity for certain groups. As movement was registered, recorded, and reported, it became an event worthy of administrative scrutiny and suspicion. Each of these events invited opportunities for bureaucratic discretion and intervention, even in the most mundane activities. In turn, this toolkit circulated between colonies during periods of crisis. Diffusion occurred through the Colonial Office, through the mimicry of laws, forms, and regulations, professional delegations that sought to emulate models of governance, and experts.

The bureaucratic toolkit of emergency and the axis of suspicion created a conceptual grid that the colonial bureaucracies employed to classify populations and control them through the monitoring of mobility. These legal-spatial systems of surveillance, established by province officials to monitor and control populations, formed practices and routines that, following independence and partition, became permit regimes that delineated the boundaries of citizenship and belonging in India and Israel through the toolkit of emergency. In both cases, state bureaucracies continued to use the colonial emergency laws that empowered ministries of home affairs, police, and military to designate belonging through the structuring of mobility. The structuring of everyday mobility would, in turn, shape the organizations, regulations, documents, and spaces that were to define the scope of political membership in the new independent states. Through disparate possibilities for mobility, bureaucrats created the differentiated order of citizens, residents, temporary residents, intruders, refugees, or stateless people.

PART III

ADMINISTRATIVE MEMORY AND THE LEGACIES OF EMERGENCY

INTRODUCTION

What were the effects of colonial rule on the making of the new states in the shadow of partition? How did decades of government through emergency laws, classifications of suspicion, and restrictions of mobility shape population management? In the aftermath of partition and independence, with the remains of the administrative structures of the British hybrid bureaucracies, in the midst of now national emergencies, both Israel and India established permit regimes to control the movement of refugees and returnees who had fled in the wake of a war of independence and the violence of partition and the Nakba. In all three states – Cyprus, India, and Israel – the making of the independent civil services was entrenched in colonial classifications of suspicion and practices of emergency. Despite the differences in the state-building trajectories of independent India, Cyprus, and Israel, the process of population classification incorporated both the categorical exclusion of those that were or became minorities and a hyper-personalized analysis of their choices, mobilities, affinities, and character. Part III excavates the relationship between colonial bureaucratic practices and their outcomes in the early years after independence. These years provide a distinctive window onto the bureaucratic making of the state, the role of the bureaucratic repertoires in the classification of civil servants, and the delineation of political membership in the period of emergency that accompanied the institutionalization of new states before their statutory laws of citizenship crystallized.[1]

As we saw in Chapter 2, the introduction of partition as a political idea brought about a flurry of population classification and grew bureaucratic discretion even further, as the stakes of matching population categories to the anticipated territorial divide exacerbated the consequences of each decision. Population categories were no longer about resources and allocations in the present but created the demographic battles of the future. Population classification pronounced communal divisions, highlighted "primordial betrayals," as Pollis writes (1973), and served to further legitimate political communities' claims to statehood, like Jews in Palestine (Robson 2017: 17) and Muslims in India (Devji 2013: 51).

After partition, the wide discretion and immense power of the home ministries meant that the identity of civil servants was a critical part of the transition to the independent state. Delineating the boundaries of citizenship, devolving "real authority onto local populations newly defined as 'national'" (Dubnov & Robson 2019: 4), was not only driven by national ideology; it was also a legacy of the axis of suspicion, especially toward those who were to be excluded as the potential citizens of the "other side" of partition (Butalia 2017).

Forged from the remains of the administrative structures of British colonial hybrid bureaucracies, the aforementioned permit regimes in India and Israel were established to control and prevent the movement of returnees that had fled the violence of partition and the Nakba. Using the bureaucratic toolkit of emergency analyzed in Chapter 3, these spatial-legal systems of surveillance and control, established at a time of emergency, were institutional mechanisms that shaped the boundaries of belonging by administrative means. The permit regimes instituted: 1) the category that the state assigned people – citizens, residents, intruders, refugees; 2) the identity document a person carried; and 3) the physical location of a person on the crucial date that determined their legal status. The permit regimes also formed ad hoc administrative structures and practices, such as forms and internal regulations intended to be temporary. As I will show, the temporary emergency measures become the very permanent foundations of new state bureaucracies and the delineation of citizenship.

In Cyprus, the regime that monitored the movement of the minority group was different. Three years after independence, during the constitutional collapse, intercommunal violence erupted throughout the island. For five years, Turkish Cypriots lived in enclaves where Greek Cypriot forces severely restricted their movement. Different from both the permit system in India and the permit regime in Israel, the Turkish Cypriots lived under a military siege. The Greek Cypriot leadership that declared Turkish Cypriot leaders to be rebels was not concerned with enumeration, surveillance, and degrees of classification whatsoever. This difference in administrative legacies underscores the central role that statutory emergency laws have in facilitating and legitimating the practices of population management in Israel and India.

The critical juncture that marked the different trajectories of bureaucratic legacy between Israel and India and Cyprus was the fate of the colonial emergency laws and the bureaucratic powers they afforded in the new states.[2] India incorporated the colonial emergency laws into its formal laws and the constitution (Kalhan 2010; Singh 2007; Baruah 2014);[3] Israel maintained the colonial emergency laws, which were also used as the legal scaffolding of a separate military government to govern the remainder of the Palestinians following the war of independence and the Nakba (Mehozay 2016; Sa'di 2016);[4] Cyprus relinquished the colonial emergency laws at independence and did not incorporate similar emergency provisions into the constitution, except to combat direct political violence.[5] In both Israel and India, emergency laws were the baseplate for the use of the bureaucratic toolkit of emergency against minorities. In Israel, emergency laws were used mostly against Palestinians: they served to control the Palestinian population during the military government from 1949 to 1966, and in 1967 were the basis for Israel's control of Palestinians in the West Bank and Gaza (Berda 2017). In India, the inherited emergency laws were used against citizens of various ethnicities and religions, including members of the Hindu majority, usually intersecting with caste, linguistic minorities, and rural areas. These laws were deployed against the Maoist insurgency, the Gurkha movement in Darjeeling, the Sikh independence movement in Punjab, in Nagaland, and in Jammu and Kashmir (Chenoy and Chenoy 2010). Prakash (2019) argues that they created the political conditions that would enable the declared Emergency in 1975.

During the period between independence and the enactment of the citizenship laws, there were fierce debates to attenuate the scope of the colonial emergency laws around the Preventive Detention Act in India,[6] and attempts to repeal the Defence (Emergency) Regulations in Israel and replace them with new security legislation.[7] Both attempts failed.

Chapter 4 compares the process of designation of civil servants that had served the colonial governments according to classifications of loyalty and suspicion. Chapter 5 compares the bureaucratic response to the return of minorities exiled or displaced by war, partition, and intercommunal violence, the establishment of mobility regimes, and the way bureaucratic methods to regulate movement determined citizenship according to the axis of suspicion. One of the most prominent features of the hybrid bureaucracy, inherited across all three colonies, was the axis of suspicion, which upended other categories of identity, creating and exacerbating fault lines between and inside communities based on identity, political affinity, and mobility.

4

Loyalty and Suspicion: The Making of the Civil Service after Independence

INTRODUCTION: INHERITING COLONIAL BUREAUCRACY'S
AXIS OF SUSPICION

During the first years of independence from British rule, the three states' determination of political membership became one of the most critical and impossible administrative tasks. The shifting location of territorial boundaries, the criteria for belonging to a population, and the legitimacy of authority were temporary and uncertain, so thousands of daily administrative decisions and classifications of belonging held far-reaching consequences for the future of individuals and communities. At this dramatic moment of transition from colonial rule, extreme violence, and uncertainty, existing administrative routines, practices, and categories provided a much-needed backbone and structure for political leadership and administration. Alongside the violence of partition and war, bureaucrats deployed their discretion through the inherited procedural violence of the colonial administration.

Retaining the colonial legacy, though, came at a heavy price. The toolkit of classification in the colonial state, which manipulated "intractably divisive primordial loyalties" (Stoler 2016: 63), had produced racial hierarchies of classification according to demographics and according to the level of threat that people once posed to British rule. The new state's bureaucracies inherited laws, administrative forms, registries, and most of the personnel to run the nascent country.

While the continuity of laws and courts following state succession is presumed to provide the scaffolding of government to run the state after regime change, sociologists of organizations have shown that organizational continuities, imprinting, and institutional logics are most prominently retained through personnel (Thornton & Ocasio 1999; Lippmann & Aldrich 2016). While organizational learning depends on lessons of experience that are maintained and accumulated within routines despite the turnover of personnel, rules, procedure technologies, beliefs, and cultures are conserved through systems of social control within the organizations. The most potent carriers of administrative memory, the agglomeration of the practices, routines, and forms from one regime to the next, were the administrators themselves. Transmission of administrative routines and forms of classification encapsulated the political regime of racial hierarchy in which they were developed, whereby administrators stretched their discretion and flexibility as much as necessary to maintain different practices and separate regulations for different populations. In the transition from British hybrid bureaucracy, administrators and their routines ensconced most of the knowledge and power of running the state.

Scholarship on the classification and categorization of populations by the colonial state examines the way in which they affected the self-understanding, social organization, and political claims of indigenous populations (Brubaker & Cooper 2000). Yet very few investigations (but see Gupta 2012; Steinmetz 2016) look at how the classification of populations shaped the governing bureaucracy itself – the state apparatus. In a hybrid bureaucracy, the organizing principle of personalism meant that the identity of the bureaucrat and the identity of the subject determined the outcome. The personalism, wide discretion, and administrative flexibility of colonial bureaucracy could be mistaken for corruption, arbitrariness, nepotism, and clientelism – evidence of a broken bureaucracy. But wide discretion and administrative flexibility were not features of a rational-legal bureaucracy gone awry or evidence of "zones of lawlessness." Wide discretion was an organizing principle that rendered administrative decrees, ad hoc decisions, and internal regulations much more prominent and powerful tools of government than published laws or judicial decisions. Determining who would be the civil servants that wielded political power was a legacy of classification according to loyalty and suspicion, which was now shaped by the new territorial boundaries of belonging.

Despite the differences in the trajectories of the civil services in independent India, Cyprus, and Israel, the process of their classification incorporated both categorical exclusion of those that were or became minorities and a hyper-personalized analysis of their choices, mobilities, affinities, and character.

This chapter focuses on the classifications and mobility of former colonial bureaucrats in the transition to the new state, as a site to examine the legacy of hybrid bureaucracy. It explores how the axis of suspicion shaped three trajectories of civil servants after the transition to states, which used similar repertoires and classifications according to loyalty and suspicion inherited from British rule, but resulted in different outcomes that were to have dramatic effects on the delineation of citizenship and the political future of minorities.

The categorization of civil servants had been a major point of contention between colonial governments and local populations before independence. As plans for partition gained momentum, the identity of civil servants became a dominant concern for communities that hoped to secure their interests and have representation in the state apparatus after independence. In Cyprus, suspicions and challenges to communal representation in the civil service were a central cause of the constitutional crisis that caused the new republic to implode only three years after its independence in 1960.

The classification of civil servants served as a communal battleground that eventually led to an administrative showdown and political implosion in Cyprus, and to a regime of suspicion and surveillance for Muslim civil servants in India. Despite its constitution that demands the representation of both Greek and Turkish Cypriots, after the crisis of 1963, Cyprus never recovered its co-religious civil service. In India, after the first decade following independence, classification and suspicion practices of civil servants stabilized to some degree. In Israel, colonial practices of suspicion were deployed against Jewish civil servants who had served the colonial government because Palestinian administrators were exiled during the war of independence, and Israeli administrators perceived those who remained as unsuitable to serve the new government of the Jewish state. The transition from colonial rule to independence in the wake of the violence of partition created massive administrative work, and despite the awareness of and public debate against the use of colonial methods of classification and discrimination, the civil services used such methods, which they justified by the emergencies that existed at the time.

In Cyprus, representation in the civil service was a constitutional imperative, a compromise to prevent partition that would rope every administrative function of the new state to the identity of its administrators and create suspicion based on categorical identities. In India, the loyalty of Muslim civil servants was determined according to their mobility across the new borders, and in Israel/Palestine, the loyalty of former Jewish civil servants of Mandate Palestine was determined according to political affiliation, while Palestinians were entirely written out of the organizational chart of the new state.

In Cyprus, the legacy of the classification of civil servants according to identity was the most prominent of all three cases, because it became the centerpiece of Cyprus's power-sharing constitution established at independence to avoid partition. The obstacles of representative administration would become a justification for the implosion of that constitution, which led to the intercommunal violence and territorial separation that preceded the de facto partition in 1974. In the constitution, the imagined resolution of the intercommunal conflict was articulated as the proportional representation of Greek and Turkish Cypriot populations. Turkish Cypriots were to hold 30 percent of the positions in the civil service and fifteen of the fifty seats in parliament, and run a communal chamber that handled issues of religion, education, and personal status. This section explores how hybrid bureaucracy's legacies of classification according to identity, loyalty, and suspicion translated into hyper-representation that affected the civil service's organization, and how their practices of classification shaped citizenship in Cyprus as one that could not be separate from communal identity. As we shall see, the battle over appointments, representation, and languages used in the civil service, framed the perception of citizenship in Cyprus as inseparable from the hyphenated identities as defined in the constitution (Constantinou 2008).

The nascent republic attempted to achieve its power-sharing through a hyper-representative system. These bureaucratic debates and negotiations on technicalities (which might seem petty or bordering on the absurd regarding the attention paid to details and paranoiac responses) were far from parochial (Markides 1998: 178). The contestations of bureaucratic appointments were testing sites for the efficacy of designated political participation, the limits of bureaucratic power, and the meaning of participation in the republic.

Independence was a strange moment for civil servants. They were both highly regarded, as representatives of their community, and held in suspicion by both Turkish Cypriot and Greek Cypriot nationalist anticolonial movements that placed little trust in those who had served the British. However, that suspicion preceded British colonial rule.

During Ottoman rule, only Turkish Muslim Cypriots could serve on the Cypriot police force. After the First World War, during British rule, recruitment to the police force gradually reflected population ratios: In 1954, 60 percent were Greek Cypriots and approximately 40 percent were Turkish Cypriots (Anderson 1993). However, during the militant campaign for *enosis* (unification with Greece) from 1955 to 1959, Turkish Cypriots were recruited en masse to the colonial police, because EOKA, the militant arm of the Greek Cypriot movement for *enosis*, targeted Greek Cypriots in the police force as being British collaborators. By 1957, the police force had doubled in size, with 51 percent Turkish Cypriots, 20 percent British officers, and only 30 percent Greek Cypriots. After independence, vigorous efforts to restore a majority of Greek Cypriots to the police were central to the bicommunal preoccupation with appointments in the struggle for control of the civil services.

Although partition was rejected in Cyprus, it played an important role in shaping the series of international agreements that birthed the new republic. In the late 1940s, Turkish Cypriot leaders had proposed *taksim*, or partition, after close contact with their counterparts in Pakistan led them to model their own future on the division of the subcontinent. *Taksim* was an opportunity to achieve political sovereignty and autonomy.[8] In the 1950s, this solution took the form of demands for "double union," or a division that would unite the newly created parts with the "motherlands" of Greece and Turkey (Bryant & Hatay 2020: 12). The Greek Cypriots accepted independence to prevent the partition of Cyprus, while the Turkish Cypriots accepted independence in order to prevent *enosis*, which was one of the main conditions in the Treaty of Guarantee, one of the three international agreements that upheld the Cypriot constitution.

The transfer of power from the colonial government to the independent republic on August 15, 1960, entrenched the dichotomy of population categories of Turkish and Greek Cypriots in the constitution. The identity of civil servants was critical because they were appointed not only to serve the republic but to represent their communities. Greek and Turkish were declared official languages of the republic in the constitution, a rule that was implemented literally – civil servants were to correspond in Greek with Greek Cypriots and in Turkish with Turkish Cypriots.[9] Government work continued in English, as it had during colonial rule, although English was no longer an officially recognized language.[10] Civil servants who spoke and wrote in their communal language were officially reprimanded for not conducting official correspondence in English, or in both Greek and Turkish.[11]

The language barrier in the civil service proved more acute than had been expected during negotiations toward independence, and issues involving the government's linguistic adaptation generated much paperwork laden with suspicion and fear. The Turkish Cypriot vice president wrote about the persistent concerns of villagers: "on many occasions, letters and forms sent to them by government offices and departments [were] in Greek and that, therefore, they [were] finding it difficult to understand their contents and to comply with them."[12] Even the names of official titles, ranks, and authorities created a crisis. For example, the mistranslation of the title of colonial district officer into *komisar* and *kaza amiri* (titles that grant greater power in Turkey) confused the Turkish Cypriot public about the scope of authority the district official actually had, resulting in frustration and suspicion that the authority of Turkish Cypriot civil servants was being curtailed.[13] Some of the linguistic controversy over the titles *komisar* and *kaza amiri* was a contestation against the continuation of the broad authority and wide discretion vested in district commissioners during colonial rule. Finally, a transitional committee decided to abolish district commissioners and replace them with district officers serving the local population who "would not, like the commissioners under the colonial regime, represent government in the districts."[14] *Kaymakam* would have been a suitable Turkish title to describe the work of the colonial district commissioner, but it did not reflect the transition to district officers. Finally, after tedious correspondence, the title agreed upon was *kaza amiri*.

The Battle over Communal Appointments

The Cypriot constitution included a communal quota of civil servants of 70 percent Greek Cypriots and 30 percent Turkish Cypriots.[15] The constitution's notorious Article 123 featured an elaborate delegation for political, judicial, and executive roles, including dividing the civil service; when it became the testing ground for the political viability of power-sharing, the 70:30 ratio in the civil service proved impossible to implement. The challenge was that Greek Cypriots claimed that they could not find enough skilled Turkish Cypriots to populate the civil service quotas, yet they refused to invest in designated capacity-building. Moreover, the ratio applied to not only every ministry but also every subdepartment.

The Public Service Commission spent inordinate amounts of time processing appeals about contested appointments, particularly from understaffed ministries pleading for allocations of personnel. The Commission was confined by rigid rules so it "[could] not take any decision relating to a Turk (even if voted for by the majority of the commission consisting of seven Greek members) without the consent of at least two out of three of its Turkish members."[16] For example, of the six administrative assistants allocated to the inundated interior ministry, only three worked due to contested appointments. A. K. Anastasiou, later director general of the Ministry of Interior, wrote a desperate request for approval for a Greek Cypriot administrator with previous experience: "There is great concern at the undue delay in posting the administrative staff, which is long overdue. Interviews with the public amount to 50 daily ... who resort to this ministry for the solution of their problems."[17] The request was denied as it did not comply with the 70:30 requirement. The senior administrative staff of the ministry who had been recruited in the 1930s and 1940s, including Anastasiou himself, and migration officers appointed in 1961 were all Greek Cypriots, so appointing another Greek Cypriot was constitutionally impossible.[18]

Greek Cypriots contested Turkish Cypriot appointments to the police force based on the ratio because Turkish Cypriots had been a majority since their recruitment during the last years of British rule. The vice president condemned the suspected political manipulation of the ratio clause that resulted in firing Turkish cleaners in the police force:

With a view to implementing the 70:30 ratio amongst the civilian staff employed in the police, certain daily paid employs, such as cleaners, were given notice. As no such similar action has been taken in other ministries where the proportion between Greeks and Turks is against the Turkish community, the vice president is very concerned that in the police and gendarmerie, where the proportion is in favor of the Turks, efforts have been made to replace Turks with Greeks.[19]

Despite the vice president's demand, Greek Cypriots went ahead and replaced the cleaners.

Preoccupation with the political representation of civil servants was evident from the lists that summarized staff identities in every department for each community.[20] G indicated Greek Cypriots and T indicated Turkish Cypriots – for example, registrars G=8, T=4; court ushers G=22, T=10. Deviations from the ratio were circled.

The ratio deficit was exacerbated by the perceived lack of trained Turkish Cypriots. Turkish Cypriot political leadership insisted that the

constitutional ratio be fulfilled, yet Greek Cypriots refused to offer training to Turkish Cypriots. The communities' racialized views about each
other, which the colonial government had cultivated, framed the perception of skills and capacities. Comparison of application forms to the
Public Service Commission reveals the differences: Turkish Cypriots
were usually educated at universities in Turkey, while Greek Cypriots
were educated at British or Greek universities. The Greek Cypriot applicants had superior experience in administration, better typing skills, and
they knew shorthand, while the Turkish Cypriots had strong educational
backgrounds but very little experience.[21]

The ratio issue was so prominent that the final examinations of pro-
spective district officers included multiple questions on managing the
communal quotas such as: "The village of Pissouri has a population of
500 Greeks and 27 Turks. The district officer has appointed five Greeks as
the Christian village commission and five Turks as the Moslem village
commission. Is the action of the district officer in accordance with the
provisions of the law?"[22] While the political contestation of the 70:30
ratio was vocal and vehement, and suspicions ran high, the tragedy was
that the statistics of civil servants show that in December 1963, just before
the implosion, the constitutional ratio in the civil service was actually very
close to fulfillment (see Figure 4).

Within three years (1960–1963), the constitutional court had to rule on
communal contestation of two thousand civil service appointments,
a preoccupation that contributed to an organizational breakdown, halting

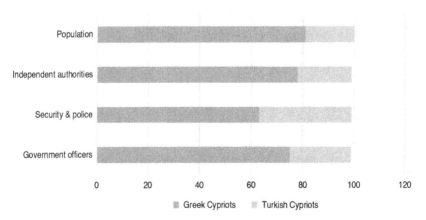

FIGURE 4 Percentage of Greek and Turkish Cypriots in the civil service,
December 1963[23]

administrative operations. In November 1963, President Archbishop Makarios submitted thirteen proposals to amend the constitution entitled "Suggested Measures for Facilitating the Smooth Functioning of the State and for the Removal of Certain Causes of Inter Communal Friction." Turkish Cypriot leadership viewed this document as a Greek Cypriot challenge to their minority rights and the very foundation of the republic.[24] Makarios justified the necessity of the measures on the grounds of the separatist nature of the constitution, which included separate municipalities and communal chambers charged with legislative and executive authorities on matters of religion, education, cultural affairs, and personal status. Some Greek Cypriots considered the provision for separate municipalities – to be elected by their respective communities – "unworkable."[25] A report of the attorney general contests the very possibility of territorial separation, echoing the Greek Cypriot rejection of partition:

> It was impossible to define the geographical areas based on communal criteria. There are not areas exclusively inhabited by Greeks or Turks, and the inhabitants are intermingled. Greeks are living side by side with the Turks, and the ownership of property does not follow the pattern of communal areas.[26]

Greek Cypriots believed that the ratio in the civil service – particularly the rigid provision whereby 30 percent of the posts in public service and 40 percent of the posts in the army were constitutionally reserved for the Turkish minority – was unfavorable to the Greek majority. Thus, measures in the thirteen-point proposal included abolishing the communal ratio in the civil service.

Following the intercommunal troubles in 1963, Turkish Cypriot civil servants left their posts in protest. Violence erupted and Turkish Cypriots first fled from mixed villages to Turkish Cypriot majority villages, and finally retreated into twenty-eight enclaves that were under siege by Greek Cypriot forces for over five years (Bryant & Hatay 2020: 10). Civil servants were classified as rebels and prevented from returning to their posts in the civil service, which created the need for a separate Turkish Cypriot administration within the twenty-eight enclaves (Navaro-Yashin 2006b: 286). In 1967, this parallel Turkish Cypriot administration was given a name: the "Transitional Cyprus Turkish Administration."[27] Navaro-Yashin claims the administration in the enclaves that were practically under siege would form the baseplate of the future administration of the "TRNC" after the Turkish invasion in 1974, both institutionally and effectively (2006b: 288). The clashes, also called the "Turkish rebellion" by the Cyprus government, changed the face of the civil service. A ministry report described the actions of the now all Greek Cypriot police: "the police force, which was seriously understaffed, comprised only of its Greek members, displayed many virtues and faced with incomparable courage, self-sacrifice and devotion, the Turkish rebels."[28]

In Cyprus, the clashes of 1963 marked the moment at which the civil service ceased to be bicommunal in any significant way. In 1964, the Supreme Court declared that the suspension of the articles in the constitution guaranteeing representation (including the 70:30 ratio) was constitutional because of a "doctrine of necessity" that justified suspension of the law for the sake of "maintaining the order of the state."[29] From that moment until the Turkish invasion and the partition of the island in 1974, Turkish Cypriots created their own civil administration that governed their enclaves and was unrecognized by the Cypriot state bureaucracy or internationally. In 1983, when the TNRC, the Northern Republic of Cyprus, declared itself as a state, recognized only by Turkey and considered illegal internationally, the civil service was transformed as settlers from Turkey joined the administration (Navaro-Yashin 2006a).

The categorical exclusion of Turkish Cypriot civil servants from the operation of the state following the violence and implosion of the constitution was entirely different from the graded suspicion deployed against Muslim civil servants, in which religious or communal identity was only one aspect of perceived loyalty or threat to independent India. The classifications of civil servants according to identity, upended by the classifications according to loyalty and suspicion, were most poignantly driven by the concern over their mobility across partition lines. Very different from the case of Cyprus, where the communal identity of civil servants was the core preoccupation with and of civil servants desperate to fulfill the constitutional quotas of representation, the classification of civil servants in India was not only based on their communal identities but mostly shaped by their patterns of mobility and how their "place" in the post-partition landscape reflected on their loyalties (Sutton 2011).

"EUROPEANS, INDIANS AND OTHERS": THE MAKING OF POST-PARTITION CITIZENSHIP IN INDIA'S CIVIL SERVICE

For the millions whose individual lives were altered by the violent transition and separation between India and Pakistan, partition was not an event but a lifelong process in which political belonging was coerced by migration.[30] Most people had very little control over the way partition would alter their life. However, for those who had served as colonial India's civil servants, not only in Bengal and the Punjab, the provinces directly partitioned, but also in areas that had larger minority populations (Gould et al. 2013: 239), partition presented a choice: to remain in India or continue with the civil service in Pakistan. The existence of this option, and the effects of civil servants' mobility across the new boundaries of partition, turned the categorization of civil servants by their communal, religious, geographic, and ethnic identities into a decision that would shape their entire lives. The anxious correspondence and negotiations around "the choice to serve in India or Pakistan" provide a site to trace the legacies of the axis of suspicion and its impact on political status, because that material and symbolic "choice" between India and Pakistan, which embodied the transition to independence and the trauma of partition, did not shape only the civil services themselves but how citizenship was visibly delineated through those who ran the state, according to a trinity of identity, loyalty, and mobility (see also Gould et al. 2013).

Classification according to identity and loyalty was rooted in the process of the Indianization of the civil service. The British had controlled the Indian bureaucracy by reserving powerful points of control for British members of the Indian Civil Service (ICS) and the IPS, or Indian Political Service, charged with foreign affairs (Potter 1973). Until the First World War, the staff for these services were British men. The process of "Indianization" of the ICS began in 1919 when the constitutional change of the Government of India Act established a diarchy that granted partial administrative autonomy to Indian ministers. The shift had a significant impact not only on allocations and appointments but also on the scope of authority and flexibility of bureaucratic discretion. Officers in the ICS believed it was necessary to retain "a strong European element" throughout the reforms but hesitated to do so publicly (Ewing 1984: 38). The Indianization of the service included requirements for recruiting Indians from minority communities (particularly Muslims) and introducing a quota of 20 percent of the ICS for promotions from civil servants of the provincial governments – a requirement that was never met. The ICS sought to recruit minorities for political reasons, to secure their allegiance against the predominantly Hindu independence movement.

The Indianization process instigated a fierce battle between groups about how recruits to the civil service were nominated and classified based on identity, and joint campaigns against the recruitment of Europeans (Potter 1973: 61). In 1935, the Government of India Act ended diarchy and introduced a constitution that included safeguards enabling the broad discretion and flexibility of the executive power of British officials in times of crisis (De 2012: 62). By 1945, as partition neared, the British government felt that the allegiance of ICS officers had shifted from the government of India to nationalist forces in India (Muslim officers to the Muslim League and Pakistan, and the rest to the Indian National Congress and independent India).[31] As the deadline for the transfer of power approached, the Indianization of the civil service accelerated. Every six months, the India Office required statistics to show the size and composition of the ICS.[32] In the reports, civil servants were categorized as Europeans, Indians, and Others.

The achievement of independence, coupled with partition, transformed the relationship between civil servants and both the new political leadership and their respective communities, while relying on the inherited institutional structure. Their relationship was narrated through very literally choosing sides: India or Pakistan. In the hurried process of dividing the assets of British India, people, animals, financial liabilities, machines, and files,[33] ICS staff and provincial government staff in Bengal and the Punjab could opt to serve in the other dominion according to their communal identity, until a deadline of six months after partition demanded the decision to be "India or Pakistan, final." Their choice was incredibly significant to the administration and the political leadership.[34]

Civil servants who had initially opted to serve in Pakistan before August 15, 1947, and later changed their minds, requesting to serve in India, were classified as suspicious, potentially disloyal, or of dubious loyalty. The inherited axis of suspicion, used to categorize people that posed a threat to colonial rule, became central to their own classification. Questions of the domicile and classification of civil servants occupied the Establishments Section of the Ministry of Home Affairs for a decade after partition, particularly when displaced persons from the other dominion applied for positions.

The Establishments Section classified ICS officers into six categories related to their status after partition. These were: Indian officers who wished to continue working in the provinces to which they belonged; European officers who wished to remain in their provinces; officers who wished to transfer to different provinces within the Indian union; officers who wished to transfer to Pakistan; officers who wished to retire but remained in the workforce temporarily due to dire need; and officers who wished to retire at the moment of partition.[35]

After everyone had filed their choice of "India or Pakistan, final," and all the officers who had chosen to leave their posts for Pakistan withdrew from their departments, an office order renamed the departments as Home Department (India) and Home Department (Pakistan).[36] Officers who had been dismissed from government service or those administrators marked as having "doubtful loyalty" suffered from mobility restrictions that ranged from the type of passport they could carry to complete refusal of passport services for travel outside of India. The ministry justified the restrictions upon the possibility that those individuals were likely to vilify or speak against the government of India in a foreign country.[37] Until the policy was amended in 1953, "doubtful loyalty" had severe implications for freedom of movement among civil servants.

While those who had initially chosen Pakistan and then opted to remain in India were held in high suspicion and suffered discrimination, those perceived as loyal to the national struggle were given support. The ministry issued an order to aid former government workers who had been previously blacklisted by the British colonial administration for political activities geared toward independence (and had consequently lost their positions) in finding government positions in the civil service after independence.[38] This order was difficult to implement because questions arose about what exactly should be classified as loyalty and/or patriotic activities (e.g., Indian National Congress activities) and what should be considered "real" subversive terrorist activities (e.g., communist or extreme right-wing activities). In 1949, the ministry decided it could not establish such a policy because it involved determining an individual's political affiliation, so they would decide on a case-by-case basis. There were civil servants who had been dismissed by the colonial government for anti-British activities related to independence that "had joined groups that were entirely objectionable" to the independent government.[39]

The question was "whether a member of a terrorist party in India [could] be treated as having participated in synergetic activities ... with the national movement for the liberation of the country for the purposes of orders regarding the grant of relief to such persons."[40] This negotiation, in which administrators determined how those who had been suspicious to the colonial government should be rewarded in the independent administration, shows an unsuccessful attempt to separate the convergence of political threat and security threat that was a hallmark of British hybrid bureaucracy. Although the debate about definitions of loyalty and suspicion was passionate and elaborate, it was not really that significant for appointment: having been blacklisted and dismissed from the colonial civil service because of political activities did not guarantee one a job, but it did open up the possibility of applying for reinstatement or accessing a small government loan.

How Mobility Defined the Loyalty of Civil Servants

For government officials, police, and the military, the decision to serve in "India or Pakistan final" was not only determined by their religion, community, or caste. By March 1948, an estimated twelve thousand Muslim government servants and policemen who had initially left India were seeking to return and aiming to be reinstated in their previous posts (Gould et al. 2013: 245). Zamindar (2007) has also shown the complex trajectories of mobility and belonging that government workers faced. The Ministry of Home Affairs considered civil servants who had opted first to serve in Pakistan and then requested positions in India as suspicious, and their loyalties were thoroughly investigated. In 1948, the ministry instituted separate specific policies to prevent their reinstatement "until their antecedents have been verified by the police."[41]

In their attempt to decide on who would be reinstated or discharged, officials engaged in deeply emotive correspondence, to create a distinction between those who "constitute[d] sufficient ground for reinstatement or discharges of such persons on security grounds." Finally, in 1949, the ministry decided upon three criteria to determine the loyalty of civil servants who had first requested a post in Pakistan and later opted for service in India. The first category was those with non-aligned political opinions. One direct consequence for determining such loyalty included removing from service those who harbored "certain political opinions". Reports did not necessarily need to identify such persons as having publicly participated in demonstrations or being formal members of political organizations that pursued an ideology "inconsistent with loyalty to India," but could include even "activities of an informal nature, such as propaganda among friends."[42] Police reports on these civil servants were formatted as intelligence reports and went much further than just checking antecedents. They also attempted to capture civil servants' political opinions, ideas, and social networks in order to assess their level of loyalty to independent India.

The second type of case involved those for whom allegations were not sufficiently specific or serious "to raise suspicions against the employees in question and render their continuance in service risky for the security point of view."[43] The report elaborates upon this category we could call "suspicious affinities": "These are cases, for instance, in which the police report that though nothing is found against them on record, they are believed to have held Muslim league views and their loyalty to India is doubtful." Apparently, their ties of kinship, affiliation, and the mobility of their family determined the level of suspicion: "If it appears that the employee has connections in Pakistan with whom he is in constant communication, if reinstated he would hold the position that could be of harm to the government of India, there will be a case for removing him."

The third class of cases placed the entire set of loyalty criteria in a peculiar light, as the emotional correspondence demonstrates that many in the leadership of the ministry seemed to think, at the end of the day, that police reports were categorically skewed and basically unreliable: "There are cases in which employees deserve reinstatement in spite of adverse police reports. Police have often taken the view that redeployment of a person is undesirable, merely because they opted provisionally for Pakistan." While the ministry understood police had a categorical bias against Muslims who had opted first for Pakistan and then for India, they still relied on the police's intelligence reports to decide whether the civil servants were suspicious or of doubtful loyalty. What may seem like a paradox of simultaneous distrust of the police reports by ministry officials and their use of them for decision-making is actually consistent with the organizing principles of personalism and flexibility that enabled officials to employ and justify a different set of practices and judgments, depending on the identities of the population in question.

In addition to classification by the three criteria, another critical factor for determining civil servants' "loyalty" involved their mobility and the location of their family during the early years of independence.[44] The Ministry of Home Affairs had demanded that all government employees in India bring their families back from Pakistan within a month, and furnish reasons to the head of their office if they were unable to do so.[45] Those who failed faced actions against them.[46]

When departments requested to know whether they could employ government workers who had opted for India but whose families had stayed in Pakistan, the ministry replied adamantly about the issue of loyalty. When administrators and military commanders asked if the civil servant's intention to settle permanently in India was enough to acquire Indian domicile, the ministry replied that it was the choice to remain in Pakistan that rendered them suspicious:[47]

The persons whose families do not wish to move from Pakistan may be categorized as doubtful. Those whose families cannot move from Pakistan, however, may be dealt with leniently, as it is only because of the compulsion of circumstances that the members of their families have not been able to migrate from Pakistan.[48]

When N. L. Nagar of the Appointments Section, in an attempt to standardize policy, stated that the intention of civil servants to bring their families from Pakistan to reside in India was not enough, he conveniently overlooked the fact that the discussion was about those who allegedly still had the right to choose "India or Pakistan, final": "Nationality and domicile are two different things. Persons who have opted to serve in India may not be Indians, and they cannot acquire Indian nationality merely by opting for service in the Indian union." Some officials retaliated against this rigid directive, calling for an approach that addressed the mayhem and uncertainties of post-partition life. They saw domicile and nationality as a "technical formality" because there was a host of legitimate reasons after partition to "persuade civil servants to leave their families in Pakistan in their ancestral homes rather than take the risk of unsettled existence." Families could lose their properties in Pakistan if they moved to India, some officials explained, and thereby "aggravate hardship and distress that the officer and his family are already put to by reason of separation."[49]

The only consensus between ministry officials was that the determining factor for appointments was "the issue of security."[50] Officials suggested relaxing the rules for determining domicile because of the uncertainty created by the mass movement of people from Pakistan to India. They suggested that only those candidates who were domiciled in Pakistan but had moved to be of service to the Indian dominion would need certificates of eligibility. Finally, the Establishments Section decided that civil servants needed certificates of eligibility if they migrated to India from Pakistan after September 30, 1948, or if they had not been continuously in government service since the day of partition, August 15, 1947. Nevertheless, Nagar reserved wide discretion for the ministry to decide. Those who served in India continuously would retain their positions "unless any of them is regarded by the authorities as unsuitable."[51]

The majority of them were Muslim. Therefore, those who had opted for "India, final" but were domiciled in Pakistan needed certificates of eligibility.[52] To obtain them, they had to provide a detailed statement and list of their family members, and the local Criminal Investigation Department (CID) and Intelligence Bureau would be consulted before each certificate the ministry issued. This meant that those who had opted to serve in Pakistan and later changed their choice would, for the most part, be considered "disloyal" and rejected.

The story of one non-Muslim clerk in the office of the Accountant General in Bombay, S. E. Cooper, who had failed to bring his family back from Pakistan, demonstrated the administrators' suspicion of both mobility across the dominions and kinship ties in "hostile" Pakistan.[53] Cooper had taken sick leave and had left to join his family in Karachi. Months had passed before he put forth a plea that no suitable accommodations were provided for his family in Bombay. He asked, for lack of any alternative, for the transfer of his service to the office of the High Commissioner for India in Pakistan. The ministry decided to discontinue the services of Mr. Cooper on the grounds of disloyalty and desertion, concluding that his plea was disingenuous. The administrators painted him as manipulative and conniving and wrote that "Mr. Cooper never thought, even in his dreams, to make India his permanent home," and that he opted provisionally for India with "definite mental reservations." Moreover, he had stalled his decision only to take advantage of his leave, and "he also committed another very serious crime of 'desertion' by slipping away surreptitiously to Pakistan, which for all practical purposes is ostensibly a hostile country. Taken with his reaction to our orders for bringing back families from West Pakistan, casts a very serious doubt on the loyalty of Mr. Cooper."[54]

The relative ease with which civil servants were declared disloyal (or of doubtful loyalty) because of their familial ties or trips taken to Pakistan in a time of turmoil, violence, and uncertainty is even more striking given the dire need for well-trained and experienced administrative personnel, who had left because of the violence. It can be better understood from the political stance of Home Minister Sardar Vallabhbhai Patel that "the Muslim personnel of the services are thoroughly disloyal to Government."[55] For Patel, the loyalty of civil servants was key to maintaining the central government's control over the provinces. It was an ethnonational loyalty because, while he was suspicious of Muslim civil servants, he battled to retain the civil servants that had served the British, against the sentiments of most of the leadership of the Congress Party, who mistrusted them for serving the colonial state.

The axis of suspicion was based on the mobility of civil servants, their actual and perceived movements, and formed perceptions of their loyalty to the new state. While trajectories of movement made civil servants suspicious, allegations of corruption and inefficiency were not charted onto the scale of loyalty and suspicion, as we shall see in the transition of the civil service from Mandate Palestine to Israel. Curiously, the loss of staff due to allegations of disloyalty is mostly absent from reports on inefficiency and corruption in the Home Ministry. Corruption and loyalty were perceived as entirely separate issues.

Why Corruption Was Not Suspicious

Until the end of 1948, the major problem in the Indian Administrative Service (IAS), the successor to the ICS, was the lack of staff. The Home Ministry's review of independent India's first year tells a tale of the loss of personnel after partition but makes no mention of how much of that loss was due to classifications of suspicion. Before the Second World War, the ICS employed more than one thousand administrators, and these numbers remained stable during the war. Despite efforts by Home Minister Sardar Vallabhbhai Patel to ensure continuity of personnel (including the British)[56] in the civil service after the transfer of power and partition – by guaranteeing their conditions and pay, many European officials retired, and "On the transfer of Muslims to Pakistan, more than 3/5 of the total number [of administrators] was lost, and the number of ICS officers today is therefore less than 400."[57]

The anxiety that central and provincial administrations would be "weakened by the loss of experienced officers" led to a campaign to ensure that members of the Secretary of State Service (India Office) would continue to serve in the government of India after the transfer of power, even though this represented a complete reversal of the Indianization of the civil service that the independence movement had fought for so bitterly.[58] The governments of Punjab, Bengal, and Sind all confirmed the terms of continuity for British officers.[59] The high regard for British expertise also solidified the routines and practices of the colonial state, particularly concerning security and surveillance, despite the vocal desire of citizens to see significant change in the everyday work of the new independent government (Gould et al. 2013).

In order to fix the shortage of administrative officials in the provinces, in March 1948, chief secretaries established a special ad hoc board for emergency recruitment.[60] Since India's constitution declared that the new state would be a federation, a large number of states were merged in the provinces and integrated into unions that would be administered by the All India Civil Service. However, the rapid expansion of the IAS was a source of anxiety for citizens who believed that corruption had risen in the wake of partition and state-making. The ministry saw the corruption as a wartime legacy:

The existence of corruption and nepotism and inefficiency in the ranks of public services cannot be denied. They are not, however, a recent or sudden growth but are more or less a legacy from the past. The situation has undoubtedly been made worse by the war and its aftermath and the rapid expansion of India's government.[61]

The Establishments branch's narrative linked corruption and nepotism to the increased workload during the Second World War that had ushered less qualified persons into government service, the recruitment and entry of Indians from lower castes, and the subsequent decline in the number of Europeans. The overworked frenzy of preparations for partition and the first months of the state created both opportunities and incentives for corruption because "The high cost of living means that there's a lot of attention government workers devote to obtain their necessities. So, they can't devote their undivided attention to their official duties."[62]

While the public demanded a transformation in the corrupt practices of the colonial bureaucracy, and ministry officials attempted to identify sources of inefficiency, they overlooked the possibility that corruption was only one source of inefficiency and disparate outcomes in the British hybrid bureaucracy. Ministry officials did not consider how hybrid bureaucracy and its racialized practices that created disparate outcomes based on identity, in relying upon flexible decision-making, dispersed authority, and the wide discretion given to European officers, had created a system of effective inefficiency necessary for controlling populations but not for its development. Instead, while retaining the organizational principles, the ministry enacted measures to combat inefficiency. It replaced unqualified recruits with more qualified people. It also reintroduced a competitive examination, which had been the traditional form of recruitment to the ICS, initially structured to keep Indian applicants out of the civil services.[63] It went to great lengths to expand registration for emergency recruitment to the IAS and Indian Police, with a great deal of patronage networks and antiminority sentiment (Gould et al. 2013). Part of this expansion was the way displaced civil servants from Pakistan were resettled, through internal regulations based on their identity.

Loyalty, Eligibility, and Resettlement of Displaced Civil Servants

After partition, the Ministry of Home Affairs placed a high priority on absorbing government employees from Pakistan, setting up four coordinating bodies for this task in two years. The Transfer Bureau was responsible for resettling the "exodus of non-Muslim provincial government employees that had fled from Pakistan to India" following the outbreak of communal riots.[64] The Transfer Bureau assisted the refugee government servants of the Northwestern Frontier Provinces, Baluchistan, and the Sind. Inundated with work, the ministry relegated placement for the refugees from West Punjab and East Bengal to the governments of the divided provinces of East Punjab and West Bengal.

Court procedures and representation by lawyers for refugees who had arrived in large numbers from Pakistan led to the establishment of the Employment Coordination Committee set up in March 1948. A Special Employment Bureau was instituted to register highly qualified refugees. In May 1948, the Employment Exchange was a fourth body charged with the task of finding employment for the lower ranks of the central government, "mainly by getting rid of people who had been recruited and were unqualified during the war."[65]

The placement of displaced civil servants highlighted the racial hierarchies of the civil service, through differentiated practices of suspicion toward those who had a relationship to Pakistan. Forms, questionnaires, and internal regulations were reinvented to facilitate the denial of placement to refugee civil servants. To be appointed to the civil service one had to be a national of the Indian dominion by birth or domicile, a person of Indian descent, a citizen of the Indian states, a citizen of the Pakistan dominion, or a citizen of any other territory adjacent to India who had a declaration of eligibility.[66] The cutoff dates of articles 5 through 9 in the Indian constitution[67] determined the citizenship of displaced government workers who migrated from Pakistan if they had resided in India six months before July 1948.

In August 1947, the ministry had declared that citizens of Pakistan could not work for the government without a certificate of eligibility, yet no one in the ministry knew what a certificate of eligibility was, what it should look like, or how to create one.[68] It was a category established to monitor Muslim government workers, but it also created an obstacle for the ministry with regard to recruiting non-Muslim civil servants who were residents of Pakistan, or who had been evacuated to India and could not be treated as citizens of India for purposes of appointment.

Therefore, while non-Muslims did not need declarations of eligibility, the ministry demanded declarations of eligibility from British subjects and Muslim citizens of Pakistan through an internal regulation: "Non-Muslims belonging to Pakistan who have migrated to India may be deemed citizens of the Indian dominion. It is not necessary to issue declarations [of eligibility] in their favor. They may be appointed straightaway."[69] K. N. Subbanna assured the Home Ministry that the Ministry of Law would not dispute "the validity of our executive order," even though it was directed only toward Muslims. In 1949, in order to make it easier to recruit non-Muslim displaced government servants from Pakistan, the ministry decided to relax the rule regarding the domicile of an applicant so that "displaced persons shall be treated as domiciled in the area where they now reside or where they intend to reside permanently."[70]

In order to avoid the glaring discrimination against Muslim refugees, the ministry created a domicile questionnaire. The elaborate list of questions that applicants were required to answer included: where their father was born; permanent residence at birth; location of father's death; if their father had ever been in East Punjab/West Bengal; had they come to East Punjab/ West Bengal for employment or other reasons?; location of their school; how often they left the province; if their parents had immovable property in East Punjab/West Bengal (and, if so, the candidates were asked to describe the property and its value); where the candidates were born; if they had ever been back to their native land; and if their wife had ever been back to their native land.[71] Each answer to the questions on domicile offered opportunities for discretion, to designate refugee applicants as unsuitable due to their doubtful or conflicting loyalties.

The domicile questionnaire had some unintended consequences. Despite the desperate need for experienced administrators, foreigners could not acquire Indian nationality by domicile because "the definition of the term 'Indian national' and the rules governing it have yet to be evolved by the constituent assembly of India,"[72] so civil servants such as those domiciled in Burma or Ceylon as well as Britain were classified as "non-Indians," because the term "British subject" did not grant status after independence.[73] Issues of identity, loyalty, and suspicion, and the distrust of civil servants from minority groups or those politically affiliated with opposition groups, continued to afflict the civil service throughout the 1950s, when both formal citizenship laws and Supreme Court decisions assuaged the blatant discrimination against displaced Muslims in the Home Ministry.

The combination of an urgent need for administrators at a time of emergency, practices of population classification based on an axis of suspicion embedded in everyday practices, and discrimination on the basis of racial and religious categories, created conditions in which the organizing principles of the hybrid colonial bureaucracy – formerly abhorred by leaders of the independence movement for their discriminatory nature – intensified under the Ministry of Home Affairs. However, the situation was very different in Palestine, where, after independence, Palestinian civil servants were not even part of the equation of potential staff. Over 90 percent of Arab civil servants were exiled or fled in the wake of the violence of the war, and others, excluding a negligible minority, were not seen as possible candidates ↗ Arabs were scratched out of the organizational chart and vanished from the potential staff lists of the new civil service in Israel, which combined those who had served the British Mandate with the administration of the Yishuv.

LOYALTY AND SUSPICION OF BRITISH CIVIL SERVANTS AT THE END OF THE MANDATE

In Palestine, the number of Jewish clerks in the colonial government had been a constant source of anxiety for the leadership of the Yishuv, which relied on them both for intelligence and to procure immigration certificates for Jews to Palestine – the principal task, after land acquisition, for growing the Jewish population in Palestine. Without a representative legislative body for colonial subjects, as there was in India, the civil servants were a key to resources and information.

Classifications based upon identity played a prominent role in encouraging Jewish recruits into the colonial government. Jewish Agency officials blamed the low ratio of Jews to the population in the civil service on British categorization according to nationality or race. In 1937, a worried David Gurevitz, head statistician of the Jewish Agency, a figure we encountered in Chapter 2 regarding the demographic battles over the Palestine census, wrote that he found that different categorizations of staff, based upon religion or nationality, made a difference in the enumeration.[74] The British categorized the civil servants as Jews, Arabs, and Others; the Jewish Agency categorized them as Jews, Arabs, Christians, and Others. Because of the discrepancies between the categories, Gurevitz's method for confirming the number of Jewish staff was to review the colonial government staff lists and identify Jews by the spelling of their name (see Figure 5).

The government apparatus, at the end of the British Mandate, encompassed approximately 29,000 permanent employees and 9,500 temporary employees – British, Arab, and Jewish. After independence and during the war in 1948, over 85 percent of government workers disappeared; 5,200 Jewish civil servants remained (4,500 clerks and service workers; 700

Category	Jews	Arabs	Other	Total
High civil servants	1,245	2,957	534	4,736
Low civil servants	1,213	7,764	2,058	11,035

FIGURE 5 Civil service staff, Mandate government of Palestine for 1937[75]

police officers). The new state apparatus needed 8,000 staff, who would come from former Mandate officials, Jewish Yishuv officials, and workers of the labor unions and parties. The civil servants that had served the Mandate were considered necessary because of their knowledge and expertise (Braun 2008: 46). But most of the political leadership believed they were not to be trusted because of their former service to the British and their lack of demonstrable loyalty to the Yishuv, and because they were perceived as corrupt. Similar to India, the discourse on the legacies of British colonial corruption was deployed by powerful members of the ruling majority party as an opportunity to maintain patronage networks and delineate the political affiliations of the independent civil service, which was now predominantly Jewish.

Exiled Palestinian and "Partially Foreign" Jewish Civil Servants: The Purification Committees

Just two days after independence, during the very first meeting of the temporary government, Bechor Shitrit, who would later serve as Minister of Police, voiced the need for a "purification" of the civil service.[76] The purification committees of the Jewish civil servants of the Mandate were not a unique witch-hunt that took place in the particular context of distrust between the three militant Jewish factions that fought the British, as some have assumed (Braun 2008). The purification committees based their activities on the colonial legacy of categories of suspicion and graded loyalties that were a prevalent feature of population management and the classification of the civil service in the British hybrid bureaucracy.

In the 1920s, only 23 percent of the officials in the Mandate were Jews, but the percentage of Jews in the upper ranks of the civil service consistently exceeded their share of the population (De Vries 1997: 375). The number of Muslim Palestinians increased during the 1930s and 1940s, but there were many more Christian Palestinians working for the colonial government in proportion to their numbers in the population (Hareuveni 1993: 109).

At the end of the Mandate, over 85 percent of the employees of the Mandatory government were exiled or fled during the war and Nakba. Of 12,000 Palestinian civil servants, some members of the upper ranks found placement in the administrative apparatus in Jordan. Although one-quarter of Palestinian civil servants in the Mandate government were from the Palestinian political elite, only some of the senior officials engaged in political activity for purely nationalist motives; only some used their positions on behalf of the national movement. The majority of the senior officials in government departments in Jerusalem had not engaged in intense national political activity when they were in the service (Al-Hout 1979) due to inter-elite rivalries (Khalidi 2007) but also because government employees were often perceived as mediators between the ruling power center and society at large, operating in parallel to the formal institutional representatives of the two national communities (De Vries 2004: 616). Almost all the Palestinian political elite were exiled or left following the violence that ensued after the UN endorsement of the plan to partition Palestine (Smith 1986).

The participation of Arab civil servants in the apparatus of the new state was unclear, but not entirely predetermined. The Mandate's last commissioner appealed to Palestinian government officers to notify him if they wished to remain in office in the successor state. According to the UN's Palestine commission, Palestinian Mandate workers were to retain their conditions after the regime change.[77] Three months before Israel declared independence, the situation committee (Vaadat Hamatzav) out-lined an emergency plan for the establishment of the apparatus of the Jewish state after its independence. Starting in February 1948, a principle guideline defined the role of Arabs in the civil service based on their loyalty to the state.[78] They agreed that Arabs could not be recruited to fill positions in the higher ranks that they had held in the Mandate govern-ment, and they would "have to be under constant supervision and surveil-lance." The government intended to announce that it would depend on "the loyalty and cooperation of the Arab administrators" to provide services to the Arab population.[79] Despite the plan to allow the Arab civil servants to remain – if they would be perceived as "loyal" – three months later, following the declaration of independence, most civil ser-vants had fled or been expelled during the Nakba in the civil war that ensued. Very few Palestinians remained in the state civil service, and those who had managed to stay found employment at local levels through appointments with the military government and ministry of minorities. This shift, from the possibility of incorporating the Palestinian civil servants of the Mandate to their elimination from the Israeli civil service, seems to be related to the different stages of the war and the Nakba. Historian Hillel Cohen argues that prior to independence, the intercommunal war was a defensive one. Four weeks after the declaration of independence, the effort turned to reducing the number of Palestinians in Jewish-controlled territories and led to mass expulsions (Cohen 2018).

The Israeli political leadership believed that former civil servants of the Mandate should remain in government service; they had the expertise and administrative knowledge, and the Jewish establishment had worked tirelessly to get them into the civil service and increase the number of Jews who ran the state.[80] However, they also harbored high suspicion of their loyalty to the British civil service, fiercely cultivated by the British officials (De Vries 2004: 616). Their neutrality and the fact they spoke mostly English, along with the British cultural markers they had acquired, turned them into partial foreigners.

The provisional government decided to halt appointments to the Israeli civil service until they could screen administrators who had served in the Mandate government so that their "ability and integrity was verified."[81] However, Jewish administrators who had worked in the Jewish establishment (the Yishuv) did not have to go through such a process, although there were numerous anonymous letters sent to the Jewish Agency claiming particular clerks of the Jewish Agency were "national traitors."[82] In January 1948, the organization of Jewish clerks in the British Mandate requested to join the ranks of the Histadrut (the most prominent workers' organization) so they could participate in the restructuring of the state administration, but the provisional government ignored the request.[83]

As the apparatus committee developed lists of personnel and offices needed for government operations, the purification committees that determined loyalty began their work, which would take two years, across the country, as thousands of former civil servants of the colonial government experienced the precarious uncertainty of being fired from their positions pending the decisions. The apparatus committee enjoyed the wide discretion given to the situation committee by the Jewish Agency to implement the transfer of power and structure the civil service. The apparatus committee created a file for each Jewish administrator in the Mandate government, including profile reports from SHAI, the secret service of the

Hagannah (the militant arm of the Yishuv).[84] The apparatus committee also invited the public to submit anonymous reports about their experience with former Mandate civil servants. Pinhas Rosenblit (later Rosen), who was to become Israel's first Minister of Justice and an influential figure in designing the state's racially differentiated citizenship regime, spearheaded the inquiry and had full discretion to decide who could continue to work in the administration, who was undesirable, and who should be prevented from working in the new state apparatus (Braun 2008: 55). Two days after the declaration of independence, Rosenblit and a group of lawyers assembled as the purification committee began to fire former civil servants of the Mandate.

In June 1948, the new People's Council, which preceded the new independent parliament before the first elections, promulgated an ordinance that declared that all administrators of the Palestine government would continue to serve temporarily in the Israeli administration, and granted authority to any minister to fire or transfer a civil servant "without declared reasons and immediately."[85] Two weeks later, the committees began vetting the "the abilities and personality of anyone intended to serve the state of Israel."[86]

Members of the investigation committees served as chosen representatives of the political factions in the People's Council. The committees had far-reaching authorities to check the bank accounts and financial details of each Mandate civil servant in order to discover "elements of corruption." A week after the appointment of the committees, an advertisement in *Haaretz*, a widely read newspaper, urged the public to supply information to the committees and aid them in their task to "evaluate the personal traits of the candidate that had served the former Government of Palestine, and decide who among them deserves to serve the government of Israel."[87] The situation committee had received both named and anonymous letters regarding civil servants' attitudes toward the transfer of power, some reporting on people who wrote they would have agreed to work for the civil service "even under the rule of the Arabs."[88]

The committees classified the candidates into three categories. The first was those against whom the committee found no evidence, doubts, or suspicions. They were appointed to the civil service. The second category included people about whom the committee had minor doubts as to whether they had accepted minor bribes in the context of the corrupt environment of the last days of the Mandate government. If they were appointed, their supervisors were instructed to surveil and scrutinize them closely. In the third category were administrators the committee had evidence against; they were fired. The evidence was not as convincing as one might expect. An illustrative example of this third category is the case of David Goldberg, who worked at the Mandate government printing agency. A secret report made a variety of allegations against him, including that he would sell his rations, supply his brothers' private press with paper from the government press, treat workers badly, speak too much English, and flatter the British.[89] These miscellaneous categories are similar to the array of reasons that landed colonial subjects on the Home Office suspect list, as we saw in Chapter 3.

Some of those fired were civil servants who had made sacrifices for the Yishuv during the confusing days of the end of the Mandate. Although they were ordered to remain steadfast in their positions and continue going to work, the Jewish Agency could neither guarantee their safety nor help if going to work breached their safety.[90]

The purification committees' secret meetings meant that civil servants did not have a chance to combat allegations against them, or even know what they were. The secret service supplied their files, including anyone on "their blacklist." A public outcry followed the decision to deny over 10 percent of Jewish civil servants' appointments and classify another 10 percent of the former civil servants as doubtful or suspicious (Braun 2008: 64).

The committees classified hundreds of former Mandate police officers in the third category and fired them. The stated reason for firing the police officers was corruption, but budgeting plans for the new Israeli police force demonstrate that downsizing the force was also a financial necessity. The police officers mounted protests and petitioned the Supreme Court against the actions of the purification committees. The Supreme Court decided that the committees' procedures were arbitrary and did not comply with fair administrative principles. When the government ignored the ruling, the fired police officers attempted, in protest, to take over the main police station in Tel Aviv. They were dispersed by tear gas and later arrested (Braun 2008: 87–88).

The effects of the purification committees, a process open to public input yet veiled in secrecy, were justified as a way of vetting former bureaucrats that had served the Mandate, according to their tendencies of heart and affinities of character, which went hand in hand with appointments according to political affinity and personalism. The making of the civil service in Israel both entailed the prevention of Palestinian participation on the national level and was also a process defined by the investigation of political affinities and behaviors, through the use of the secret service and the discretion of party officials.

THE LEGACIES OF COLONIAL CATEGORIES OF SUSPICION AFTER INDEPENDENCE IN CYPRUS, ISRAEL/PALESTINE, AND INDIA

Examination of the classification and plight of civil servants during the transition from colonial rule to independent state, in the wake of plans for partition, produces very different insights from research that focuses on the state-building actions the civil service performed. Classification of civil servants was critical because of the inherited principles of hybrid bureaucracy – administrative flexibility, wide discretion, and personalism – which meant that the identity of the official was a determining factor for any administrative outcome.

Turning our gaze on the way their administrations viewed civil servants underscores the effects of the axis of suspicion inherited from British hybrid bureaucracy, which were different in each case. In India, minority civil servants underwent a regime of suspicion and doubt based upon their communal belonging, yet during the first decade after independence, many found employment possibilities in the independent republic. In Israel, where a military government ruled the Palestinian minority until 1966, the role of Palestinian civil servants was negligible, usually made possible only if they were considered collaborators or useful to the Jewish state establishment. Palestinian civil servants of the Mandate government had left in the wake of the violence in 1948 and including the remainder of the Palestinian citizens in Israel was a slow administrative process. Despite affirmative action plans, Palestinian citizens of Israel to date comprise only 6 percent of the civil service – mostly in the lower ranks – although they constitute 20 percent of Israel's population. In Cyprus, the clashes of 1963 ended the participation of Turkish Cypriots in the civil service. After the Turkish invasion, partition, and establishment of the Turkish Republic of North Cyprus in 1974, the Turkish Cypriot administration assumed positions within the new state that was recognized only by Turkey.

CONCLUSION

This chapter investigated two of the three population categories that the colonial governments created and that the independent administrations adopted: forming an axis of suspicion alongside classification to make the population legible and classifying civil servants as a state-building project of and for the new majority following partition, independence, and Nakba. As the new states struggled with the necessity for administrative structure and routine, the legacies of the colonial administration that each had inherited to varying degrees, burdened them. In India and Cyprus, the classification of civil servants served as a communal battleground that eventually led to the collapse of the state machinery in Cyprus, and to a regime of suspicion and surveillance for Muslim civil servants in India. However, in India, after the first decade following independence, the classification and suspicion practices toward civil servants stabilized. In Israel, those very practices of suspicion were deployed against Jewish civil servants who had served the colonial government, since Palestinian administrators had fled during the war of independence, and those who remained were not considered suitable to serve the new government of the Jewish state. The purification committees marked a painful episode in the making of the Israeli civil service and the way the practices of classification according to suspicion shaped the transfer of power in the transition from colonial rule to an independent administration. In Cyprus, similar to India, the majority suspected civil servants from religious or caste minority groups, but in Israel, the Palestinians had not been considered part of the relevant pool of candidates for civil service, and practices of classification and suspicion were directed internally, within the rival Jewish factions. Classifying former civil servants of the colonial government as suspicious or of dubious loyalty was directly related to their pre-state organizational affiliations and commitment to the institutions of the Yishuv. These tests of loyalty and commitment to the Israeli national agenda were different from the way the administrative leadership treated those who had served in the colonial civil service in India and Cyprus during the transition to an independent administration. In India and Cyprus, public perception of the colonial civil service was apolitical and professional, imbued with the corruption of the racial hierarchies of colonial rule. Questions of loyalty and suspicion were directly linked to communal identity and religion, exacerbated by partition plans. In Israel, the state did not include Palestinians in its classification of loyal civil servants; as we shall see, at best, the state viewed Palestinians as collaborators and enablers rather than loyal subjects.

The transition from colonial rule to independence in the wake of the violence of partition created massive administrative work, and despite the awareness of and public debate against the use of colonial methods of classification and discrimination, these were used within the civil services and consistently justified by the conditions of emergency that existed at the time. The delineation of political affiliations, perceived loyalties, and the mobility of civil servants was part of the larger project of the delineation of the political community, through the monitoring of mobility according to the axis of suspicion.

5

How Hybrid Bureaucracy and Permit Regimes Made Citizenship

INTRODUCTION

In the dramatic violence of partition, war, and Nakba in 1947 and 1948, people fled India, Pakistan, and Palestine/Israel. In Cyprus, following intercommunal violence in 1963, Turkish Cypriots fled to enclaves, creating a territorial separation that has been called "the first partition" (Droussiotis 2005; Triminkliotis 2009). That flight and forced exile would become defining events for the designation of the political status of those who fled or were exiled (Sen 2018; Khalidi 2005; Masalha 1997).

But it was not the violence and exile themselves that created the long-term impact on political status and the making of citizenship (Cohen 2018). Rather, it was the bureaucratic response to the violence, subsequent exile, and population transfer that ensued – the institutional routines in their aftermath that created differentiated regimes of citizenship for those who were designated as belonging to the "other side" of partition, whether in another state or one that was not yet created (Kimmerling 1977: 172; Butalia 2017; Bryant 2012: 333).

Two groundbreaking studies mark the turn of attention from the debate on the violence of partition and independence and the causes of displacement, to their long aftermath of regime change that structured the citizenship of minorities (Bashkin 2020; Ramnath 2021). Vazira Zamindar (2007) invites us to understand the "long partition" of India and Pakistan not as an event but as a process,[1] in which nationality and belonging were framed through mobility restrictions and attempts to control the movement of millions of displaced persons. Shira Robinson (2013) shows how Israel's campaign against the return of refugees, through the establishment of mobility restrictions on the Palestinian remainder after the Nakba,[2] constructed their status as "citizen strangers" of a formally liberal state and subjects of a settler colonial regime through the use of emergency laws and the establishment of a military government.

In India and Israel/Palestine, powerful home ministries and other organizations deployed restrictions on mobility and spatial designations to monitor the movement of subject populations in order to control or prevent the return of minorities who had fled the violence of partition and the war. As they attempted to go back to their homes, permit regimes were enacted to block their return: a permit system on India's western frontier with Pakistan and a permit regime in the "security zones" of the military government in Israel established to control the remaining Palestinian population. Virtually overnight, people who had been colonial subjects became refugees who would be classified as intruders, infiltrators, undesirables, and security threats.

This chapter builds upon these studies to advance the claim that the bureaucratic mobility regimes the new states used to manage populations in flight were inherited from the British hybrid bureaucracy and created an organizational template that continues to shape the way citizenship is practiced and experienced in the present day. Initially justified as security measures, they created the conditions in which official documents that enabled mobility became necessary means for survival. The mobility regimes across the partition lines became the organizational building blocks of national belonging and citizenship. The implementation of the bureaucratic toolkit relied on the continuity of colonial emergency laws that the independent states chose to incorporate into the new regime.

During the early years of the states, the absence of formal citizenship and nationality laws made it possible for bureaucrats to determine political membership in Israel and India through designations of mobility and suspicion. The permit regimes themselves were unplanned and unforeseen. This was an example of one of the features of British hybrid bureaucracy – the routinization of emergency, which occurs when the administration creates an ad hoc response to a problem and then that practice is solidified and institutionalized into administrative regulations, justified politically and institutionally by both the emergency and the racial hierarchy ingrained in the administrative toolkit of separate practices for separate populations.

The first section of this chapter returns to the overarching argument of the book, outlining the way that bureaucratic practices affected political membership in the new states, using the inherited colonial bureaucratic toolkit of emergency (Chapter 3) and the axis of loyalty and suspicion

(Chapter 4) through its classifications of mobility, based on identity and suspicion (Chapter 2). It marshals the similarities between the permit regimes in India and Israel, and the divergent outcome in Cyprus, discussed in the following empirical sections, to show that inheritance of the tools of racialized bureaucracy, the two powerful tools of empires (as in Arendt), were contingent on the continuity of the colonial emergency laws and the sphere of bureaucratic power it produced to shape political categories (as in Hussain). The second section, on the permit regime in India, juxtaposes the bureaucratic development of a mobility regime to regulate entry from Pakistan on the western border, which would become a mechanism to curtail Muslim claims for citizenship, with a surveillance mechanism on the eastern border. The third section traces how the military government developed a set of mobility restrictions to control the remaining Palestinian population, which were gradually used to differentiate between Palestinians and prevent claims to citizenship. The fourth section, on Cyprus, discusses its divergent path following the abolition of the emergency laws at independence, the attempt to rid the new civil service of features of hybrid bureaucracy in the first three years of the republic, and the very different mobility regime that developed after the implosion of the constitution. The analysis provides the link between the practices of hybrid bureaucracy and the way they created a conceptual grid that structured citizenship, not as an abstract membership in the community or access to tangible rights but as one defined by an individual's trajectory for mobility.

MOBILITY REGIMES TO RESTRICT TRANSITION FROM SUBJECTS TO CITIZENS

While the motivations to institute the permit regimes were different in Israel and India, the bureaucratic technologies of the permit regime were based on the bureaucratic toolkit of emergency developed in the interwar period. As we saw in Chapter 3, these were initially practices based on the agglomeration of technologies of surveillance and calculations of risk formed during times of crisis, what Foucault (2007: 21) called the "dispositif of security," but gradually institutionalized into the daily fabric of colonial bureaucracy through the routinization of emergency. The array of emergency restrictions solidified and became an apparatus to control movement across frontiers and within restricted areas, which included the designation of disturbed or dangerous areas, permits needed to travel, daily demands for registration, and detention.

In turn, these repertoires, which were contingent on the continuity of the colonial emergency laws, were used by home ministries and other bodies to control, prevent, and monitor the movement of minority populations during their early years of crisis. The bureaucratic routines that assigned permits for mobility gradually solidified the statuses of stateless, refugees, infiltrators, internally displaced, residents, or citizens.[3] These classifications were to shape a differentiated regime of citizenship on a graded scale of suspicion based on mobility, rather than one of rights.

While in the metropole, emergency meant that the governments had to suspend citizens' rights, in the independent postimperial states, citizenship rights had yet to be carved out of an emergency state that had ruled subjects. Therefore, with continuity of emergency laws, the administration did not have to strip people of their citizenship to deny them rights; they had only to prevent people from gaining status as citizens or residents.

The permit regimes had transformed colonial practices of population management that had originated in the interwar emergency laws into a method of administrative exclusion, reducing the number of those who could claim citizenship once the statutory laws were enacted and enabling citizenship as a differentiated structure of domination for those who would (Tatour 2019: 13).

Told separately, the histories of preventing the return of refugees who fled or were exiled because of intercommunal violence at partition in India/Pakistan, war and dispossession in Israel/Palestine, or the constitutional implosion of Cyprus inform national claims for sovereignty, belonging, return, and reparations. The stories of exclusion, domination, dispossession, and subjugation of those who attempted to return also help us understand the disparate political regime of each new nation-state in the aftermath of the racial ordering of empire.[4]

The bureaucratic regime to govern mobility and prevent return, and the making of political status were also means to achieve the goals of accumulation, dispossession, and repossession of land and property (Tatour 2019: 20; Bhandar 2018: 151–153; Sabbagh-Khoury 2021) and to perpetuate the racialized separation of labor (Shafir 1996; Nuriely 2019).[5] While the mobility regimes served the trinity of goals to regulate land, labor, and political status, the effort here is focused on the latter, from the standpoint that population management and land and property acquisition were managed by different organizations within the state bureaucracy.

Investigated together, the shared and connected histories of bureaucratic practices to restrict mobility that enabled the differentiated regime of citizenship, provide three points for theoretical intervention from an organizational perspective: the first is to highlight the role of bureaucratic practices in shaping political status; the second is the way colonial bureaucracy shaped the nation-states; and the third is to challenge the idea of neutral bureaucracy – that the machinery of the state will continue to function similarly, regardless of regime change, through the divergence of the trajectories in Israel/Palestine and India, on one hand, and Cyprus, on the other.

EMERGENCY LAWS AS A CONDITION FOR INHERITED HYBRID BUREAUCRACY

The critical juncture that marked the different trajectories of bureaucratic legacy between Israel and India and Cyprus was the fate of the colonial emergency laws and the bureaucratic powers they afforded in the new states.[6] India incorporated the colonial emergency laws into its formal laws and the constitution (Kalhan et al. 2006; Singh 2007; Baruah 2014); Israel maintained the colonial emergency laws, also used as the legal scaffolding of a separate military government to govern the remainder of the Palestinians following the war of independence and the Nakba (Mehozay 2016; Sa'di 2016).[7] Cyprus relinquished the colonial emergency laws at independence and did not incorporate similar emergency provisions in the constitution, except to combat direct political violence.[8] In both Israel and India, emergency laws were the baseplate for the use of the bureaucratic toolkit of emergency against minorities. In Israel, they served to control the Palestinian population during the military government from 1949 to 1966, and in 1967 were the basis for Israel's control of Palestinians in the West Bank and Gaza (Berda 2017). In India, the emergency laws would create the conditions for the declared Emergency in 1975 (Prakash 2019).

As we shall see, in Cyprus, where colonial emergency laws were relinquished at independence, the response to intercommunal violence and constitutional collapse led to an entirely different regime of constitutional exception (Constantinou 2008): the creation of a state within a state (Bryant & Hatay 2020).[9] This divergence highlights the choice to retain the colonial emergency laws as the decisive factor through which bureaucracy in the new states amassed the power and authority to shape political outcomes, including political membership. The reasons for this difference, the establishment of the Cypriot Republic as an international arrangement to avoid partition, and the temporal epoch of Cypriot independence in the era of decolonization and human rights are discussed later in this chapter.

The continuity of colonial emergency laws did not only provide the legal authority to deploy measures for the surveillance and control of the population within specific territories. Rouhana and Sabbagh-Khoury (2015) claim that emergency laws provided a framework for the enactment of multiple citizenship regimes, including "settler colonial citizenship" for Palestinians. Their insight on the role of colonial emergency laws can be broadened to situate citizenship regimes in the bureaucratic and legal aftermath of British imperial rule (Bhambra 2015), because the emergency laws were the vehicle that enabled the establishment of separate administrative practices for different populations within a modern liberal legal order.[10] The emergency laws provided the method for differentiation between populations by bureaucratic means so returning minorities were managed through administrative regulations, routines, and evidentiary demands.

BUREAUCRATIC POWER AND ENTREPRENEURSHIP IN THE FIRST YEARS

The permit regimes were developed through bureaucratic entrepreneurship, ad hoc solutions, and contradictory decisions. The anxious tensions of hybrid bureaucracy were a perpetual negotiation between those who wished to "keep the letter of the law" and those who wished to expand executive authority to "get the job done" – a negotiation that demanded constant bureaucratic innovation of documents, regulations, designations of territory, and classifications.

The permit regime that would delineate those who had "a right to have rights" on one side of the new border was not the product of a deliberate policy to define differentiated racialized citizenship through mobility restrictions. The differentiation was to be defined gradually by the documents, the checkpoints, the classification of the type of returnee one was, by registration and the absence of it, and by the distinctions of suspicion. Ad hoc measures that were at first justified by security reasons and emergency following the movement of populations, became institutionalized into classifications of political status, based on temporal and spatial restrictions on mobility. Shifting from the initial focus on security, the primary goal of these technologies was to bureaucratically prevent people from having documents, the evidence with which to claim their political belonging. The labyrinthine bureaucracy was complex, but the method of exclusion was simple: the permit regimes created a variety of identity documents and registries. If people could not get the identity documents they needed as evidence to prove their rights as citizens, they could be classified as residents, aliens, or infiltrators, with a constant contingency of their status. As the legislation of citizenship laws neared, the bureaucratic toolkit of emergency was no longer reserved for the purposes of surveillance, population legibility, and management, but was used to solidify the borders of the nation against those who were perceived as "enemies."

BUREAUCRATIC LOGICS OF SUSPICION: SIMILARITIES BETWEEN ISRAEL AND INDIA

As we shall see, Palestinians in Israel and Muslims and other minorities in India received citizenship based on the documents that enabled mobility during the permit regimes. The documents and classifications used during the permit regimes provided the material means to stay when citizenship laws were enacted. That legal inclusion of citizenship for "suspect" populations prevented their deportation. The rationale of suspicion in both countries was similar but had different applications in Israel and India. In India, intelligence reports claimed that some returning Muslim refugees could be made into loyal citizens, while others were "potential saboteurs and fifth columnists" who needed to be quarantined and policed. Indian officials feared the creation of "mini Pakistans" and that the "influx of many Muslims to this place is due to a deep conspiracy aimed at the establishment of a Muslim rule."[11] Thus, in India, Muslims were suspects, but they enjoyed the hypothetical possibility of being loyal citizens. Whereas in Israel, the scale of suspicion for Palestinians was clearer and harsher. At best, they could be collaborators with the military government, but even then, they remained suspect. As Robinson (2013: 10) shows, this was because, to secure its wartime territorial gains and simultaneously maintain international legitimacy as a democratic state, Israel had to assign political membership to some of the population that opposed the establishment of the state.

The primary similarity between the permit regimes in Israel and India beyond the continuity of emergency laws, was the prominence of the population registry and the specific fluidity of the categories of refugees and "infiltrators" based on a graded axis of suspicion. Both governments arranged for an urgent population census and specifically enumerated the displaced persons or refugees.

In September 1948, the Israeli military government orchestrated a special census because not all the Arabs had been included in the general census. The Israeli government ordered that Arab inhabitants be counted quickly so authorities could assess population numbers after the massive flights and expulsions, and also to help locate infiltrators who had returned after the census in order to expel them (Leibler & Breslau 2005). The newly founded ministry of rehabilitation in India, similarly, took a special census[12] of 5 million displaced persons from West Pakistan in October 1948 and 1.95 million from East Pakistan in July 1949.[13]

In India and Israel, voting preceded citizenship. The mobility regimes relied on the census registries conducted for the elections. Shani shows how the expansion of electoral rolls to universal franchise for the election in 1951, and particularly the bureaucratic effort to register partition refugees who were in a state of legal limbo, would create India's citizenship regime (Shani 2017: 5). In its first elections, Israel faced the fundamental quandary of meeting increasingly explicit international standards for political inclusion and democratic representation, while simultaneously appropriating Palestinian territory and ensuring the ethnocommunal character of the Jewish state. The inclusion of Palestinians in the vote was the result of what Shira Robinson calls "the unprecedented colonial bargain that its government believed it had to strike in order to gain international recognition in 1949 – to grant Palestinians the right to vote in the midst of its ongoing quest for their land" (Robinson 2013: 55).

In Cyprus, there was no registration or attempt at enumeration of the general population of the republic. Each community – Greek Cypriots and Turkish Cypriots – enumerated themselves as part of the demographic battle for municipal autonomy.[14] Population registers had been separate since 1956 and served as the basis for electoral rolls after independence.[15]

The second similarity between the permit regimes is the coupling of two related but different goals: the first, to survey and monitor the "suspicious" and "dangerous" Muslim population, which may be a "fifth column," in order to reduce "the growing menace of enemy espionage" and the pressure on the population caused by "one-way traffic" (Zamindar 2007: 94), and the second goal, to prevent the physical return of refugees by blocking their legal claims for citizenship through bureaucratic means. Each goal perpetuated a different set of bureaucratic practices and routines. The surveillance apparatus was directly inherited from the colonial regime, as Home Ministry officials and legal advisers "cut and pasted"

(Berda 2017) ordinances, practices, and document templates. Administrative exclusion from citizenship was an institutional innovation in which categorical suspicion was deployed by the bureaucracy, not only to curb mobility in the present but also to deny rights presciently.

As we shall see, in the Israeli permit regime, the military government worked toward both goals because the mobility regime was necessary to enable the takeover of Palestinian lands through the state and other pre-state organizations (Robinson 2013; Sa'di 2014). In India, however, surveillance and exclusion practices were carried out differently on the frontiers of West and East Pakistan. In the West, the focus was on excluding the population from citizenship. In the East, they focused on surveillance. The next section examines the administrative discourse on two separate frontiers – the permit system in East Punjab on the border with West Pakistan and attempts at surveillance and border controls in West Bengal on the border with East Pakistan – to understand the administrative mechanisms and negotiations between the ministries of Home Affairs and External Affairs. The organizational vantage point, which traces the institutional impact of racial hierarchy and the wide administrative discretion granted through routinized emergency, provides a distinctively different account of the ways that "managed mobilities" (Stoler 2012) of colonial rule delineated citizenship.

THE PERMIT REGIME IN INDIA

The Unplanned Permit Regime and the Axis of Suspicion

The partition and the transfer of power were meticulously planned and debated in India, by committees,[16] commissions,[17] and cartographers, as the national bodies of each community prepared for the exit of the British. The permit regime was not planned or foreseen in these debates, although, as we saw in Chapters 2 and 3, their institutional foundation of population management and political justification of territorial separation had developed for over a decade.

Initially, the partition plan had called for open borders and free movement across the dominions. The partition council thought there was even no necessity to distribute passports because partition was not to have any effect on nationality. This was not simply a declarative position. The partition council, charged with the administrative implementation of the partition plan, received a report from the Expert Committee (#8) on Domicile. The Expert Committee had recommended that Indians and

Pakistanis should be exempted from any impediments to freedom of movement, or visa restriction, because "the committee came to the conclusion that partition by itself will effect no change in nationality."[18] The committee recommended a mutual mobility regime:

A suitable adaption of the passport rules should be carried out under which the inhabitants of each dominion will be exempted from the passport regulations of the other dominion ... at the start there are no passport restrictions between the two dominions. The Dominion governments can later carry out such modifications, as they consider necessary.[19]

Despite the recommendation to the partition council and its initial implementation regarding the civil service, whose members were to choose to serve in Pakistan or India, the permit system was enacted shortly thereafter.

On July 14, 1948, the government of India announced it would establish a permit system for people coming across its western frontier with Pakistan as an emergency measure. It promulgated the Influx from Pakistan (Control) Ordinance, which determined that entering India from Pakistan without a permit was a criminal offense. Three months later, in October 1948, the government of Pakistan enacted a parallel permit system:[20] the Pakistan (Control of Entry) Ordinance 1948, in both East Bengal[21] and West Punjab.[22] This system controlled the movement of people across the borders until 1952, when special passports for travel between India and Pakistan were distributed. Established in 1948, the organization of the permit system was a massive, convoluted patchwork of changing administrative practices, technologies, and evidentiary demands "needed to enforce the system on the frontier."[23]

Building on Vazira Zamindar's study of the permit regime on the western border, this section investigates the debates to forgo the permit regime in the East, to highlight how bureaucrats negotiated and developed the mobility restriction. In particular, this debate on "why not to create a permit regime" underscores the elasticity of the terms "security," "emergency," and "suspicious populations" and the way the axis of suspicion justified administrative flexibility and differentiation based on the identity and location of the population.

The central government was deeply concerned that granting permits to Muslims who wished to return to India, estimated to be between thirty and forty thousand per month,[24] would result in their demand for citizenship and nationality. The Home Office justified the necessity of the permit regime because of suspicion against people perceived as possible security risks, and the initial goal of the permit regime was to block refugees' return as a new demographic threat, in which yesterday's residents became alleged enemy agents.

Strangely enough, despite the security threat posed by the influx of returnees, the Ministry of Finance decided not to implement a permit system on the mammoth eastern border despite the insistence of the ministries of Interior and External Affairs on population crossing as a security threat on the eastern border.

The paper trail of border security and monitoring in West Bengal demonstrates a stark difference between the way the practices and routines of border surveillance evolved within the administrative departments for the frontiers of East Punjab with West Pakistan and West Bengal's frontier with East Pakistan.[25] (See the map of post-partition India in Figure 6.) The initial position of the Ministry of Home Affairs (following

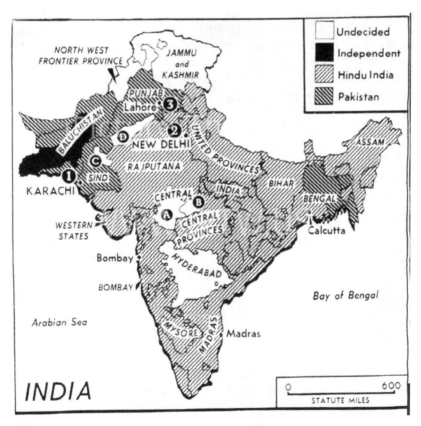

FIGURE 6 Post-partition India[26]

the partition council) was that any type of documentary surveillance on population movement between the two dominions was both illegitimate and unfeasible.

In view of the agreement recently reached between India and Pakistan ... The proposal to have a regular system of passports or visas or permits between the two dominions or the setting up of police posts in all road and rail crossings of the border for the purpose of checking all passengers crossing the border seems to be out of the question.²⁷

However, gradually, over the course of a few months, demands within the ministry and security forces for establishing an "unobtrusive watch" on population movement across the borders turned into security checks and an elaborate surveillance system.

The surveillance system was established because foreigners still had to be checked, so the Intelligence Bureau (DIB) in the Ministry of Home Affairs devised a scheme to circumvent the interdominion agreement on the freedom of movement. They would quietly issue "Separate instructions to the local police authorities concerned explaining that it would be desirable in the interest of security, to check all persons whether foreigners or others entering India from Pakistan and vice versa. This can easily be done under the cover of checking passports of foreigners entering India from Pakistan."²⁸

In the exchange within the Home Ministry, there was a fiery negotiation between officials who wished to "keep the letter of the law" and those who wished to expand executive authority to "get the job done," through forms of bureaucratic entrepreneurship to collect and classify the returning populations:

It is quite essential that we shall have some idea of the numbers of Muslims returning to India and the numbers of non-Muslims leaving Pakistan for India. This object will be served by means of an unobtrusive watch kept by the police in uniform, as well as plainclothes at the frontier of posts and at airports and seaports. ... Delhi police are reporting in the daily reports on the approximate number of Muslims coming into and leaving Delhi. Such a watch can be maintained without violating the spirit or the letter of inter-dominion agreement.²⁹

R. N. Banerjee was worried about the impact of the surveillance on individual rights. "My feeling is that in practice, subordinate police officers ... may start a system of interrogation, which may inevitably prove to be inquisitorial."³⁰ His fears of border securitization were confirmed by the undersecretary of the home department, Fateh Singh, who also suggested the Home Ministry rely on the permit system on the western border and relinquish the plan for a system of surveillance on the eastern border because of a lack of staff:

The East Punjab government and the chief Commissioner in Delhi have intimated that they are maintaining some sort of watch on suspects entering India from Pakistan. Because the permit system has since been introduced in respect of the movement of persons between India and Pakistan, I do not think that any further action is necessary in this respect.[31]

B. Shukla, undersecretary of the West Bengal government,[32] explained that the West Bengal plan for border control surveillance was met with skepticism from the Ministry of Finance, which found it to be outrageously expensive compared with the permit regime on the western border, shrugging off the attempt to turn surveillance of the eastern border into a national concern.

From the All-India point of view, they wrote, "we have our central intelligence organization that are expanding the activities on various Indo Pakistan frontiers and are watching the activities of such political parties and of persons entering India." Finally, the Intelligence Bureau proposed a plan by which the passport-checking posts would be merged with the land customs stations, and that there would be eleven such stations in West Bengal, significantly fewer than the twenty-three stations proposed by the West Bengal government.

As various government departments deployed the security argument to negotiate for resources, it became clear that the border with East Pakistan was not a security concern but an economic one. The border remained open until 1952, when the active prevention of the return of Hindu refugees to West Bengal was carried out through both policies to provide relief, but not rehabilitation, and a growing set of documentary demands to differentiate between economic and political refugees (Roy 2012: 189).

The situation on the western border was entirely different, not least because of the scale of partition atrocities which claimed the lives of hundreds of thousands in the Punjab[33] and the low-grade, protracted violent encounters that fed the slower migration from the eastern border (Chatterji 2007: 105–106).

The correspondence that led to the abandonment of the permit regime in the East strengthens the argument that the goal of the permit system in the West was not simply to maintain order and security but to prevent Muslims who had fled to West Pakistan from returning and claiming citizenship in India.

THE FILE AND THE CHECKPOINT: THE PAPER LABYRINTH
OF IDENTITY

The permit system attempted to control a border that was both an international border between India and West Pakistan, and an internal border[34] between the majority and the non-Muslim minority, their loyalty and legitimacy questioned by the conflation of their religious and ethnic identities with classifications of suspicion. As we saw in Chapter 4, ascriptions of loyalty and suspicion were designated by one's mobility, particularly when attempting to return after the initial flight from violence. The axis of suspicion used to classify civil servants was like the graded scale used to designate permits.

As the permit system expanded in its scope and sophistication, it used the bureaucratic toolkit of emergency to create a new administrative grammar of mobility, linking the category of population to evidentiary demands that determined mobility, which would eventually culminate in political status. But new national subcategories of loyalty and suspicion created a cascade of new documents and classifications. The Indian High Commission in Pakistan began to issue five different kinds of permits to regulate movement temporally: (1) temporary visits; (2) permanent return to India; (3) repeated journeys for businessmen and officials; (4) transit travel for traveling across the two halves of Pakistan; and (5) permanent resettlement for Hindus who wanted to migrate to India.[35] The different types of forms and classifications were matched to the applicant's identity.[36] For the most part, resettlement was an option only for Hindus, and it granted them access to refugee rehabilitation programs. Returnees could convert the resettlement permit into a long-term visa that was renewed from year to year until they applied for citizenship. Permanent return was for Muslim refugees, who had to navigate a bureaucratic labyrinth of uncertainty in which requests took years (sometimes decades in courts) to get past the administrative filters.

Resettlement for Hindus was only relatively easy compared with the plight of Muslims attempting to return. However, those classified as "Hindu Pakistani Nationals" underwent a difficult process because of their questionable loyalty. They had to apply for short-term documents for entry, valid for only two to three months, before receiving a permit to stay for a year on the way to resettlement. Until 1953, these requirements had changed five or six times.

The permit regime divided Muslim families. Some stayed behind in Delhi to protect homes or businesses; others left their families behind and went to Pakistan in search of employment. This latter group included many Muslim civil servants[37] who opted to work in the new Pakistan government but keep their homes and families in India.

Discretionary Documents and Bureaucratic Inventions of Status

Bureaucratic anxieties about the ineffectiveness of the permit system and the urgent need to restrict the return of Muslim refugees led to repeated attempts to improve its techniques. This meant that Muslims who were moving were subjected to increasing regimes of control and surveillance. New categories of population and new classifications of risk increased resources for enforcement along the border and through surveillance methods.

These difficulties also created a black market of permits and forgeries. Forgeries created a problem of misclassification or misidentification in the "micro politics of identification" (Kim 2016: 12) that perpetuated a new set of regulations which criminalized counterfeiting practices and demanded higher burdens of proof for identity documents. These burdens of proof escalated over the years. Someone was suspect if they had lived in Pakistan, worked in Pakistan, or had family in Pakistan, but the official dealing with the case had the discretion to determine the degree of suspicion and decide on the classification.[38]

The burden of proof grew heavier, as did the policing methods and the criminalization of people who had not succeeded in obtaining permits, to the point where any Muslim living in India who wanted to visit Pakistan had to establish that they belonged to India in order to avoid being prevented from returning. They had to obtain a "no objection certificate" from the police and district magistrate before leaving India, which provided another chance for surveillance of mobility. Later, those visiting from or going to Pakistan were required to report to the police station on their arrival. These demands were based on the colonial Registration of Foreigners Act and Rules 1939, and the Foreigners Act 1946, which granted full discretion to Home Ministry officials to define, demand registration, and control the territories where one could go.[39]

Muslims returning to India were most affected by these new policies, and a significant number of people were arrested for overstaying their temporary permits. Because of the increase in arrests and court cases, citizenship provisions (articles 5 to 9) in the constitution were put in force in November 1949, in advance of the Indian Constitution itself. (See also Shani 2017.)

Despite targeting them, the permit system was not a master plan for excluding Muslims. It developed gradually through a series of emergencies that were routinized. The response to new needs and bureaucratic anxieties to regulate movement was ordered by the inherited administrative racial hierarchy of separate practices for separate populations. With each new institutionalized adjustment, the permit system created paper artifacts, discretionary documents, and bureaucratic inventions that had a political life, embodying the relationship between a person's status, their degree of loyalty or suspicion, and what would be their future claim to citizenship.

An example of how artifacts grew from such ad hoc solutions is the invention and implementation of the "passport of restricted validity." This type of passport was issued in cases in which there was a doubt regarding the Indian nationality of an applicant for an Indo-Pakistani passport. The document's lifespan was uncertain as the ministry had full discretion concerning the timeframe of its validity; it was defined as "a passport for a period that in the opinion of the state government is sufficient for the purpose of the holder."[40]

The use of such ad hoc solutions and innovations perpetuated a constant exercise of defining and redefining the status of citizenship and belonging in India, deciding who was part of the republic's new polity, and under what conditions or restrictions, and who was not. The restricted validity passport, for example, raised both technical and constitutional dilemmas regarding the national status of such passport holders. As a result, mid-tier bureaucrats innovated and created a new legal status of political belonging: "As the national status of such person is in doubt, it is clear that under the column 'national status' on page 1 of the India Pakistan Passport booklet; his status cannot be described as an Indian citizen."[41] In an attempt to address the gap between the political status and the indecision regarding their loyalties, the Ministry of External Affairs offered to register such a passport holder as a "citizen of India under naturalization." Nevertheless, undersecretary Fateh Singh refuted this idea and decided to invent another travel document instead of establishing a hybrid legal status:

I do not think the description "citizen of India under a naturalization" would be quite correct. Secondly, we may not accept them as Indian citizen in the long run. In such cases, they may have either to return to Pakistan, or obtain Pakistan passport in India.

The best course would be to grant them some temporary travel document to enable them to go to Pakistan .... We may describe them exactly as is done in the emergency certificate.[42]

New legal status, or its prevention, led to the formation of more emergency and intermediate documents, which continued the permit system de facto, long after passports were distributed in 1955, and even after the citizenship act and rules were to fix and crystallize the relationship between rights, political status, and official documents.

Negotiations between the Ministry of External Affairs, which was primarily interested in security, and the Ministry of Home Affairs, whose priority was to reduce the number of returning Muslim refugees, disclose that there was no explicit official decision to exclude Muslims from becoming Indian citizens. Nonetheless, that gradually became the major goal of the permit regime. Different administrative departments at the outset of the permit regime deployed the axis of suspicion differently, but the security and exclusion rationales merged over time into a procedural prevention of claims to citizenship.

As the statutory citizenship law was enacted, the goal of exclusion through practices became clearer to the political establishment, as did the role that bureaucratic discretion had played in shaping the content of citizenship. In 1956, Prime Minister Jawaharlal Nehru intervened in a case in which a person was denied permits, and later a long-term visa, even though he was cleared from classification based on suspicion. Nehru wrote, "Under our new nationality law, a person can become an Indian citizen if he has been a resident for a certain number of years and is otherwise qualified. That means that we permit him to reside here for that number of years. If we don't permit him to do so, then no foreigner can qualify under that rule."[43] He failed to understand the confusing policies of the Ministry of Home Affairs on the matter. Nehru was well versed in issues of classification of the population for the purposes of citizenship, and he was especially concerned with the classification of Indians who were overseas or beyond India's territory.[44] In the months that followed the enactment of the citizenship act and rules, it became clearer to all politicians, from both the Congress and the opposition, that while they knew of the importance of the Home Ministry in matters of political membership, they had not been aware of the scope and substantive power of the ministry to make laws and deny rights. Besides Sardar Patel, India's first home minister and conservative leader in the Indian National Congress, who had closely followed the growth of India's mobility regime and the way it was affecting differentiated rehabilitation and citizenship, many politicians did not grasp the extent of the effect that administrative innovations in the inherited bureaucracy had on political membership in the new republic. This is not to claim that officials invented policy or rebelled against political will. On the contrary, they aligned with what they perceived as political will, but did so in such a way that procedure, rather than policy, shaped political status.

In Israel, where the permit regime was also forged through the exigencies of bureaucratic anxieties and entrepreneurship, the goals of the political leadership to achieve a Jewish majority were more explicitly articulated to the military government that established the Israeli permit regime over the remainder of the Palestinians in 1949.[45]

THE ISRAELI PERMIT REGIME

The permit regime in Israel also defined the population it monitored and attempted to exclude as "infiltrators," "intruders," and "fifth column" through an array of documents that were necessary for survival, first to ensure mobility and later to claim citizenship.

The similarity between the bureaucratic development of the permit regime to prevent returnees in Israel and the one in India is more striking because of the different political conditions of the partition that did not happen in Palestine. The displacement of Palestinians during the 1948 war was not a population transfer to or toward their own state, but the result of military conquest driving them from their native lands, beyond the border of the designated Jewish state. The mass displacement of Palestinians from their land during and after the war (Sa'di & Abu Lughod 2007) was to advance the goal of a Jewish majority that had not been achieved prior to partition (Shafir & Peled 2002; Rishmawi 1987). While there is little doubt that the mass displacement of Palestinians to secure a Jewish majority was planned even in the first stage of the Yishuv's defensive war (Cohen 2018), let alone after Israel declared independence, the bureaucratic apparatus to consolidate the gains of displacement during the war was not.

The permit regime that controlled the mobility of the remainder of Palestinians and prevented refugees from returning was developed during the early years of the state, when nearly three quarters of a million Palestinians were displaced, and the same number of Jewish immigrants, both Holocaust survivors and Mizrahi Jews from Arab countries, were settlers in the new state (Cohen & Gordon 2018; Cohen 2002).

As with the permit regime in India, there was no master plan for bureaucratic exclusion from citizenship based on mobility regulation prior to independence.[46] The practices of the permit regime grew from a series of emergency administrative decisions and decrees, based on the British colonial Defence (Emergency) Regulations, as a response to individual and collective resistance to the restrictions. This routinization of emergency gradually ballooned into a bureaucratic apparatus whose purpose was not only to control the influx of returnees but to prevent refugees and returnees from claiming citizenship. Like in India, alongside the permit regime to prevent return, general elections were held before the enactment of citizenship laws that were based on residency.

Whereas in India the permit regime developed on the margins of the new state, the role of the permit regime was central to the making of Israel's hybrid political regime. The central government incorporated the institutions of the Zionist Yishuv, together with legal and administrative structures of the British Mandate, into formal democratic institutions. The military government, based on the Defence (Emergency) Regulations,[47] ruled over the remaining Palestinian population in the administered territories that were not internationally recognized as part of the state, because they were on the "other side" of the partition plan that the Palestinians had rejected. There was no official map of the borders of the military government because it was not a stable jurisdiction of a particular territory, but of a particular population. However, maps were consistently referred to in military court cases. Wherever there were Palestinian civilians, the military government operated. It effectively ruled over 90 percent of the Palestinian population, with the remaining 10 percent in mixed towns (Sabbagh-Khoury 2021).

Earlier studies have focused on the military government's agglomeration of methods of colonial control, surveillance, and monitoring as internal colonialism (Zureik 2003) or as methods of counterinsurgency, policing, and coercion to induce collaboration with security forces (Sa'di 2003, 2016) and methods of criminalization of political dissent (Korn 2003). More recent studies have shown how the military government was formative to Israeli state-making, setting clear boundaries of belonging and spatial segregation based on race and suspicion (Shafir 2018), and constituting what Shira Robinson describes as a "Settler colonial liberal state" (Robinson 2013: 8; see also Degani 2015), which designated the "settler colonial citizenship" of Palestinians through the emergency laws (Rouhana and Sabbagh-Khoury 2015). Tatour (2019) shows how citizenship was granted to those who remained to exclude others from return. Building on these insights, the aim of this section is to trace the development of the permit regime, in the early years of the state, based on the inherited bureaucratic toolkit of emergency that turned restrictions on mobility into the designation of political status. In this organizational portrait, we see how the permit regime was not an extraordinary, incoherent, or corrupt regime, but featured the organizing principles of hybrid bureaucracy: racial hierarchy, wide discretion and administrative flexibility, the creation of exceptions through a proliferation of documents, and secret and shifting regulations.

Closure and the Necessity of Documents for Movement

Immediately after the Israeli War of Independence, the Israeli administration was preoccupied with blocking Palestinians who wished to return to their homes, as refugee property was classified as "absentee property" and confiscated by the state (Zureik 1979; Forman & Kedar 2003). Initially justified for security reasons, to prevent refugees and displaced persons from returning to their lands, the military government established an apparatus to control the movement of the Palestinian population that would later turn into a tool used by the Ministry of Interior and other bodies to assign or deny political membership. The bureaucratic toolkit of emergency, developed and deployed during the Mandate (most prominently in 1936–1939 and from 1945 until the end of British rule), analyzed in Chapter 3, was used both as the governing apparatus to confine the Palestinians who remained and to prevent the return of those who had fled. It was a bureaucratic regime that regulated mobility through documents, violence, and the threat of violence (Saban 2011). It created the conditions for identity documents to become an artifact critical for survival. Regulations 109 and 125 prevented entry to areas classified as "closed military zones"[48] (Jiryis 1976) and regulations 110, 111, and 114 allowed the military governor to prevent or limit the movement of subjects under his authority. Regulation 125 was the source of most of the restrictions. This regulation was like "the power to make orders" in the Foreigners Act in India.[49] The wide discretion to limit movement afforded to the military governors was coupled with the powers to deport or detain anyone suspected of incitement (Nasasra 2020).

A major objective of the permit regime was to survey and prevent changes in residency from one area of the military government to the other. This was essential to prevent the return of internal refugees, displaced during the war (Masalha 1997), to their abandoned villages, or to prevent the return of land that had been declared Absentee Land, now in the custody of the state. Some of these practices aimed to control the flooding of the employment market in Jewish areas (Nuriely 2005) or to prevent Arabs from working in areas declared as security zones. Economic segregation had been central to the constitution of Yishuv settler society (Shafir 1996), but the declaration of "closed zones" (Figure 7) facilitated the enforcement of spatial economic segregation because people needed to obtain permits not only to travel to other areas but also to leave their zones (Masalha 2003; Sabbagh-Khoury 2011).

Monitoring movement, employment, and the ownership of property, the permit regime enabled almost constant surveillance of the population. The surveillance was despite the fact that Israeli army officials agreed that the population under its direct control were mostly peaceful civilians.[50] The security fears were not of the population of residents but of attacks by returnees on the new immigrant settlements that had been established on the new frontiers (Rozin 2016: 454). The justification for the general

FIGURE 7 Map of military government and closure of northern districts ISA Gimel 5/ 2263 courtesy of Akevot

closure and control over civilians was that "prevention of infiltration with intention to settle, cannot be achieved or controlled without supervision and restriction of movement in the territories liable to this infiltration."[51]

The permit regime developed differently in the northern, central, and southern districts of the military government (Figure 8), through the wide discretion of officials and the invention of rules, documents, and punishment for those who lacked them. Repeated attempts to standardize practices, documents, and punishment across the different districts of the military government, which had been managed, as one officer commented, "as if they were different countries,"[52] were unsuccessful. The

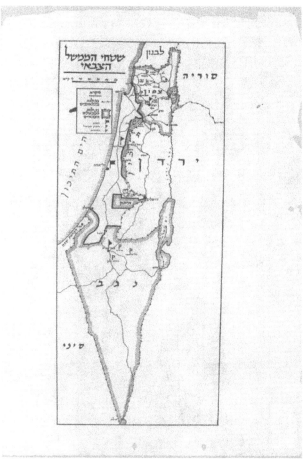

FIGURE 8 Map of military government territories: north, central, and south ISA GL4/17005 Courtesy of Akevot

wide discretion and administrative flexibility, as well as unpublished regulations, made standardization difficult.

The bureaucratic labyrinth people encountered when applying for a permit reflected bureaucratic indecision and uncertainty about the status of residents. The most vulnerable were Palestinians who were refugees that had left families during the Nakba and tried to return, those who had managed to return but had no legal status and were hunted by security forces (Robinson 2013: 81), and the internally displaced who had managed to remain in what was now Israel without legal status or official documents. Intense correspondence during the first two years of the military government depicts the military government's preoccupation with a group of four hundred people they called "chronic infiltrators" who entered frequently to visit their families and later requested family unification. The correspondence shows the shift in the bureaucratic perception of monitoring the movement of "suspicious" people, to focusing on blocking their future requests for family unification as a gateway to citizenship. "Chronic infiltration" was a form of resistance to the permit regime. Similar to the permit regime in India, Palestinians had an active role in shaping the bureaucracy and its enforcement through their resistance to it, individually and collectively, through direct political protest, circumventing the military government in daily and mundane activities, through the direct relationships they formed with officials, and most of all through the practice of returning again and again, despite their expulsion (Robinson 2013; Darweish & Sellick 2017).

The graded classification according to the axis of suspicion grew as networks of collaboration with and resistance to the military regime solidified in Palestinian communities. Rigid classifications designated the entire population as suspicious, graded by region.[53] Wide discretion made legal entry into Israeli-held territories increasingly complex. It is indeed surprising how many people did manage to receive some type of identity document. Exiting the country, however, was an entirely different story. Facilitating exile was a goal of the military government; those who wished to leave the country were encouraged to do so by simplified bureaucratic procedures, such as immediately granting exit permits, having security forces escort persons to the borders,[54] and transferring their possessions out of the country.

The ministries of interior, minorities, and immigration were all involved in the administrative war on returning refugees who were now classified as "infiltrators" and intruders, and created classifications and templates that would enable their exclusion from future citizenship by bureaucratic means.

The time and place of residency were critical to distinguish between residents and refugees, which would translate into categories of lawful residency or illegal infiltration (Leibler & Breslau 2005; Tatour 2019). In January 1949, the military government took a special administrative census of Arab inhabitants,[55] so authorities could assess population numbers after the massive flights and expulsions and to help security forces locate Palestinians perceived as "infiltrators," who had returned after the census, and expel them.

Like in India, the time and place of people's return would be the defining features of their potential to obtain status, and their movements after those dates designated them as suspicious. During 1949, an array of different, sometimes contradictory, documents of identification for Palestinian residents was distributed by different bodies, which had different lengths of validity. Finally, in order to standardize the validity of identity documents people held, and render others invalid, June 1, 1949, was set as the date to distinguish between those who had entered "the security zones" and held valid documents and those who had entered after that date and would be considered infiltrators, regardless of the documents they carried.[56] Those who entered after the date could apply to the exceptional committee to try to obtain valid documents.

The expansion of classifications and categories of population and suspicion, the means to document and verify identity, and the perception of the Palestinians as a security or demographic threat fluctuated and changed frequently, as the permit regime grew in sophistication in its efforts to prevent return. A rare document both in its detail and in its successful outcome, the following application for a permit highlights the level of enforcement of mobility restrictions alongside the wide discretion to assign status. On September 4, 1950, the military governor of the Galilee recommended the committee grant a temporary permit to Yousef Assad Kides, fifty-five years old, who was married without children and was what the military government called "a chronic infiltrator":

I was born in Ein al Sit and stayed there with my family until March 1948. Then I moved the family to Majd al-Krum and remained there until the army conquered the village.

A few days after the occupation of the village, I was sent by the labor office to Lyd to work in the fields. I stayed there for a few days and then returned. Two months after the village was occupied, there was a search, and I was taken with the rest and expelled to Jenin.[57] I stayed in Jenin one month and returned after that.

After six months, there was another search in the village. I was caught and expelled to Jenin for a second time. I stayed in Jenin three days and returned. Since then I stayed in Majd al-Krum without leaving. My wife moved to Acca and received an ID card.

The military governor who recommended that Kides receive a permit was later reprimanded because the applicant was a returnee who had been expelled multiple times. Returnees were locked into a permanent state of illegality – if they were expelled and then requested a permit, the request was refused because they were illegal, yet those who applied for temporary permits were those who were unregistered or had been expelled.

From Mobility Permits to the Invention of Temporary Residency

The transition from governing mobility to prevent return, to the designation of differentiated documents in order to prevent future claims of citizenship, was complicated by officials who were concerned about adhering to standards of international law, and the problem of international legitimacy.

What the military establishment called "the war on infiltration" was a political problem for the government. Israel had declared in the UN that it would grant citizenship to Palestinians who were enumerated in the census of 1948 and committed itself to repatriating 100,000 refugees out of an estimated 700,000 (Robinson 2013: 29; but see Bracha 1997).[58] The attempts to expel so-called infiltrators, Palestinians who had fled their homes during the war and attempted to return, and deny their status as residents and subsequently citizens required the creation of a bureaucratic exception.

The administrative solution to the political and legal problem of expelling returnees was the invention of a temporary residency permit instead of ID cards for certain Palestinians who were deemed less desirable as potential citizens.[59] The solution was the bureaucratic invention of an exceptional identity document, with an indeterminant political status, that would allow them to be included in the registry, but prevent the use of the document as evidence to claim citizenship in due course.

Yehoshua Palmon, the Prime Minister's Advisor for Arab Affairs, was a central player in the transition of the permit regime from a system that monitored mobility to an administrative apparatus with the goal of preventing as many Palestinians as possible from claiming citizenship.[60] Palmon explained why the ID card was not just a document but embodied the claim to citizenship: "The ID card, even if it is just a method of identification according to the law, is a document, through which one gets a ration card, is evidence for the legal residency of its holder in the state and can be used to achieve citizenship." One proposed method was amending discretionary powers in the colonial population registry ordinance. But the attorney general warned that it was illegal for the Ministry of Interior to deliberately exclude residents from the ID registry. There was also the possibility that such an amendment would motivate a petition to the supreme court. The invention of temporary residency raised a controversy common to hybrid bureaucracy, between civil servants wishing to adhere to legal standards and officials seeking the executive means to get the job done.[61]

Finally, Maximilian (Meir) Hartglass, the ministry's legal adviser, found a creative solution for the impasse: Why amend the law when they could carry out their policy through bureaucratic means?[62] He suggested the Department of General Administration issue an internal directive to the registration offices that would allow the distribution of temporary IDs.[63] That internal regulation founded the permit regime.

In September 1949 the administration distributed temporary residence permits to Palestinians who, because they were not enumerated in the census and were considered absentees, were most vulnerable to the shifting and sliding scales of suspicion and classification that restricted or prevented movement.

The Administrative Flexibility of Suspicion

Temporary IDs were distributed so "their loyalty to the state" could be examined.[64] Various agents in the military government apparatus had discretion to decide who was loyal or suspicious, but there were no clear guidelines. Affiliations with powerful bodies such as the Histadrut (the most prominent workers' organizations) or political connections to Mapai (Israel's ruling party) improved one's chances of family unification or receiving a permit (Degani 2020: 14).

Temporary IDs provided opportunities to rope in populations that were illegible to bureaucracy and offer opportunities for dependence on military government officials. The classifications of suspicion were prevalent in every procedure. Hartglass suggested that when "intruders" came to register their families at the registration offices, officials should call the police to arrest them, or provide them with a written recommendation, if they deserved it, without which giving Palestinians ID cards was like "giving the fifth column bread and butter through ration cards … Aiding their struggle against 'our state.'"[65]

Returnees needed to apply for a permit from the military government, which sent the application to a special committee attached to the Immigration Office, in charge of requests for entry from Palestinians or foreigners. The committee granted a temporary permit for thirty days, pending a decision on their three-month permit. People could only apply if they had a recommendation from a regional military governor, and the latter were instructed to only recommend Palestinians who could be of use to the military government.[66]

After the initial recommendation, at the discretion of the military officials, the permit application then had to be endorsed by both the police and the secret service. Temporary permits were given for three months, and each renewal of a permit was a surveillance opportunity for the police and secret service because the military governor could cancel the permit and with it the right to "temporary residence." Palmon explained that "the period that the permit is in effect is an examination. The behavior of the permit holder can influence the renewal, annulment or exchange with formal ID card."[67] It was an opportunity to examine "their true nature." The type of suspicion designated a status category: temporary ID holders held in suspicion who had to be cleared by the security service or "Communists from Gaza, who have found their asylum here, and whom we do not wish to turn over to the Egyptian police."[68] Coupling categories of suspicion with the distribution of temporary permits in order to diminish the number of people who entered the country grew into a central goal of registration practices: "The objective of the military governors should be to minimize … and disencumber the state of the presence of people whose past, and their behavior in the present do not guarantee that they will be peaceful residents in the country."[69]

The military regime strove to enforce the distinction between Arabs with Israeli IDs or permits and those they called "infiltrators." The anxieties were not only about returnees coming in, but also about residents of the military government that would venture to enemy Arab countries and return to Israel.[70] The biggest threat was those that could serve as guides for other groups of returnees. When they could not prevent movement to combat the mobility across the border, because people had permits and ID cards, they decided to request the Custodian of Absentee Property to confiscate the property of those who had left and crossed into an enemy country, even if they had done so with the intention to return.[71]

Detention was another site for differentiation between Palestinians who held permits and returnees. While officially the separation was intended to prevent information exchange between residents and returnees, this practice established a hierarchy of suspicion and branded returned refugees as perceived enemy agents.[72] Ballas (2020) shows how most of the returnees, called infiltrators, were deported because the project to incarcerate detainees had failed.

The Bureaucratic Differentiation between Palestinians

By 1950, the military government faced severe delegitimization by Israeli political elites who called it a "free for all," "mayhem," operated by "a corrupt bunch of brutes," and a "colonial government par excellence."[73] The military government had to justify the practices of the permit regime following allegations of corruption[74] and an evolving black market for permits[75] that produced counterfeit documents. Politicians had discovered that the military government operated based on the Defence (Emergency) Regulations without formal legal authority to govern civilians: sentences were passed, movement was restricted, curfews were imposed, infiltrators detained and expelled, activities, such as commerce and union activity, were limited, etc.

The emergency regulations were used to constitute the permit regime, but the authority of the military government had not been legally established and the was no official map of its territorial jurisdiction. Officials agreed that it was necessary to establish legal authority and that using the Defence (Emergency) Regulations was preferable to new legislation, which would not only lead to lengthy discussions in parliament but might hamper some of the executive authorities granted by the 1945 emergency laws (Berda 2020).[76]

By the time any inquiries were made into the legalities of the military government, the toolkit of emergency had already served its purpose to delineate, reduce, and differentiate between Palestinians in different spaces, based on mobility restrictions, and their claims to citizenship and residency in the state. Lana Tatour shows how the Israeli cabinet drew on distinctions of citizenship from other settler colonies, not only to differentiate the status of Jews and Palestinians but also to use citizenship laws to differentiate who was legal and who was illegal (Tatour 2019: 24). Citizenship laws would provide the means to deport those who were deemed illegal and did not have the evidentiary claims to citizenship.

As was the case in India, in the very first years following the violence of independence, the military government and the Ministry of Interior forged and innovated upon the colonial toolkit of population management, and adapted it into a new set of colonial practices, this time of the majority ruling the remaining minority through executive power. Through the designation of closed military zones and demands for permits to exit and enter or to move one's residence, a mobility regime was established for the surveillance and control of the population. The early stage of the mobility regime was to prevent the return of refugees to the administered territories and the return of the displaced to their villages. As bureaucratic control of mobility became institutionalized through the routinization of emergency, the classifications and practices created during the emergency, translated into permanent practices of the Ministry of Interior and Ministry of Home Affairs. Through bureaucratic entrepreneurship and the invention of hybrid statuses such as "temporary resident" and an array of identity documents, exceptional committees, and procedures, the permit regime differentiated between legal and illegal Palestinian residents. In turn, the designation of documents based on mobility, the logic of classification at the border or frontier, became the classification of the entire minority population.

Between 1950 and 1953 Israel legislated three laws that constructed the Israeli citizenship regime. The Law of Return enacted in 1950[77] provided automatic citizenship rights to Jews who immigrated to Israel and was the "statutory manifestation of Israel's commitment to its Jewish moral purpose" (Peled 1992). The citizenship law of 1952 was to govern the citizenship of Palestinians and other non-Jews and the Law of Entry 1952 regulated the status of residents and foreigners and the designated criminality of illegal entry.

This legal complex meant that Palestinians who had managed to remain, despite the permit regime, were granted a status of non-deportability. All others, those who had been prevented from returning, would continue to have a relationship to the state, and the borders of partition, through mobility regimes.

How did the permit regime and the hybrid bureaucracy in the military government shape political membership? To answer this question, one must revisit the rich debate on Palestinian citizenship, which has seen it described as hollow citizenship (Jamal 2007), nominal citizenship (Plonski 2017), formal citizenship in an ethnocratic regime (Yiftachel 2009), second-class citizenship (Rouhana 1997), conditional citizenship (Blecher 2005), and settler colonial citizenship (Rouhana & Sabbagh-Khoury 2015), assuming a categorical effect on all Palestinian citizens of Israel, pertaining to the measure of their rights and the limits of membership in political communities within the Jewish state. Yet a closer look at the practices of the military government and its permit regime highlights that the most crucial aspect of Palestinian citizenship in Israel is a form of non-deportability and restricted mobility. Rather than a categorical type of citizenship based on ethnicity or nationality, securing mobility based on a graded scale of suspicion captures the practicality of the political status of Palestinians that granted mobility, and not necessarily rights.

From an organizational perspective, the officials that developed the permit regime did not articulate its goals; these were broadly defined by the political leadership. Rather, they provided the method by which to achieve them. However, they did not simply execute policy: the bureaucratic toolkit of emergency was a weapon of racial differentiation, which embodied the organizing principles of hybrid bureaucracy and forged the institutional logic that would continue to define the relationship of Palestinians to the state through their possibilities for mobility, and in relation to the border of partition. The mobility regime would serve to regulate the status and relationship to the Israeli state of Palestinians in East Jerusalem, the West Bank, and Gaza after the occupation of those territories in 1967. It would serve as the template for Israel's mobility restrictions in the West Bank and Gaza from the early 1990s (Berda 2017).

The similarities between the permit regimes in India and Israel were conditional on the continuity of the British colonial emergency laws. What would have happened if the inherited bureaucratic toolkit of emergency was not retained? In Cyprus, colonial emergency laws were relinquished in the political arrangement to avoid partition. In the absence of the bureaucratic toolkit of emergency, the legacy of British rule was a preoccupation with classification and the outcome was entirely different, as the new republic attempted to decolonize from the hybrid bureaucracy, producing an another kind of regime of emergency. The subsequent de facto partition and exceptional regime in Cyprus was not a remnant of colonial bureaucracy but a result of the attempt to break away from it.

THE REPUBLIC OF CYPRUS: THE ATTEMPTED ESCAPE FROM COLONIAL BUREAUCRACY

The administrative response of the Greek Cypriot majority to the flight of Turkish Cypriots into the enclaves during the "first partition" of 1963 was entirely different from the population management policies and mobility regimes that developed in India and Israel/Palestine.

In this study, the divergent trajectory in Cyprus, which, contrary to India and Israel/Palestine, abolished the colonial emergency laws at independence and with them the burgeoning executive powers to control the target population, underscores the definitive role of colonial emergency laws as the legal grid that facilitated the inheritance of hybrid bureaucracy and differentiated population management practices applied to minorities in the new states.

This section outlines the divergence of bureaucratic legacies in Cyprus, where partition was rejected but did eventually take place, and where an exceptional regime created an entirely different administrative response to the minority population, which was no longer governed by the independent republic but created its own administration. First, it examines attempts by the nascent Cypriot administration to eradicate the principles of hybrid bureaucracy – wide discretion and the creation of exceptions – until 1963, then turns to the intercommunal violence in that year and the subsequent siege on the Turkish Cypriots that ensued as a different type of mobility regime, and finally outlines the different type of legal emergency in Cyprus-the suspension of the bicommunal constitution, to show how the exceptional regime in Cyprus was not a remnant of the iron cage of colonial rule but a result of the attempt to break free from it.

The Impossible Bargain to Avoid Partition

The independence of the Republic of Cyprus was born out of an impossible bargain to end civil war and colonial rule, and avoided the solutions preferred by the nationalist movements – *enosis* (unification with Greece) or partition (Constantinou 2008; Xydis 2017: 369). The 1960 constitution established a bicommunal system of governance in which both communities would share power on equal terms. The rejection of partition entailed a rejection of majority powers (Papastylianos 2018: 114). The bargain specified that "the two Motherlands" along with Britain would serve as "guarantors" to the power-sharing political regime that was established in the constitution. The guarantee was of neither union with Greece nor the partition of the island without the concurrence of Turkey and Greece. The close ties to the motherlands[78] and the language of the constitution were a rejection of the possibility of a single Cypriot identity based on territorial belonging to the island (Loizos 1976). The constitution created a binary of identity: one had to belong to either the Greek Cypriot community or the Turkish Cypriot community, so collective rights of other minorities were effectively denied (Varnava 2010). The series of public and secret treaties that birthed the republic also enabled the British to remain sovereign on military bases on the island and to retain imperial power on part of the territory, without any responsibility toward the population (Constantinou & Richmond 2005: 68). Most important for our story, it included relinquishing the colonial emergency laws and substituting them with a clause in the constitution that required the cooperation of both communities to declare a state of emergency.[79]

The abolition of colonial emergency laws and the dependence of any declaration of the state of emergency on the cooperation of the Turkish vice president are usually explained as a result of the deep suspicion of the communities of each other, particularly the Turkish Cypriot minority, which also produced a rigid bicommunal system of checks on the separation of powers (Papastylianos 2018: 115). This explanation sits within the Greek Cypriot critique of the "unworkability" of the communal arrangements because there was no legal solution for the situation in which the two communities would cease to cooperate.

But there was another aspect to relinquishing the emergency laws: breaking away from the bureaucratic toolkit of emergency that had been so devastatingly deployed during the Cyprus Emergency, which was both an anticolonial militant campaign against the British and a civil war between the militant arms of Greek and Turkish Cypriots. During the Emergency from 1955 to 1959, the British had enacted seventy-six laws that granted the police, military, and clerks wide discretion to control movement through the designation of "protected areas," to arrest, detain without trial, deport, exile, and interrogate. The legal fight against the colonial emergency regulations had been central to the Greek Cypriot anticolonial campaign (French 2015: 199). Lawyers mobilized both to represent detainees and to lobby the British parliament and petition the European Commission of Human Rights. The Cyprus law association turned advocacy for detainee rights into a form of resistance to British rule, which they framed as human rights activism (Drohan 2018: 16–17). The legal battle against the emergency regulations was considered inseparable from the insurgency and was a matter of Greek Cypriot national pride.

However, the decision to relinquish the colonial emergency laws meant that the new republic had done away with the repertoire of administrative tools for the majority to manage the minority, control movement, detain without trial, and prevent its political organization. In contrast, despite controversial debates in India and Israel on the continuity of emergency laws that were viewed by the oppositions to the ruling parties as the very embodiment of colonial government (Berda 2020), the political choice was to retain the executive powers they afforded the state to manage those minority populations that had been designated by the state as a "political problem."

The rejection of the emergency laws and the bureaucratic toolkit of emergency were coupled with efforts to curb the administration of surplus executive powers to legislate, judge, and impose duties on citizens.

"Decolonizing" Hybrid Bureaucracy, 1960–1963

In the short-lived constitutional republic of Cyprus, the three years in which the two communities shared power in the functions of the state, besides spending inordinate resources to fulfill the rigid representation requirements of the constitution in the civil service, as discussed in Chapter 2, significant attempts were made by the Ministry of Interior to establish separation of powers and curb some of the features of hybrid bureaucracy. In the practice of making a bicommunal state, a flurry of directives, office instructions, negotiations, and reprimands attempted to delimit the wide discretion of officials, personalism, the use of unpublished regulations, the creation of exceptions to rules, and the practical feature of the principle of racial hierarchy – the application of separate practices to different populations according to their identity. While many of these interventions were directly related to communal representation, they were articulated as a commitment to break with colonial rule and its surplus executive powers.

First and foremost was the warning that administrators could not make law. It was reiterated repeatedly to every district and department, that administrative documents and circulars could not create substantive law, suspend rights, or impose duties on people that were outside the public service.[80]

On August 15, 1960, the first act of the commissioner of the district of Limassol was the circulation of a set of office instructions, defining his own transition from "district commissioner" to district officer.[81] The change was not semantic, but to establish a separation of powers and abolish the post of colonial district commissioner, who held wide discretion to make regulations and preside as judge. "District officers would not, like the commissioners in the colonial regime, represent government in the districts ... they would represent the ministry of interior."[82]

Officials deliberated the translation of the term "district officer" into Turkish, which went on for a few months and charted the scope of discretion officials had in Turkey, in provinces or districts, in comparison with the British colonial district commissioners. The problem was that the proper definition of district officer, *kaymakam*, conveyed higher authority because it literally meant "the governor of a district"[83] who would also "perform the duties of a judge."[84] Public confusion regarding the title of the district official was a problem because it indicated wide discretion and defied the purpose of arresting the scope of power.[85] Finally, it was decided that district officers would be *kaza amiri*, a term that helped Turkish Cypriots understand the change from colonial district commissioner to "district officer."

For the first year after independence, any remnant of the colonial defense regulations, used through transitional powers to maintain technical regulations for licensing and supplies until primary legislation was enacted, was heavily monitored to avoid "the many abuses which may occur between introduction of the bill and its enactment."[86] In another transition away from the uncertainty and precarity Cypriots had experienced as British subjects, the constitution granted all citizens the right to request or complain to any public authority and receive a response within thirty days. As various districts established their procedures for complaints, including strict timelines and rigid limits on designation of discretion, they culminated in a motivational statement on the historic significance of bureaucratic reform: "after centuries of rule from the outside, Cyprus achieves its independence and the reins of administration are taken over by the government elected by its own people."[87]

In the early years of the state, the Ministry of Interior made efforts to implement the bicommunal constitution, but also to rid the bureaucracy of some of the legacies of colonial order. Because the history of the conflict in Cyprus is marked by the implosion of the power-sharing republic in 1963, and the way the impasse of the civil service contributed to the constitutional crises, these early attempts to institute a new bureaucratic order are only viewed in light of their failure.

Constitutional Implosion: Another Type of Emergency

The story of the constitutional crisis and the violence that erupted as a result is told from the Greek Cypriot perspective as an impasse, because the rigidity of the political arrangement that was imposed prevented change. The binary structure created a complex system of proportional representation in all branches of government that required a ratio of 70:30 Greek to Turkish Cypriots in the administration and civil service, discussed in Chapter 2, and provided for separate municipalities,[88] which the Turkish Cypriot leadership at the time called "municipal partition."[89]

In 1963, the president of the republic and the archbishop of the Greek Orthodox Church proposed to amend the constitution's power-sharing mechanism, which Greek Cypriots saw as unworkable. The amendments were meant to dismantle some of the power-sharing safeguards and Turkish Cypriot representation.

Turkish Cypriots walked out of parliament in protest. Violence exploded into a civil war from December 1963 to August 1964, during which over 90 percent of Turkish Cypriots retreated to armed enclaves (Bryant & Hatay 2020: 10). However, no state of emergency was declared because the constitution required the agreement of the vice president of the republic, a Turkish Cypriot, for its enactment.

Greek Cypriots declared the Turkish Cypriots rebels ר and abolished the bicommunal arrangements, including the right to separate elections of the vice president and Turkish Cypriot representatives. Effectively, these actions prevented the Turkish Cypriots from returning to parliament and their posts in the civil service (see Bryant & Hatay 2020: 10).[90]

In 1964 the supreme court enabled the legal suspension of the constitution's bicommunal arrangements, through "a doctrine of necessity" that did not allow the burgeoning of executive powers at the expense of the legislative branch, but rather legalized the function of state bodies, regardless of the bicommunal arrangements that could not be fulfilled due to the prevention of Turkish Cypriots returning to their posts (Emilianides 2019: 115–124). The doctrine of necessity enabled the continued function of the state bodies, while suspending the *raison d'être* of the constitutional order: the bicommunal power-sharing political order.

The correspondence in the Ministry of Interior state archives reflects the implosion of the bicommunal arrangements. All correspondence was in English or Greek; government departments that were now on the Turkish side of Nicosia housed records that the Greek Cypriot administration did not have access to, which included registration of land and population.[91] There is scant mention of Turkish Cypriots, beyond reports on unidentified crimes attributed to "Turkish Cypriot rebels" and the retention of records. The nearly total unmixing of the population wiped the trace of Turkish Cypriots from government work, including population registries. In the enclaves, a separate Turkish Cypriot administration was created to coordinate the twenty-eight enclaves that remained under siege until 1968.

Bryant and Hatay (2020) provide the first comprehensive account of the institutionalization of the Turkish Cypriot administration in the enclaves during the siege. The Greek Cypriots established a siege to prevent Turkish Cypriots from living in the enclaves. The siege turned the consequences of the violence and exile into a long-term condition that was a de facto partition (Kliot & Mansfield 1997: 497), but was not a mobility regime to control populations, did not engage in mapping or surveillance of the population, and did not produce documents that were necessary for movement.

A Different Mobility Regime: The Siege on the Turkish Cypriot Enclaves

Turkish Cypriots fled to the enclaves (Figure 9) during the last days of December 1963, as intercommunal violence spread to a civil war. They had expected that their flight to the enclaves would be temporary. But the government of Cyprus set up barricades around the enclaves, cut telephone lines, and surrounded villages and areas (Patrick & Bater 1976: 49). Turkish Cypriots barricaded themselves inside and were prevented from leaving the enclaves from the outside.

The siege on the Turkish Cypriot enclaves was initially organized as a military operation, a method to separate populations in a civil war, and gradually developed into an economic siege in the summer of 1964.[92] The siege did not regulate population movement but did regulate supplies and goods that were designated as "strategic materials," which were forbidden to enter the enclaves (Strong 1999).

In the winter of 1964, the Turkish Cypriot administration established a permit system for men of military age who were leaving the enclaves. These permits had two justifications: to monitor the population's movement in order to ensure their safety and security from Greek Cypriot interception and arrest by the Greek Cypriots, and to prevent desertion by military-aged males.[93] This system of permissions was not standardized and, once a permit was issued, the movement of the person carrying the permit was not monitored or registered anyway. Permits for leaving the enclaves became increasingly important when the number of missing persons escalated due to encounters with Greek Cypriots.[94]

The Greek Cypriot military forces and police established checkpoints and roadblocks around all Turkish Cypriot enclaves. Yet, in the archives,

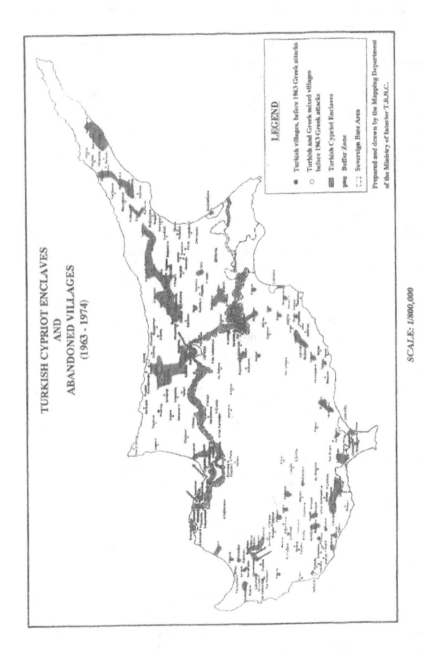

FIGURE 9 Map of Turkish Cypriot enclaves (Source: TRNC Public Information Office)

there are only scarce references to these measures by the Ministry of Interior and police, who were mostly concerned with the image of the republic as a police state in the eyes of tourists and visitors who encountered the checkpoints and roadblocks. When asked to supply a list of roadblocks for visitors to the island, the Ministry of Interior replied that it could not gather the information.[95]

The siege on the Turkish Cypriot enclaves was fashioned by a military logic of separation, not one of population management. There is no evidence that Greek Cypriot forces and police were concerned with enumerating and classifying the Turkish Cypriot civilian population. The Ministry of Interior of the Republic of Cyprus did not attempt to conduct a census of displaced Turkish Cypriots, or to register the population at all. The movement of Turkish Cypriots was monitored by military means, not administrative ones. The territorial separation and unmixing of the population meant that Turkish Cypriots were no longer perceived as a minority within the republic that needed to be managed and governed. Bryant and Hatay (2020: 11) provide the first comprehensive history of the making of the Turkish Cypriot institutions within the enclaves, which included the government offices and departments from which they had withdrawn and employed the civil servants who had been prevented from returning to their posts. Building alternative institutions affected the remainder of Turkish Cypriots outside the enclaves, who refused government services, as that would have been an acceptance of Greek Cypriot control of the republic (Bryant & Hatay 2020; see Patrick & Bater 1976).

Despite the spatial impediments to movement and the state of emergency, there is no paper trail of an institutional legacy of colonial population management practices or any relationship between the permits to move during the siege and the access to citizenship. The colonial emergency laws roped in populations through the bureaucratic regimes of control that maintained a perpetual relationship between subjects of registration and surveillance and the colonial state. This effect remained after independence in Israel and India, as the toolkit of emergency enabled the bureaucracy to designate and govern the minorities' relationship to the state through mobility restriction.

In Cyprus, the emergency state did the opposite. The doctrine of necessity severed the connection between the Turkish Cypriot population and the state, with no method of roping people in. Turkish Cypriots formally remained citizens of the Republic of Cyprus but could not maintain any effective relationship with the state, due to violence and the creation of the Turkish Cypriot "state within a state" (Navaro-Yashin 2007: 90). In December 1967, the provisional Turkish Cypriot adminis-tration announced that all Turkish Cypriots would be governed by the administration until the 1960 constitutional arrangement was restored (Patrick & Bater 1976: 169).

In 1974, the island was partitioned into two separate ethnic zones. Reacting against a Greek coup aimed at uniting the island with Greece, Turkey sent its army on July 15, 1974, and in two military operations partitioned the island into separate ethnic zones. A third of the Greek Cypriot population was forced to abandon their homes and properties. Since then, Greek Cypriot leaders' attempts to reunify the island have championed the right of the refugees to return to their homes. By contrast, the partition of 1974 conferred substantial secur-ity for Turkish Cypriots and was welcomed by most of them (Papadakis 2005).

In 1983, the "Turkish Republic of North Cyprus" declared sover-eignty over half of the island, but is still not recognized internationally, except by Turkey. Movement across the partition "green line" was forbidden by the TRNC and monitored by checkpoints from 1974 to 2003 (Krasniqi 2019). During the entire period, Turkish Cypriots retained their rights to citizenship. Following the opening of the check-points, Turkish Cypriots applied to Greek Cypriot authorities in the Republic of Cyprus to obtain them. The Ministry of Interior and regis-tration departments facilitated access to identity documents and citizen-ship (Navaro-Yashin 2007: 91).

In Cyprus, the prominent legacy of partition, forged through the colonial practices of classification based on identity and suspicion, was not translated into a bureaucratic repertoire of population management and monitoring of mobility, used by the majority against the minority that belonged "on the other side," as in India or Israel/Palestine. The bureaucratic toolkit of emergency was used to exclude, control, or dominate those that wished to belong and to remain in the territory. When the Turkish Cypriots actively created a separate "de facto" state in 1963, quickly simulating sovereignty and the functions of their own government, roping in Turkish Cypriots as belonging to a separate "state within a state" until they would receive full representation, they rendered the bureaucratic repertoire to manage populations redundant. They did not seek to return to their territories, but awaited recognition and the possibility of restoring the bicommunal republic or continuing with partition.

CONCLUSION: THE ROLE OF BUREAUCRATIC POWER
AND LEGACIES OF MOBILITY REGIMES

What role did British hybrid bureaucracy play in the shaping of political belonging in the new states?

Establishing control over moving populations after partition was a critical part of state consolidation during the transition from British colonial rule to the Indian dominion, and from Mandate Palestine to Israel. Most central was the sorting of those who would be able to return to India after their flight to Pakistan, and the prevention of the return of Palestinians. Initially framed as regimes of security at the new fluctuating borders, the mobility regimes were based on the colonial repertoire of emergency laws and classifications based on suspicion. These gradually became sorting mechanisms between those that could legally reenter and remain in the new state and those that had liminal status with regard to the state.

This chapter outlined the shared institutional logics of the permit regimes in India and Israel, based on colonial emergency laws, and shaped by the organizing principles of hybrid bureaucracy in response to and during the contingencies of partition, violence, and mass exile. The divergent outcome in Cyprus, where the attempt to reject both partition and legacies of hybrid bureaucracy resulted in an exceptional legal regime of separation, provided an example where the outcomes were a result of the political system created during colonial rule, and not its bureaucratic repertoire.

In India five categories of permits designated different outcomes for their bearers, based on their identity, mobility, and suspicion.

In Israel, documents were given on a temporary basis to provide more opportunities for bureaucratic intervention, and police and security examinations. The temporary documents were considered examination periods, and they separated different kinds of Palestinians based on their registration, classification, and degrees of suspicion.

If citizenship is a regime of closure, in the realities of partition, and before the solidification of legal citizenship, bureaucratic regimes of mobility provided the mechanism for exclusion that was not based on political belonging, but on the relationship to the state and territory as defined by the bureaucrats who designated mobility documents. The transition from subjects to citizens or suspects was not the work of a defined set of experts that shared technical knowledge and applied it to political ends. While bureaucrats used the bureaucratic toolkit of emergency from suspect lists to "closed" or "protected zones" to permits for entry and exit and practices of daily registration, the permit regimes in the aftermath of empire were no longer in place only as mechanisms of control and surveillance to maintain colonial rule. Officials used those documents and classifications as methods to differentiate between claims of belonging to the state. Through the discretionary work of bureaucrats, the mobility regimes produced documents and a set of classifications that were perceived as containing within them the political significance of membership. Navaro-Yashin (2007) suggests that identity documents – the material objects of law and government – are physically charged phenomena that effect affect. For the officials, mobility documents provided the site for exercising the ultimate executive power: the delineation of the political community.

The mobility documents were not only legal evidence of identity but were also evidence of a relationship to the state – any relationship to the state – being roped into its political order through bureaucratic procedure, despite their legal status. Therefore, for example, stateless Palestinians who had been denied reentry, and given temporary permits that were subsequently annulled, retained their relationship to the Israeli state, as those that were excluded. In India, Muslims who held temporary permits spent decades in courts to regain their citizenship.

The legacies of colonial population management practices and the shaping of citizenship as a mobility regime are more evident in Israel/Palestine, where the colonial defense regulations continue to serve as the legal baseplate for the most prominent population management system in the world for Palestinians under military occupation in Gaza and the West Bank, residents of East Jerusalem, and those of foreign nationality prevented from entry. In India, the institutional legacies of hybrid bureaucracy are more prominently visible but in the last two decades, the bureaucratic toolkit of emergency has been redeployed to transform India's citizenship regime through restrictions of mobility and classifications of identity and suspicion. These remnants of British colonial hybrid bureaucracy have created contemporary citizenship as a mobility regime.

Conclusion: The File and the Checkpoint – Colonial Bureaucracy and the Making of Contemporary Citizenship

The file and the checkpoint, the definitive artifacts of emergency mobility regimes and the hallmarks of population management in modern empires, once again have become central to daily life. The experience of Palestinians over the last two decades of a harsh mobility regime and the recent attack on the mobility and political membership of Muslim minorities in India are not solely the result of political programs, but the long-term outcomes of institutional structures created during colonial rule. This book has traced how colonial bureaucratic practices, namely state classification of populations based on suspicion and the ordering of mobility through emergency laws, have contributed to the making of citizenship in the long aftermath of partition. Although the book traces historical processes from the interwar period, through independence and partition, to the first decade across India, Israel/Palestine, and Cyprus, the analysis of micro bureaucratic practices offers a framework with which to understand the contemporary role of bureaucratic legacies, against the backdrop of macro historical processes transforming citizenship. That are transforming the political regimes and in which the bureaucratic practices and colonial laws are used once again to redefine national boundaries through classifications and restrictions of mobility.

How are colonial bureaucratic legacies relevant for the making of political membership today? What understanding have we gained by the organizational vantage point, focusing on administrative practices across time and space, instead of following constitutions, parliamentary legislation, or court decisions? How does the historical analysis of institutional legacies, namely the way the colonial repertoire of bureaucratic practices shaped the conceptual grid of state agents and organizations about political status, shift our understanding of the long-term effects of organizational practices on the shaping of the political life of the state and its regime of citizenship? While the book draws definitive conclusions about the historical legacies of colonial bureaucracy, perhaps the most important question is one it cannot answer: What do bureaucratic legacy and its production of the "state effect" tell us about the potential to imagine other possible futures?

Before attempting to answer these questions, through the conclusions offered by this book, I want to briefly situate the contemporary moment: the last few years of the battles over political membership by bureaucratic means in Israel/Palestine, India, and Cyprus.

On December 12, 2019, the Citizenship Amendment Act (CAA) amended India's citizenship law from 1955 (see Roy 2010). The CAA redefined access to Indian citizenship on ethnoreligious grounds by providing a fast track to Indian citizenship for Hindus, Parsis, Sikhs, Jains, Buddhists, and Christians from Afghanistan, Bangladesh, and Pakistan while excluding Muslims from these countries (Chawla et al. 2020).

The promulgation of the CAA brought to light the pivotal role of the National Registry of Citizens (NRC), a labyrinthine bureaucratic process carried out in India's northeastern state of Assam from 2013 to August 2019 to identify and deport "foreigners." Forcing people to produce documentary evidence of belonging going back several generations, the NRC relies on voter registration lists to identify "doubtful" voters. Classification according to loyalty and suspicion was a central feature of British colonial classification of populations and civil servants, as we saw in Chapters 2 and 4. Those without sufficient paperwork proving their long, uninterrupted presence within the territorial boundaries of the Indian state were left out of the registry. They were then compelled to make counterclaims before "foreigners' tribunals," notorious for their lack of procedural or substantive standards (Roy & Singh 2009). The roots of the practices around the NRC are based on the Foreigners' Acts that served as the foundation of the bureaucratic toolkit of emergency, discussed in Chapter 3.

In 2018, the Israeli government promulgated a constitutional law called Basic Law: Israel as the Nation-State of the Jewish People, declaring that only Jews have a right to self-determination in Israel, which legally enshrined the racial hierarchy practiced for over seven decades that preferred and promoted Jewish settlement into a constitutional law. Moreover, the law defined Israel as a "supra national entity" that represented Jews everywhere, irrespective of their citizenship, and removed Arabic as a formal language (Sa'di 2019). In 2020, US President Donald Trump announced a unilateral plan with Israel to create a state out of a collection of Palestinian enclaves, enabling partial annexation of the occupied Palestinian territories. The plan also included a population transfer of Palestinian citizens of Israel to the territorial enclaves of the Palestinian state.

Scholars have attributed these two major political shifts in the delineation of citizenship to the ethnonationalist and authoritarian politics of the leadership and political parties that promulgated them (Jabareen & Bishara 2019; Jamal 2019; Yadgar 2020). Other analyses view these events as direct legacies of settler colonial rule or religious and casteist supremacy that has prevailed since the earliest days of independence, Nakba, and partition in Israel/Palestine and India (Sa'di 2019; Ben-Youssef & Tamari 2018; Jayal 2019; Carswell et al. 2019).

Explanations for the contemporary attack on universal citizenship, ranging from political authoritarianism to the rise of majoritarian nationalism or settler colonial structures, can benefit from contextualization within a macro historical, relational process of regime change from British colonial rule to independence. Instead of relying on political and ideological explanations, I have traced the bureaucratic micro institutional practices driven by emergency laws that forged boundaries of citizenship through the construction of mobility regimes. The bureaucratic toolkits of emergency classified populations based on suspicion, restricting mobility according to that classification. In turn, nascent states prevented members of those turned into minorities by partition from gaining access to citizenship by monitoring and preventing their movement in the early years of the state. In this respect, the legacy of British colonial rule by emergency was that it provided the baseplate for structuring citizenship on the restricted mobility of minorities, or remainder populations, who allegedly belonged on the "other side" of the partition lines.

EMERGENCY, BUREAUCRACY, AND RACE: COLONIAL LEGACY FROM AN ORGANIZATIONAL PERSPECTIVE

A focus on bureaucratic routines and legacies in three former territories of the British Empire demands a study designed to see the administration of the new states in relation to their imperial pasts, without assuming continuity of the imperial structures and practices, while neither assuming a single isomorphic model of colonial statecraft, nor assuming the exceptionality of each case. Briefly returning to the propositions of research, I outline how the analysis contributes to an understanding of the effects of colonial bureaucratic practices on contemporary political outcomes.

First, instead of taking for granted that each new state had its own trajectory for regime change and focusing on their structural differences, I analyze their shared set of institutional practices. Contrary to those that view the colonial state as an ad hoc enterprise without a particular institutional theory, I suggest a set of organizing principles of hybrid bureaucracy based on practices and their justification by colonial bureaucrats. This synthetic set of principles enables the empirical study of both the origins of the bureaucratic practices and the similar trajectories and divergent outcomes of the three cases, which were dependent upon the continuity of emergency law after independence. Colonial administrators relied on the coupling of racial hierarchies and rule by emergency in their attempts to govern the colonies. They did so by using flexibility, secrecy, and personalism to create and justify separate practices for different populations in the same territory. The organizing principles of hybrid bureaucracy offer a synthetic model to address the way racialized state bureaucracies operate, without the declared myth of equality and impersonality. Because the colonial state permanently failed in its project of legitimacy in the eyes of the colonizers, the bureaucracy included pronounced racial hierarchies into the naturalization of the categories constituted and reconstructed by the state. Refuting both the modernist interpretations of Weber that hold the rule of law as the central component of rational-legal bureaucracy and those that reject the Weberian framework for its race blindness and European focus, I show how the illiberal nature of the rule of law and its sustained breach of universalistic applications to administration ordered by racial hierarchy do not render a system of rule into one that is lawless, broken, or corrupt. The very breach of the liberal rule of law, through the bureaucratic routinizing of emergency, becomes a powerful tool of executive power that might seem inefficient, but is effective in its mission to contain and control minority or remainder populations. The organizing principles of hybrid bureaucracy in British colonies escape the binaries of liberal critiques of administration as being legal/illegal or efficient/inefficient. Far from an alternative institutional chart of colonial states, these principles evade the binary juxtaposition between modern liberal bureaucracies and other bureaucracies, previously conceived as invariably different from their counterparts in colonial/postcolonial settings. The contours of hybrid bureaucracy reflect the ways that both societies with pronounced racial hierarchies and modern liberal states justify the rule of law and equality before the law, while maintaining structural inequalities and differentiated administrative repertoires based on hierarchies of worth.

The organizing principles of hybrid bureaucracy (Chapter 1), and the focus on the colonial legacies of classifying populations based on suspicion (Chapter 2) and the extensive use of the bureaucratic toolkit of emergency (Chapter 3) provide new directions for political theorists, legal scholars, and sociologists and anthropologists to rethink the colonial state and its deep impact on new states through its bureaucratic practices, and to understand contemporary modes of state power in societies with pronounced racial hierarchies. The study contributes a conceptual framework to study bureaucratic power across the divide between global north and south, building an organizational and institutional component to complement legal historians of empire, who have shown the colonial and imperial origins of modern government in the metropole.

Legal histories of empire point to the central role of policing but largely overlook the ways colonial governmentality was predicated on emergency laws, and how its operation created an axis of suspicion deployed through bureaucratic classification. As I show in Chapters 2 and 3, using emergency laws as the connected point of departure in the three cases, the axis of suspicion upended other types of classification, creating a bureaucratic arsenal for managing perceived "dangerous populations."

Second, by investigating the bureaucratic toolkit of emergency, the study offers an alternative view on the legacies of colonial rule. The study of administrative correspondence and institutional practices, not as outcomes of policy decisions and political discourse, has required me to temporarily suspend the national narratives, mostly driven by political leadership and state historians, and usually divided along lines of national or nationalist affiliations. Similarly, my investigation of administrative practice independently from the contemporaneous decisions of the supreme courts, in order to temporarily suspend the prominence of jurisprudence in legal history, has facilitated a focus on bureaucratic negotiations that tell us an entirely different administrative story of the relationships between political membership, rights, and the state. I trace the origins and genesis of the toolkits of emergency: the implementation of the Foreigners Acts, blacklists, and classification according to degrees of loyalty and threat to the state follow the formation of a powerful administrative arsenal that routinized emergency and classified "dangerous populations," which in turn would employ emergency laws to define citizenship in the independent state. The trajectory of the bureaucratic toolkit of emergency was fueled by the belief that any form of political activism toward liberation from British colonial rule was a threat to "peace and good government," which led colonial governments to develop a set of bureaucratic practices of population control and surveillance through emergency laws. During anticolonial insurgencies and intercommunal violence, from the Quit India movement to the Arab Revolt in Mandatory Palestine in 1936–1939 and the Cyprus Emergency, the classification of political activists and militants, coupled with various counterinsurgency activities, augmented the enforcement of emergency laws on mass civilian populations.

Following Israel's independence and the Nakba, these practices became an "administrative toolkit of suspicion" for the military government's relations with the remaining Palestinians, as we saw in Chapter 5. In India, a similar toolkit shaped the relationship between citizenship, political opposition, and political violence, establishing a distinction between the sovereign people as a political community endowed with rights and those engaged in political violence who were governed by emergency laws sanctioned by the constitution (see Samaddar 2006) and excluded from the political community. Even those who held formal citizenship became a class whose rights were at the discretion of bureaucratic officials.

Tracing this trajectory provides an alternative history of the infrastructure of citizenship, similar to emerging scholarship in historical sociology (Kim 2016) and political anthropology of the state (Mathur 2018) that investigates the role of bureaucratic practices in structuring political membership. If one suspends the state narrative of equality – what Brubaker (2014: 805) calls the "statist logic of citizenship" – as well as scholarly accounts on the ways the supreme courts protected individual rights during the very early days of the new states, we can trace the contours of political membership not to rights but to what these narratives overlook: possibilities for mobility, as I show in Chapter 4. The content of political membership and differentiation between types of political status shifts when one studies the bureaucratic constructions of citizenship, instead of assuming that a particular status entails rights.

Third, instead of viewing partition as a historical event or a characteristic of the state, I build upon the innovative scholarship that views partition as a process that shaped political and social trajectories, showing how partition configured practices in state administrations from the very point of its introduction as an idea, through its violent aftermath in the wars of independence. Beyond the lasting effects of partition that constrain political imagination, create mnemonic communities of belonging, and define territorial disputes, partition defined bureaucratic practices restricting mobility that divide across legal or imagined partition lines. India made a decisive choice to grant citizenship based on territorial ties rather than lineage. Seeking economic survival during colonial rule, millions of Indians were dispersed throughout the British Empire as indentured laborers or as permanent second-class citizens in other countries (Tinker 1977). These millions were not present in India at the time of independence and partition. The territorial definitions also meant that mobility into the territory of independent India was critical for attaining citizenship. That mobility was mediated by the permit regime, which, as I show in Chapter 5, differentiated between Hindus and Muslims who attempted to return to India after the initial waves of violence of partition.

Israel, as a Jewish state, developed two paths to citizenship. The first was through lineage. One had to be of Jewish heritage, as defined in the Law of Return. The second path to citizenship was the naturalization of the remainder Palestinian population after independence and the Nakba.

In Cyprus, citizenship was granted to those with Cypriot heritage in its nationality law enacted in 1967. Effectively, following the Turkish occupation of Northern Cyprus in 1974 and the de facto partition, Turkish Cypriots continued to have citizenship, but many of their rights were curtailed because of their restricted mobility, because they could not cross from the TRNC into Cyprus until 2003, and because official documents of the TNRC are not recognized.

In all three cases, citizenship was shaped by the macro historical politics of partition, self-determination, and population transfer, as well as the micro bureaucratic practices of population management, intrinsically linked to the legacies of colonial classification and perceptions of loyalty.

Fourth, by introducing the "axis of suspicion" as the core of population classification and control in the colonial state, I situate the role of emergency and the repertoires of suspicion not as a Schmittian binary of distinction between friend and foe, but as a process that weaves suspicion into the very distinctions that were the hallmark of colonial governmentalities based on racial divides. The colonial state used categorization as a political and administrative tool to manage populations, which had its greatest ramifications on population mobility. Classifying groups in colonies fraught with intercommunal divisions often solidified communal identities, accentuated differences, and turned old racial and religious disputes into violent conflicts. In

Chapter 2, I show how two types of population categories created by the colonial governments were later adopted by independent administrations that classified populations on an axis of suspicion alongside attempts to render the population legible. The new states also used the classification of civil servants based on loyalty and suspicion as a state-building project of and for the new majority following partition, independence, and the Nakba. As I show in Chapter 4, the classification of civil servants served as a communal battleground that eventually led to the collapse of the state machinery in Cyprus, and to a regime of suspicion and surveillance of Muslim civil servants in India for the republic's first turbulent decade. In Israel, those very practices of suspicion were deployed against Jewish civil servants who had served the colonial government, since Palestinian administrators had fled during the war of independence and those who remained were not considered suitable to serve the new government of the Jewish state.

The axis of suspicion, stemming from rule by emergency, steers away from the neat divisions between settler and native, and enables the analysis of population management as a dynamic field which helps explain the way the state bureaucracy maintains and constitutes other inequalities, even within the ethno-majorities.

Fifth, a study of the bureaucratization of emergency laws as a way of tracing colonial continuities facilitates an institutional view of colonial legacy that is contingent upon the legal vehicle of emergency. The difference in the formalization of colonial emergency laws in the new states accounts for their divergent outcomes.

The practices and documents that grew the permit regimes into powerful institutions in both Israel and India after independence originated in colonial administrative practices of classification and surveillance, developed to implement spatial-legal measures in counterinsurgencies, and gradually led to a routinization of emergency. The practices that developed in India during the interwar period – preventative detention, closed zones, exit permits, daily monitoring of movement of foreigners, and the impunity of security forces – evolved into a formidable repertoire of procedural violence that diffused to Mandate Palestine and Cyprus when the colonial governments responded to anticolonial campaigns by local nationalist movements.

The institutionalization of the colonial emergency laws into the independent regimes had a critical effect on the way the states would manage the minority population after partition, and it accounts for the difference in the case of Cyprus, where security laws did not shape citizenship even when the republic was torn apart by ethnic violence, analyzed in Chapter 5.

Following independence, both India and Israel inherited the bureaucratic toolkit of emergency measures – comprising laws, maps, statistics, equipment, and bureaucratic forms that had been deployed against those opposed to British rule – but each formalized these powers differently, demarcating boundaries of national belonging that legitimated the differentiated use of executive power against different types of citizens. The wars over partition had transformed Muslims and other minorities in India, and Palestinians in Israel, into aliens of a sort, belonging to a separate political entity in the eyes of the bureaucracies and security forces of their respective countries. They became suspects a priori and enemies de facto. Once they were perceived in this way, the bureaucratic toolbox embedded a political logic of suspicion that legitimized the use of colonial measures against the new "minorities" who remained in both India and Israel. Bureaucrats used a classification matrix of loyal and suspicious populations to produce maps of danger zones, borderlands, and areas of infiltration, which determined the limits of mobility in tandem with the boundaries of political membership in the community. Notwithstanding the fact that partition never materialized in Israel/ Palestine, and despite the difference between the political regimes of Israel and India, in both cases, permit regimes based on emergency laws were one of the methods deployed to prevent refugees from returning to their homes, alongside the massive taking over of land and homes, to fuel the Jewish settlement which replaced the Palestinian population that had been exiled and the influx of Hindu refugees from Pakistan. Returning refugees were termed "infiltrators" in Israel and "spies" in India. In Israel, this spatial-legal system was a mechanism that used administrative means to shape the boundaries of political belonging and prevent Palestinians from returning and claiming residency and then citizenship. The categories by which Israel classified subjects (as citizens, residents, refugees, or infiltrators) were institutionalized through the permit regime. The type of permit one held infused legal and political meaning into one's location (for example, in India during the first population census in 1951) and determined one's status. Thus, temporary emergency decrees that prevented mobility became the foundations for the categorization of minority citizenship

As I show in Chapter 5, the similarity between the permit regimes in India and Israel reflects the legal-spatial methods that gradually shaped the goals of the population management systems, which were not articulated as official policy at the outset. Both regimes were first geared to survey and monitor the "suspicious" and "dangerous" Muslim population, which may have been a "fifth column," and second, to prevent the physical return of refugees by blocking their legal claims for citizenship through bureaucratic means. Each goal perpetuated a different set of bureaucratic practices and routines. Partition plans played a crucial role in shifting the foci of the colonial practices away from surveillance and intelligence-gathering for the purpose of monitoring and controlling the population and preventing opposition to an existential goal of achieving or maintaining a demographic majority. While in the metropole emergency meant that the government had to suspend citizens' rights, in the independent postimperial state, citizenship rights had yet to be carved out. Therefore, in order to deny rights, the administration did not have to suspend them, but had only to prevent people from gaining status as citizens or residents.

In Israel, exclusion was structural and included two types of political regime: a colonial regime that ruled the remaining Palestinian population in the administered territories, and a postcolonial state that incorporated much of the legal and administrative structures of the British Mandate in what was to become a permanent legal state of emergency. India's citizenship regime was more complex, as massive efforts were made to grant rights and political participation through the largest organization of democratic franchise in the world, while at the same time preventing the return of minorities who had fled in the wake of the partition violence.

Despite the shared legacy of colonial emergency regulations, the relationship between citizenship and security laws in the two countries evolved differently. In India, inherited colonial laws were used against citizens of various ethnicities and religions, including members of the Hindu majority, usually intersecting with caste, linguistic minorities, and rural areas. These laws were deployed against the Maoist insurgency, the Gurkha movement in Darjeeling, the Sikh independence movement in Punjab, in Nagaland, and in Jammu and Kashmir. In Israel, emergency laws served as the backbone of the colonial military government from 1949 to 1966 to control Palestinians perceived as an enemy population. In 1952, Palestinians were legally granted citizenship, yet the practicable rights of the Palestinian minority came into effect de facto only when the military regime was dismantled in 1966. From 1967 onwards, the Defence (Emergency) Regulations were also used as the legal infrastructure for governing Palestinians in the Occupied Territories.

The absence of formal citizenship and nationality laws made it possible for the bureaucratic powers to determine political membership in Israel and India. Instead, powerful home ministries and intricate permit regimes governed the lives of minorities in the postcolonial states. While the labyrinth of bureaucracy was complex and sophisticated, the method of exclusion was simple: the permit regimes created a variety of identity documents and registries. If people could not get the identity documents they needed as evidence to prove their rights as citizens, they could be classified as residents, aliens, or infiltrators. For the minorities, administrative practices that developed during the colonial era through emergency laws dictated the boundaries of political membership. These practices were no longer reserved for the purposes of population legibility and management but were instead used to solidify the borders of the nation against those who were perceived as enemies.

SHARED HISTORIES AND DIVERGENT OUTCOMES: HOW BUREAUCRACY MAKES CITIZENSHIP

In Chapters 4 and 5, I show how powerful state bureaucracies used administrative routines to *structure* rather than just administer political policies, and reconfigure the political membership of the population, while legal citizenship remained indeterminate, before formal citizenship laws were enacted. Accordingly, rather than being tools to suppress the rights of citizens, security emergency laws, through the conceptual legal-spatial methods they created, created differentiated political statuses based on identity, region, and mobility.

Hybrid bureaucracy enabled wide discretion, flexibility, and secrecy, which configured a powerful, autonomous, and almost sovereign bureaucracy that ran the ministries of interior and other bodies that managed the population such as the Ministry of Rehabilitation in India and the military government in Israel. While in India the continuity of the Indian Civil Service after the regime change accounted for the persistence of the emergency repertoire, in Israel a separate apparatus – entirely structured as a colonial government – controlled the remainder of the Arab population, while most of the administration of Israel's Jewish population was carried out by civil servants who had worked for the Yishuv, Israel's pre-state administrative institutions.

In Cyprus, where the new state bureaucracy did not partake in the classification and administration of citizenship, colonial emergency laws were annulled at independence. If bureaucratic repertoires need a legal anchor to survive regime change, then in Cyprus there was no such legal anchor, and there is no evidence of the use of the colonial bureaucratic toolkit of emergency during the Cyprus conflict after the collapse of the republic in 1963. In Israel and India, colonial emergency laws provided the legal anchor of the survival and continuity of the bureaucratic toolkit of emergency.

The military government and its permit system that monitored and controlled the movement of Palestinians created the documents that were necessary for claiming citizenship. Yet this military bureaucracy transformed political membership in the new Israeli state into one in which a person's classification – in degrees of loyalty and suspicion – determined their range of mobility. Similar to the mobility regime for Muslims in India in the very first years following the violence of independence, the British colonial toolkit of population management in Mandate Palestine was adapted into a new set of colonial practices, this time of the majority ruling the minority, the survivors who remained within the boundaries of the independent state following the Nakba. As control of suspicious and dangerous populations became institutionalized, the temporary classifications and practices created during the emergency transformed into permanent practices of the Ministry of Interior and Ministry of Home Affairs. The Israeli permit regime transformed the colonial practices of population management into a method of administrative exclusion, reducing the number of Palestinians entitled to claim citizenship once the statutory laws were enacted. For Jews, citizenship entailed access to rights, effected and scaled by racial classifications, which were deployed through a separate mechanism of the developmental state. For Palestinians, citizenship was a mobility regime that granted nondeportability and protection from exile, though not from internal displacement.

The striking similarities between the Israeli military government's surveillance of mobility and the permit system on India's western border with Pakistan, underscore how ad hoc measures that were initially justified by security reasons following the influx and movement of populations became institutionalized into administrative routines that, in turn, shaped the definitions of the political communities of the new states. Restricting the mobility of those colonial subjects who had become minority populations after partition and the Nakba was central to the remaking of the relationship between authority, territory, and population in independent India and Israel. Although some scholars perceive restrictions of mobility as either security measures or methods to ensure territorial expansion in a settler colony, researchers have overlooked how the bureaucratic policing movement constructed citizenship in the aftermath of empire. Yet analysis that focuses on ethnonationalism has severe limitations, not least because it assumes that the state apparatus is a neutral apparatus working to achieve ethnonational goals. If bureaucracy is a neutral apparatus that carries out ethnonational policies, then it also follows that representation is the central method to ensure that equality exists. While minority representation can be significant, it cannot singly change the organizing principles and the embedded political and racial hierarchies that shape daily administration.

CITIZENSHIP AS MOBILITY

What does the investigation of bureaucratic practices of managing populations tell us about the relationship between citizenship and mobility? The history of bureaucratic routines illuminates the practical experience of dispossessed minorities. Security laws and perceptions of suspicion and threat carve out people's movements within the state while preventing their deportations from it. Acquiring the document that prevents their deportation also ropes them in and binds them to a surveillance system that subjects their rights to bureaucratic discretion based on loyalty. This practical experience of precarity, uncertainty, and exclusion highlights the way that bureaucratic practices create the materialities of political status. Bureaucratic practices and organizational formations can no longer be treated as arenas of implementation, or as "red tape" and the "banalities of evil," because of their formative weight in the making of contemporary legal and political status.

A comparative study against the backdrop of partition highlights the ways territory and political membership are mediated through bureaucratic means but can be transferred to other sites of investigation beyond former British colonies, using the concept of citizenship as a mobility regime. In this study, because citizenship was based on one's physical location, in India as well as for the Palestinian remainder who resided in Israel, the permit regimes purposefully shaped access to citizenship. For the colonial state apparatus, mobility was dangerous. In the independent state, however, citizenship rather than mobility presented danger. The evidence regarding the Israeli state organizations and military government points to this conclusion explicitly, while in India, the separate spatial-legal measures for Muslims presents implicit evidence. Thus, the monitoring of mobilities – which had been a central feature of colonial governmentality – developed into the bureaucratic implementation of emergency laws. These mobility regimes subsequently demarcated different kinds of citizens.

Citizenship as mobility becomes visible when we interrogate the bureaucratic toolkit of the state while muting its constitutional debates, parliamentary inquiries, and even supreme court judgments. This is not because the state was managing a cover-up operation; it is because everyone thought formal citizenship necessarily meant that citizens have rights, including the bureaucrats in the military government and the Home Office who were trying their best to fight the returnees and infiltrators and doing everything possible to create evidentiary obstacles to citizenship. Because many of the state's agents believed that citizenship granted the "bundle of civil and political rights" (Shafir & Peled 1998) and that the formal laws determined citizenship, albeit unequal citizenship, they pursued two types of actions to prevent the damage of the citizenship laws to the ethnonational project through bureaucratic and administrative means and, at the same time, to create practices that rendered citizenship devoid of rights because of its subordination to a bureaucratic regime that held separate practices for different populations.

Understanding citizenship as a mobility regime does not challenge the legality of formal citizenship or the perception of citizenship as a liberal bundle of rights, a civic status, or a birthright. On the contrary, it enables a richer analysis of differentiation between populations on an institutional level, without equating differentiated regimes of citizenship simply because of variegated ethnicities, which are so prevalent in the modern state. Citizenship as mobility allows us to understand how political membership functions in regimes of pronounced inequalities, when we no longer uphold the imaginary hierarchy between rights and the mundane bureaucratic processes that prevent them.

Notes

INTRODUCTION: THE SPECTACLE OF INDEPENDENCE AND THE SPECTER OF BUREAUCRACY

1. Excerpt from the "Tryst with Destiny" speech by Jawaharlal Nehru, first prime minister of India, in the Constituent Assembly at midnight of August 15, 1947, http://nehrumemorial.nic.in/en/component/content/article/79-nmml/214-tryst-with-destiny-speech-text.html.
2. India embarked on the largest project of universal franchise before its first elections, which Ornit Shani (2017) views as the administrative path to democracy, through the work of inclusion in the electoral rolls and registries. See De (2018).
3. Gyan Pandey (2001) describes partition as rupture, a critical juncture that created a binary of two nations.
4. NAI MHA 170/5/47 ESTS. P. V. R. Rao, Joint Secretary to the Government of India, memo to the Home Department, July 26, 1947. Historian William Gould and anthropologist Vazira Zamindar both write of this decision as a moment that encapsulates the contradictions and ambiguities of the making of citizenship in partition (Zamindar 2007; Gould 2010).
5. Zamindar 2007, Chapter 6; Sriraman 2018, Roy 2012
6. Lord Curzon, then Viceroy of India, first introduced the concept of partition in 1905 as an administrative necessity to organize the province of Bengal. Partition was envisaged as an extreme but necessary tool of controlling and managing the population. Decades of historiography have been devoted to arguments about the origins and "smoking guns" of ideas of partition (Chatterji 2007) and the instigators of division and exclusion of native minorities from citizenship, which have been central to the experience of postcolonial state building. For some, the British are at fault; others blame elites from majority communities, such as the upper-caste Hindus in Bengal (Chatterji 2002) or the Palestinian leadership (Mattar 1992). Others focus on the role of religious and national ideologies such as Zionism (Khalidi 2007), the irredentist Megali idea of Hellenic power in

Cyprus (Loizides 2007), Palestinian Christian sectarianism (Robson 2011), or religious political convictions in India and Palestine (Devji 2013). In the 1990s, studies of partition in India, suspicious of official sources, privileged oral history and memory studies over administrative files. Yet these sensitive narratives mirrored the tendency of the subjects of research to look back at partition as a history of an "inexplicable catastrophe" (Chatterji 2009). A third wave of studies of partition (Khan 2017; Ansari 2005; Zamindar 2007) has focused on its aftermath and takes an approach that considers the narratives of individuals and communities, as well as political elites, in shaping political trajectories of nationalism and citizenship.

7. The epistemological divide between social scientists who perceive the inheritance of colonial rule as an asset or a burden is both political and disciplinary, between those who focus on imperial rule as a project of progress, broadly defined, that ended with decolonization, and those who perceive the ongoing destructive elements of imperial rule as a continuous present. Social scientists who see colonial administrative structures as assets explore the impact of colonial legacies in order to understand how colonial regimes have shaped trajectories of development in terms of democratization, economic growth, the rule of law, and gender equality (Mahoney 2003; Iyer 2010; Lange 2009; Halliday et al. 2012). Most of this work, however, treats bureaucracy as one variable of many, mainly differentiating between direct and indirect colonial rule. They have not distinguished types of bureaucracies or the ways the state actually organized the means of administration.

8. The vast scholarship on impediments on movement usually separate between detention and confinement and mobility restrictions. Dayan terms these colonial repertoires as regimes of separation. See Dayan (2009).

9. The exemplary sociological study of comparative colonial administration is George Steinmetz's *The Devil's Handwriting* (2008a), in which he investigates the formation of native policy through ethnographic knowledge and intra-elite competition between administrators. The effort of this study is different, hence the focus on the routines and practices themselves rather than the competition and relationships between administrators within the "social field of the colonial state."

10. IOR R/20/A/2451 p. 16. Form T 7912/473/378, January 17, 1933, a "Declaration to be made by colored seaman claiming to be a British subject or British protected person and applying for a special certificate of nationality," included a box marked "character."

11. The omission of imperial and colonial histories from organizations theory was due to both the history of its development, including the Parsonian translation of Weber (Shenhav 2003; Loveman 2005) and what Julian Go calls "the imperial episteme" in sociology (Go 2020). Some exceptions are Nkomo (1992), Prasad (2003), Banerjee et al. (2009), and Victor Ray (2019) on a theory of race and organizations.

12. Max Weber rejected "race" as a viable sociological variable of analysis of social closure, arguing that race is a superfluous category that overlaps with other variables of inequality. Weber explained racial hierarchy as a form or method for creating social closures. See also Brubaker (2014).

13. Note on archival research: Archival research on Palestine from the introduction of the partition plan in 1937 until the withdrawal of the British mandate included correspondence of the Department of Immigration and Statistics with the High Commissioner of Palestine, the General Secretary, the Border Police, and the Office of Passport Control, as well as correspondence on population statistics from the central Zionist archive. For the transition from the British mandate to the enactment of Israel's citizenship laws, documents from the interim government decisions on immigration and population classification, files from the Ministry of Interior-Central Office (until 1965) and the Ministry of Minorities (until 1949), correspondence with the military government on citizenship and residency status, intruders, aliens and immigrants, and suspicious persons. Archival research in Cyprus from 1950 until independence in 1960 included files of the Administrative Secretary, the Secretary for Immigration, the Statistical Officer, and District Commissioners' files relating to classification of persons. Documents from the Ministry of Interior from 1960 to 1964, the period of independence through the collapse of the republic's constitutional arrangements. From November 1963 to 1965, the Ministry of Interior of the Republic did not effectively administer the Turkish Cypriot population. The Turkish Republic of North Cyprus Archive in Kyrenia does not contain primary sources of documents prior to 1974. For the years from 1963 to 1974, I conducted six structured interviews with former members of the Turkish Cypriot administration and used secondary sources. I relied on the Nancy Crawshaw papers at the MNSC library at Princeton University, and a dissertation conducted at the time (1963–71) that serves as a historical resource: Patrick (1976). I also rely heavily on Bryant and Hatay (2020) and their groundbreaking historical research and analysis on the making of the Turkish Cypriot administration, as well as conversations with legal scholars and anthropologists to reconstruct the administrative history for this period. Archival research in India included correspondence of the home department until 1946, and the political and secret document collection of the India Office in the British Library. Documents from between 1952 and 1956 included correspondence from the Ministries of Interior and External Affairs related to population classification, civil servants, and border control.

14. Primary sources for the synthetic model of hybrid bureaucracy in Chapter 1 include documents written by imperial officials, none of whom wrote as systematically as did Lord Cromer, Proconsul of Egypt. Working closely with Yehouda Shenhav (Shenhav and Berda 2009, Shenhav 2013) I chose Cromer as a main source of data because of his distinct influence on the practical and theoretical knowledge about colonial administration that diffused across the British Empire during and after the First World War. Starting with Cromer, and the imperial bureaucrats who worked and corresponded with him, I searched and coded the materials of official and unofficial writings, correspondence, and opinions using seven concepts or their cognates: organization, bureaucracy, government, governance, administration, structure, and race. I found twenty-two British colonial bureaucrats who worked at different levels both in India and across the British Empire, who are listed in the table below. I defined the officials' connections to each other according to evidence of one of the following four indicators: mentor

and mentee relationships; when one official's writing was cited as an inspiration for another's practice or writing (for example, Hastings for Cromer); shared experiences in a single location; and when officials who were structural equivalents held similar concurrent positions in different locations.

Serial	Name	Location	No. of major works
1	Alfred Milner	Egypt, South Africa	
2	Carthill (Joseph Fuller)	India	9
3	Charles Somerset	Cape	
4	Curzon	India	
5	Edward Cecil	Sudan, Egypt, South Africa	1
6	Francis Campbell Balfour	Sudan & India	
7	Fredrick Lugard	Nigeria, Hong Kong,	4
8	J. S. Furnivall	Burma	11
9	George Grey	New Zealand	
10	Harold MacMichael	Sudan	
11	Harry Smith	South Africa, India	1
12	Herbert Kitchener	Egypt	
13	Hugh Shakespeare Barnes	Baluchistan	
14	James Shaw Hay	Gambia	
15	Jameson (Leander Starr)	South Africa	
16	Lord Cromer (Evelyn Baring)	Egypt	5
17	Marshall Clark	South Africa, Lesotho	
18	Northbrook	India	
19	Rhodes	Cape	
20	Ripon (George Robinson)	India	
21	Robert Lytton	India, Afghanistan	
22	Warren Hastings	India	

1 THE EFFECTIVE DISORDER OF HYBRID BUREAUCRACY

1. In 1883, Evelyn Baring, Lord Cromer, became the British Consul-General of Egypt after several formative years of service in India. He was the first British bureaucrat to collate a theory of imperial bureaucracy, in "The government of subject races" (1908) and in *Modern Egypt* ([1908] 2010).

2. Roger Owen(2004: 362) pointed out that "'The government of subject races' presented materials which were removed from earlier drafts of *Modern Egypt*, in the guise of a review of a book on the decline of the Roman Empire."

3. Cromer quoted in Arendt (1951: 310).

4. The rule of law was perceived as a safeguard against instrumental rationality and the "legal" breach of rule of law that enabled it. For instance, in Franz Neumann's *Behemoth* (1942), he distinguished rule of law from "rule by law" to depict the disastrous connection between efficient bureaucracy and the loosely integrated legal apparatuses of the Nazi state.

5. Even staunch critics of this epistemology, which places the rational model of bureaucracy within historical and cultural contexts, remain anchored in assumptions about the rule of law as the primary definer of legitimate action. Among these postulations, one may find: (1) neo-Marxists (e.g., Edwards 1979), who study rational-legal rule as a means of labor control and the resistance it entails; (2) neo-institutionalists (e.g., Dobbin 1994; DiMaggio & Powell 1991; Scott & Meyer 1994; Friedland & Alford 1991; Adler & Borys 1996), who examine ceremonial and institutionalized sources of rational-legal bureaucratic rule; (3) proponents of post-bureaucracy (e.g., Ouchi 1980; du Gay 2000; Ashcraft 2001; Courpasson & Clegg 2006); (4) Holocaust researchers (e.g., Bauman 2000; see also Shenhav 2013), who attribute atrocities to a rational-legal bureaucracy gone astray when driven by a strong culture of "instrumental rationality"; (5) poststructuralist critics (e.g., Tsoukas & Knudsen 2003; Shenhav 1999), who deconstruct bureaucratic rationality yet continue to adhere to western assumptions about the rule of law; and, lastly, (6) studies of bureaucracy in post-colonial societies (e.g., Singhi 1974; Farazmand 2009) that criticize the rational-legal ideal type but at the same time use it as a yardstick for analysis. Eventually, these studies, despite their criticism, canonize and reify the ideal type of bureaucracy under rational-legal domination, positioning it as historical and universal (see also Courpasson & Clegg 2006).

6. From functionalist perspectives such as Thomas Merton (1963/1939) or the early critique of Michel Crozier (1964), whose method of research was to attend to the dysfunctionalities of bureaucracy to decipher its apparatuses.

7. Bourdieu warns that one cannot think about the state beyond the categories that have been produced and maintained by the state, particularly about its form of organization (Bourdieu 1994). The suggested organizing principles of hybrid bureaucracy, extracted from the writing of bureaucrats themselves, are an attempt to use the perceptions of the bureaucrats of explicitly racialized systems as the building blocks of the model, not only as a tool of critique of historical racialized bureaucracies and their direct legacies but also of contemporary bureaucracies governed by what is perceived as the liberal "rule of law."

8. An alternative model of hybrid bureaucracy would not be considered by Weber as dysfunctional or illegitimate. Weber did not incorporate into his model an epistemological sphere of illegitimacy (Mommsen 1974: 83; see also Titunik 2005: 145). He seemed to assume that any "stable" political structure is legitimate. Therefore, the failure to gain legitimacy in the eyes of the

"subject races" would not have entailed an inherent violation of the model of legitimacy (but see Steinmetz 2008b: 592).

9. Weber did not develop a consistent theory of imperialism or imperial bureaucracy (Mommsen 1984) yet in his sociology of law, he devoted much attention to the concept of "imperium," which denotes authoritarian power held by, for example, a prince, the master of a household, magistrates, or bureaucratic officials (Swedberg 2005: 123; Weber 1978: 839).

10. During this period, bureaucratic solutions to the political and moral challenge of imperial legitimacy were not confined to British rule. The Dutch reformed their bureaucracies to form what Locher-Scholten (1994) calls "ethical imperialism."

11. The term "personalism" indicates the way personal relationships and identity were decisive to administrative interaction in hybrid bureaucracy and does not refer to a belief in personalist philosophy. Personalism, juxtaposed with "impersonality" in the rational-legal model of bureaucracy, represents traditional authority and patrimonial arrangements (Rudolph & Rudolph 1979).

12. Cromer was inspired by the administrative solutions Warren Hastings attempted in India and applied similar measures in Egypt. See the review of Cromer's report on the administration of Egypt in 1899 in West (1900).

13. Hussain (2003) traces the genealogy of Hastings's position to his correspondence with John Malcolm, an East India Company agent and later governor of Bombay, who was a strong proponent of the use of despotic authority, rather than a set of codified, published, and abstract laws.

14. Furnivall was a staunch critic of the paradoxes of British colonial administration, evidenced in his study of the early administration of Burma. See also Rutherford (2012).

15. TNA CO 537/6244. Minute, Bennet, Colonial Office response on Standardization of Emergency Measures in the colonies, draft letter to Governor of Cyprus, April 20, 1950.

16. A well-known example of the diffusion of policing methods is Charles Tegart, who served as police commissioner in Calcutta and was recruited to aid in the repression of the Arab Revolt in Mandate Palestine because of his notoriously effective methods for interrogating suspects. See "Charles Tegart of the Indian Police": an unpublished biography by Lady Tegart; IOR MSS Eur C235. For Tegart's legacy in contemporary Israel/Palestine see El Rifai et al. (2017).

17. ISA M/5134/10 is a file of miscellaneous forms for use in the Immigration Department in Palestine, which included a number of forms from India, two of which had a category of "race or caste or tribe and sub tribe" that were crossed out.

18. TNA CO/733/315/2 Part II, 1936. Pamphlet and corresponding minutes.

19. The modernist interpretation of Weber's model offers three historical, consecutive, and progressive phases of legitimacy – charismatic (personal), traditional, and legal – although Weber did not perceive them as linear or exclusive, but suggested the possibility of mixed types of legitimate domination (Mommsen 1974; Shenhav & Berda 2009).

20. Weber was well aware of the dubious possibilities created by the subjective reasoning of the state: "The sure instincts of the bureaucracy for the

conditions of maintaining its own power in the home state are inseparably fused with this canonization of the abstraction of objective idea of reasons of state" (Weber 1978: 980).

21. Fortress colonies were Cyprus, Malta, Gibraltar, Aden, Kenya, Hong Kong, and Singapore (Porter & Stockwell 1989: 494). Colonial Secretary Alan Lenox Boyd used the term "fortress colonies" in a speech he made in 1958 to indicate territories that were "vital to the free world."

22. The consistent creation of uncertainty as a form of control was not exclusive to colonial bureaucracy. Yehouda Shenhav (1994) shows how managers have used uncertainty as a strategy to increase control over subordinates; for contemporary analysis on fostering ambiguity in bureaucracy see Best (2012).

2 FORMS OF SUSPICION: MOBILITY AS THREAT, CENSUS AS BATTLEGROUND

1. *Thugee* and *Goonda* were terms used to categorize and to describe "criminal types" and "minor security threats." The first Goonda law appeared in the Punjab in 1923, for the control of "dangerous and disorderly persons," authorizing police to act with force, sometimes permitting officers to shoot on sight.

2. IOR R/20/A/2451 p. 16, January 17, 1933. Form T 7912/473/378, a "Declaration to be made by colored seaman claiming to be a British subject or British protected person and applying for a special certificate of nationality," included a box marked "character."

3. NAI HD 19/51/41 political external. Letter to provincial governments from political external dept. regarding application procedures for passports and naturalization, November 15, 1941. Those of doubtful loyalty were classified as category B on applications for passports and other naturalization documents. Checking antecedents for this category was more elaborate. The registering officer had to corroborate the details of the application with the authority in their province of residence, and the province of their birth.

4. Passports were not officially introduced for Britons until 1915; nevertheless, since then, applications for travel were of interest to the Colonial Office, the Foreign Office, and the India Office. See Fisher (2007) and Mongia (2018).

5. The Criminal Tribes Act of 1871 provided for the "registration, surveillance and control of certain tribes designated criminal." The act also empowered local governments to designate any gang, tribe, or class of persons as a "criminal tribe" if "they were addicted to the systemic commission of offences without bail."

6. For a critical stance on millet as a technology of rule to maintain tolerance, see Makdisi (2000).

7. Julian Go, referring to fluctuating definitions of race in the context of American empire, suggests that race should be understood as "code," a category that acquires meaning within local spatial and temporal contexts (Go 2008).

8. The British kept an important feature of millet governance: the autonomy of educational institutions. It would become an arena for battling official categories because of funding allocations based on population classification. Colonial reports, Annual no. 1025 Cyprus (1920 CMD 508–9), pp. 5–6, House of Commons Parliamentary Papers online, 1917–18.
9. Rebecca Bryant, the partition project, "The Leftover Community: Demography and Anxiety in a Society Under Siege," manuscript in progress, p. 17.
10. According to census data from the following sources: the Cyprus government; *The Cyprus Blue Book, 1946* (Nicosia: Govt. Printing Office, 1948); census of Cyprus, 1881. *Report on the census of Cyprus 1881, with appendix. By Fredrick W. Barry, superintendent of the Government of Cyprus,* House Of Commons Parliamentary Papers online, 1884–85.
11. Religion was the sixth category on the census schedule and mother tongue the seventh. Prior to these were name; relation to head of family; conjugal condition; sex; and age. Following religion and language were place of birth; and occupation.
12. TNA CO 67/264/10 1936a, Governor Richmond Palmer.
13. CSA/SA1/1322/50. Cyprus Census Office Minute by Mr. Percival, February 18, 1950. *Mukhtars* were village headmen, who were under the payroll of the colonial government and represented the district commissioner in the village.
14. CSA/MI/223/1960/1, p. 63. Letter from registration officer to Interior Ministry, October 13, 1960.
15. CSA/MI/82/1960, p. 22. Submission to Council of Ministers, November 25, 1960.
16. CSA/MI/178/1960/2.
17. CSA/MI/82/1960, p. 19. Letter from Department of Lands and Surveys (G. P. H. Avramides), April 28, 1964.
18. W. Chichele Plowden, *Report on the Census of British India taken on 17 February 1881* (London: Eyre and Spottiswoode, 1883), p. 101.
19. India, Census Commissioner, *Census of India, 1911* (Calcutta: Superintendent Government Printing, India, 1912).
20. The political debate on the term Adivasis and its relationship to claims of indigeneity, land, and cultural rights began in the 1930 census debates and continues to be salient to this day, because of shifting claims of Hindu nationalism and challenges to universal citizenship. See Karlsson and Subba (2006).
21. For a rich discussion of debates around the classification of Adivasis as "original inhabitants" vs. "indigenous peoples" see Parmar (2015: 6–7).
22. NAI HD public branch file 2/1/41/pub.
23. Ibid.
24. Census 1941, vol. 1, Tables 1943, p. 9.
25. W. Yeatts (1943), "The Indian Census of 1941," *Journal of the Royal Society of Arts*, 91 (4634), 182–194, www.jstor.org/stable/41363062 (accessed January 31, 2020).
26. Ibid.
27. NAI MHA 2/18/48. Letter from M. W. M Yeatts to the Ministry of Home Affairs regarding the appointment of a Registrar General for vital statistics, September 19, 1948.

28. NAI MHA 15/43/48. Public Letter from Census Commissioner M. Yeatts regarding major changes to the first census questionnaire in Independent India, to Ministry of Home Affairs, March 9, 1948.
29. NAI MHA file 2/14/1948. Memo of M. W. M. Yeatts, Census Commissioner for India, September 3, 1948.
30. NAI MHA file 2/14/1948, pp. 2–3. List of questions issued in accordance with section 8 of the Census Act of 1948, September 4, 1948.
31. Palestine, *Report and General Abstract of the Census, 1922* (Jerusalem: Greek Convent Press, 1923).
32. Palestine, *Census of Palestine, 1931* (Alexandria: Government of Palestine, 1933).
33. TNA CO 733/206/5a. Questionnaire Schedule for enumerators Palestine census 1931.
34. Ibid.
35. TNA CO 733/206/5a, pp. 63–64. Instructions for enumerators: rules for filling up the schedule.
36. The Hope Simpson Commission was established after the bloody intercommunal riot/uprising of 1929 to address immigration, land settlement, and development issues, and tied Jewish immigration to economic growth capacities. For analysis of the riots/uprising, see Cohen (2015) and Barakat (2019).
37. TNA CO 733/206/5a, p. 33. Extract from Hebrew press survey no. 40.
38. Ibid.
39. TNA CO 733/206/5a, p. 51. Letter from E. Mills, Superintendent of Census to Chief Secretary, June 16, 1931.
40. Palestine Royal Commission Report. Cmd, 5479, London, July 1937, p. 139.
41. Head of the National Health Services after Israeli independence.
42. Fuad Saba was a well-known accountant, auditor for the British government, and part of the group of Palestinian businessmen interested in developing the Palestinian economy. In 1937, he was deported by the British for aiding the Arab Revolt. See Seikaly (2015: 26–27, 51).
43. TNA CO 733/206/5a, pp. 51–54. Letter from E. Mills, Superintendent of Census to Chief Secretary, June 16, 1931.
44. TNA CO 733/206/5a. Letter from John Robert Chancellor, High Commissioner of Palestine to Sir John Shuckburgh.
45. TNA CO 733/206/5a p. 75. Minutes of the meeting of the Jewish advisory sub-committee to the census.
46. TNA CO 733/206/5a. Minutes of the meeting of the Jewish Advisory Committee, July 8, 1931.
47. Ibid., p. 99.
48. Ibid., p. 101.
49. Historians Shira Robinson (2013) and Laura Robson (2011) claim that the Jewish community agreed to the racial/national distinction of Jew and Arab. My research shows there was a deep practical concern in the Jewish Agency at the binary categorization of population introduced by the Mandate government in the 1930s, since officials believed that categorization based on religion allowed the Jewish Agency more negotiating power with regard to posts in the civil service and other issues.

50. The Shaw commission of 1929 wrote that, despite the efforts of the colonial administration to balance the numbers of administrators in proportion to the size of their community in the population, there were 1,111 junior administrators who were Muslim Arabs and 1,176 Christian Arabs, although Christians comprised about 10 percent of the Arab population of Palestine (Shaw 1930: Vol. 2, Exhibit 56).
51. CZA S19 – 302. Letter to the Chief Secretary, March 27, 1944.
52. CZA S19 – 302. Letter from Gurevitz to Yizhak Luria, December 2, 1947.

3 THE BUREAUCRATIC TOOLKIT OF EMERGENCY

1. The continuity of emergency laws followed different patterns in each state. In Cyprus, colonial emergency laws survived through the Supplies and Services (Transitional Powers Continuation) Laws. In Israel, the entirety of colonial laws was inherited through the Law and Administration Ordinance of 1948, which transferred power from the colonial government to Israel's provisional government. www.knesset.gov.il/review/data/eng/law/knso_govt-justi ce_eng.pdf.
2. See also Kolsky (2005).
3. Permit regimes for monitoring the movement of populations were an old British colonial method. Timothy Mitchell (2002) writes about a permit regime enacted in Egypt for economic reasons in the late nineteenth century to prevent workers from leaving plantations. Lauren Benton (1999) has written about the Cape of Good Hope, where colonial officials authorized travel passes to monitor the movement of the Khoikhoi people in order to survey areas that had become "frontiers of lawlessness." Every European settler had the right to stop a Khoi traveler, inspect their pass, and arrest them if they did not carry it.
4. Memorandum No. F.653-G/40 from the Undersecretary to the Government of India in the External Affairs Department, with the subject "Application for passport facilities," dated November 15, 1941.
5. Franz Neumann differentiates between the rule of law, in which the executive power adhered to the principles of the rule of law, and "rule by law," which he uses to describe the legal system of the Nazi state that used the law instrumentally.
6. While some political theorists claim that the colonial state used the state of exception to extend sovereign power outside the law (Mbembe 2013), the uses of sovereign power were very much part of the law, even within the boundaries of internal regulations and guidelines (Kolsky 2015).
7. The legal histories on the codependency and justifications of legal distinction in the use of state violence between metropole and colony, are beyond the scope of this study. Some important accounts of these debates are Sutton (2009); Anghie (2007); Benton (2009); Mantena (2010).
8. Attorney General Donald Somerville reprimanded the military authorities for their demand for executive powers by declaration of martial law. "In the event of war or open rebellion, troops may, by common law, employ all powers necessary to suppress the disturbance, but the legality of the powers is

determined by the necessity of the case. Even at the time of the Jacobite risings in 1715 and 1745 no such powers were ever claimed by the armed forces of the crown as those recommended by the military forces." TNA CO 733/315/2 Part I, pp. 31–32. Note of conference held at the Colonial Office, September 1936.

9. 4 & 5 Geo. V.C 29, August 8, 1914.

10. The emergency regulations, a variation of the Defence of India Rules that were adopted in Mandate Palestine and Cyprus, were drafted after a template devised by an interdepartmental committee on the defense regulations for the British Home Office (headed by Sir Claud Schuster, permanent secretary of the Lord Chancellor) that were to be implemented in India and Burma. IOR L/P&J (S)/1925, p. 13.

11. For example, India's United Provinces Disturbed Areas (Special Powers of Armed Forces) Ordinance, 1947, article 2 (b) and (c). From NAI HD file 453/47, political internal division.

12. Northwest Frontier Province Disturbed Areas (Special Powers of Armed Forces) Ordinance, 1947 was concerned with giving policing powers to military personnel, extending the reach of the emergency laws.

13. See, in Palestine, Defence (Emergency) Regulations, 1945 Articles 108–110; Defence of India Rules, 1915; Cyprus Emergency Regulations of 1955.

14. NAI HD (political external branch) 59/43. Report of Security Control Office Calcutta – sent from the Home Department of the Government of Bengal to the Central Government Home Department.

15. NAI MHA 13/3/47 Political External Branch. Instruction for use of the Home Office Suspect Index written by W. R. Perks on 25 November 1946.

16. NAI 13/3/47 Political External. Example of suspect list for March 1946.

17. By 1940, suspect lists were incorporated into the fortnightly reports sent by the local CID (Criminal Investigation Department) to police commissioners and reports sent by district commissioners to the Ministry of Interior. Official copies of the Home suspect index were numbered and were kept under lock and key. Upon receipt of the new suspect list, the old one would be returned to the Home Office. NAI HD 22/3/41 (political external). Minutes regarding dispatch of warning circulars for 1941.

18. NAI HD file 111/44 political external. Notes October 13, 1944.

19. IOR L/P&J/8/&36.

20. NAI HD 39/55/44, political internal, p. 10. Policy for treatment of recovered Indian and Nepali (Gurkha) P.W & civilians at holding camp Jhingergacha.

21. NAI HD 39/30/44 poll (I). Letter from R. Tottenham, additional secretary, February 22, 1944, on machinery set up for examining refugees coming into India from the eastern frontier.

22. NAI HD 39/55/44, political internal, p. 10. Policy for treatment of recovered Indian and Gurkha P.W & civilians at holding camp Jhingergacha.

23. NAI HD 21/15/45 poll (I). Report on status and release of security prisoners 1945.

24. NAI HD 39/70/45 poll (I). Restriction order of S. Vailu to Madras for 2 months, by joint Secretary Cracknell, July 20, 1945.

25. HD 39/24/45, political internal. Letter from political department to Rajputna on the repatriation of security prisoners classified "grey" to their home in Indian States, June 14, 1945.

26. NAI HD 21/15/45, political internal. Orders of chief of staff to Eastern command and Home Department on powers of final classification and disposal – civilians, December 15, 1945.

27. NAI HD 44/13/45, POLL (I). Classification of prisoners was critical to their release. An unclassified security detainee could not be released until categorical information was received by the Home Department.

28. NAI HD 22/7/45, political internal 6. Letter from Joint Secretary of the Govt. of Bengal to Home Department, February 1, 1945. In Bengal in 1944, there were 2,700 Goondas, of whom 2,281 were in detention without trial.

29. NAI HD 44/13/ A 45, political internal. Letter from Viceroy's assistant to Sir Francis Mudie of the Home Department, July 11, 1945.

30. NAI HD 44/5/44, political internal 1, minutes, p. 1.

31. NAI HD 44/13/A 45, p. 34 Letter from Sir Evan Jenkins to Home Department, November 3, 1945.

32. NAI HD Public Branch file 67/4 1941. Annual report of the Home Department.

33. NAI MHA 67–5/1947 Police A; MHA 7–1/1947 A& G, p. 9. The political external war branch worked on the monitoring of enemy foreigners and political suspects. After independence, the political external war department became the foreigners' section of the Home Office that was in charge of citizenship and nationality issues.

34. During the war, the Home Department was preoccupied by the surveillance of foreigners and frequently amended the Foreigners Act, the Registration of Foreigners Rules, and the Enemy Foreigners Order.

35. NAI Home Department file, Political external Branch 1/14/41. An administrative discussion about the proposed amendment of rule 11/13/C of the Foreigners Registration Rules 1939.

36. NAI HD 1/14/41 political external. File on the proposed amendment to the registration of foreigners rules 1939 so as to make it applicable to foreigners who are constantly traveling. Minutes and correspondence, pp. 13–53.

37. NAI HD 4/1/44, Assam & Bengal. H. G. Dennehy, Chief Secretary of the Government of Assam writes to the Deputy Inspector General of Police in Assam and all registration officers on July 11, 1941, regarding the procedure for travel permits for enemy aliens. This procedure is established in paragraph 4 of the Enemy Foreigners Order and paragraph 18 (1) of the Provisional Instructions for the Control of Foreigners in War.

38. NAI HD 4/1/44, Assam & Bengal.

39. NAI HD 25/4/47, political internal.

40. NAI HD 1/4/47. The article was often used in particular neighborhoods in Calcutta. "The Commissioner of Police in Calcutta and District Magistrate [had powers to] order [that] . . . . No person present within any area specified in the order shall between such hours as may be specified in the order, be out of doors except under the authority of a written permit granted by specified authority of a person."

41. HD 13/9/46 – 49 B p. 2–3 minutes of the Home Department, July 7, 1947.
42. NAI HD 20/41. Political external branch.
43. NAI HD 1/4/47. Minutes from 25th of April 1941. An elaborate permit system for enemy foreigners was established in 1941 to prevent leakage of information. Secretary Hampton of the Home Department sketched the permit system for enemy foreigners: "I have suggested the possibility of the introduction of a unified permit system for European non British subjects. The actual permit to be in three parts: 1) 'no objection certificate' from the military authorities where required; 2) 'no objection certificate' from the reserve Bank; 3) permit based upon these two certificates and issued after passport issuing authorities are satisfied and have endorsed the passport."
44. Anarchical and Revolutionary Crimes Act, 1919 (Act No. 11 (Ind.)).
45. Bengal Criminal Law Amendment Act, 1930, Act No. 6.
46. Quoted in Kalhan et al. (2006: 129 n.).
47. NAI HD file 8/17/46, political internal branch. From question 69 to Council of State.
48. These acts were not identical. The Punjab Public Safety Ordinance of 1946 was considered more drastic in its targeting of political activities than other Public Safety laws. See memo from G. V. Bedekar to legislative dept., October 10, 1946. NAI HD file 6/2/1946, political 1 branch.
49. NAI HD 21/9/45. Memo on Postwar Emergency Powers, F. G. Cracknell, Deputy secretary, political branch I, Home Department.
50. NAI HD file 21/30/46. Letter from P. Mason, War Dept. secretary to Home Dept. of Bombay government regarding the enactment of martial law explaining that the intention of the AFPSA was external security and not internal security and could not be used to establish martial law, February 9, 1946.
51. NAI HD 21/9/45. Memo on Postwar Emergency Powers, F. G. Cracknell, Deputy secretary, political branch I, Home Department. Apparently, the Home Department drafted an Emergency Powers Ordinance to go alongside the Defence of India Rules, but decided to incorporate the measure into the local Public Safety Acts to avoid public debate.
52. Item 1 of List 2 of Seventh Schedule of the Government of India Act, 1935 (26 Geo. 5 Ch. 2).
53. The PDA had been so heavily debated in the Lok Sabha (India's lower house of parliament) in 1950 and 1951 that the Home Minister promised to bring a resolution in 1953 for open debate as to the "necessity of continuing to make use of the preventative detention act" in order to prevent the debate in 1952. NAI MHA 44/22/52, political 1 branch. Memo of H. V. R. Iyengar, August 4, 1952.
54. NAI MHA File 8/17/46. Question 69 of Raja Dutt Singh on November 15, 1946.
55. A. K. Gopalan *v.* The State of Madras. May 19, 1950. 1950 AIR 27, 1950 SCR 88.
56. Ordinance XLI of 1942.
57. NAI HD File 21/30/46, political 1 branch.

58. Paragraph 9(b) of the Internal Security Instruction 1937. NAI HD 52/7/47. Home Department political branch I reply to Govt. of Bengal, March 20, 1946.

59. NAI MHA 64/47, police branch. The Ordinance of 1942 was extended until 1946 because of police demands, despite the Legislative Department's attempt to repeal it. See NAI HD file 21/25/46 political internal. Political Department memo on November 7, 1946.

60. "The only case ... that a 'shoot on sight' order would be perfectly legal is where martial law has been declared." NAI HD 21/25/46, p. 26.

61. NAI HD 21/25/46, November 8, 1946. Wakely to political branch of Home Department.

62. www.constitution.org/cons/india/po3034.html.

63. Assam state introduced two acts based on the order: the Assam Maintenance of Public Order (Autonomous Districts) Act, 1953 and the Assam Disturbed Areas Act, 1955.

64. NAI MHA file 453/47. Draft of United Provinces Disturbed Areas (Special Powers of Armed Forces) Ordinance 1947 article 3 determines that legal proceeding against any person (not only soldiers) acting under authority of the government in a disturbed area, demand prior central government sanction.

65. Diffusion between postcolonial states that share a common past is of much greater interest than the circulation of laws within an imperial framework to social scientists. Likhovski (2009) suggests that legal transplants are a form of signaling desire for membership of or belonging to a particular political order; Kedar (2014) shows how diffusion of definitions of absentee and evacuee migrated from draft Pakistani law to Israeli law, to support his argument that comparative law is central to the study of critical legal geography.

66. ISA M/5134/10. A file of miscellaneous forms for use in the Immigration Dept. in Palestine included several forms from India, "two of which had a category of race or case or tribe and subtribe" which were crossed out.

67. TNA CO 733/315/2 Part II 1936. Pamphlet and corresponding minutes.

68. ISA M/5135/5 Dept. of immigration, government of Palestine. Chief secretary to representative of the government of Palestine in Cairo, February 6, 1947 I/ 962/46

69. In my survey of the twenty-two imperial bureaucrats to outline their under-standing of their bureaucratic model of government, specific practices were rarely referred to, unless in response to critique.

70. A colonial office file on martial law and disturbances in Palestine 1936, TNA CO 733/315/2 Part II, included the pamphlet of Bengali emergency laws that had served as a template to copy and paste from, or adapt to the circumstances in Palestine, as the note and markings show.

71. TNA CO 733/320/15, Palestine Martial Law (Defense) Order in Council of 23 July 1936, 3 Government of Palestine 19 Ordinances, 259, Supp. No. 2 to Palestine Gazette Extraordinary No. 584, 19 April 1936.

72. The Defence (Emergency) Regulations were applied in Palestine (and on Cyprus) based on a formula created by an interministerial committee to be

applied in India and in Burma. India Office Records (IOR) Public & Judicial P&J (S)/1925, p. 13.

73. TNA CO 733/320/15. On April 19, 1936, under article IV of the Order of 1931, the High Commissioner of Mandate Palestine made a set of regulations. Presumably because of some unease over the unpublished order of 1931, a new Order in Council was made, namely the Palestine Martial Law (Defence) Order in Council of July 23, 1936. 3 Government of Palestine Ordinances, 259, Supp. No. 2 to Palestine Gazette Extraordinary No. 584 (Apr. 19, 1936).

74. TNA WO 191/88 Notes on Operations in Palestine November 1937 and December 1939, pp. 2–3.

75. IOR L/ PS/ 12/ 3344– 45 Telegram, High Commissioner Palestine to Secretary of State for Colonies, 22 May 1936: Palestine Situation.

76. TNA CO 733/312/4, pp. 19–20. Secret letter to commanding officer of British forces on Departure from Palestine Ordinance (1936), September 23, 1936.

77. ISA M/236/65. Lletter from Criminal Investigation Department to chief secretary, 495/13/GS.

78. TNA WO 275/114. Operation Agatha report. See also Wagner (2008).

79. TNA WO 208/1706. Measures against terrorism.

80. TNA CO 67/277/15 1937 Cyprus. Richard St. John Omerod Wayne, district commissioner, Paphos, report on the administrative and political situation in the district of Paphos (May 8, 1937), enclosure in governor's secret dispatch, May 20.

81. For an account of international pressure on Britain against emergency measures through human rights bodies during the Cyprus Emergency, see Drohan (2018: 16–46).

82. CSA/SA 1689/50. Attorney general to colonial secretary John Fletcher Cook, July 26, 1950.

83. TNA CO 537/6244. Minute, Bennet in a draft letter to Governor of Cyprus, April 20, 1950.

84. Ibid.

85. TNA MED 469/67/01(CO/926/561).

86. Ibid, p. 53.

87. TNA MED 469/64/01 Part II. Secret telegram from Governor's deputy to Secretary of State for the Colonies, June 5, 1956.

88. Ibid, p. 106.

89. TNA MED 374/04 (CO 926/1016), p. 24. Letter to Colonial Office, January 1958.

4 LOYALTY AND SUSPICION: THE MAKING OF THE CIVIL SERVICE AFTER INDEPENDENCE

1. In India, the Citizenship Act was enacted in 1955. In Israel, a trio of laws defined the range of political membership: the Citizenship Law of 1952, the Entry into Israel Law of 1952, and the Law of Return, enacted in 1950, which defined the right of those of Jewish descent to gain citizenship in Israel. See Peled (1992: 435).

2. I do not claim that abolition of the emergency laws was the only cause of the different outcome in Cyprus, because it was part of a set of intertwined political constraints, and each one could be seen as a cause for divergence from the other two cases. I see it as a deterministic critical juncture (Slater and Simmons 2010) because it prevented the use of the repertoire for population management against the minority, as it was deployed in Israel and India.

3. Despite the shared legacy of colonial emergency regulations, the relationship between citizenship and security laws in the two countries evolved differently: In Israel, emergency laws served as the backbone of the colonial military government from 1949 to 1966 to control Palestinians perceived as enemy population (Sa'di, 2016).

4. In Israel, the Mandatory regulations have the status of primary laws; they apply notwithstanding any law, and they may amend any law with and without modification. They also remain in force with no time limit, and they are valid regardless of whether a state of emergency has been formally declared. See Mehozay (2016) for a comprehensive analysis of Israel's multiple bodies of emergency laws.

5. Article 183 of the Cyprus constitution outlines the state of emergency as one that affords measures to combat political violence. Although the constitution is based on the cooperation of both communities, it contained no safeguards in the event of refusal of the power-sharing structure itself, which happened in the crisis of 1963. (See Constantinou 2008; Papastylianos 2018: 116; Lerner 2011: 30–51.)

6. Preventative detention (second amendment) Act, 1952. NAI MHA 44/22/52 Political 1. Home Secretary memo section 18, August 18, 1953.

7. On December 16, 1951, the Israeli government decided to form an interministerial committee that would develop security and emergency legislation to replace the Defence (Emergency) Regulations, 1945. ISA/56/G/2199/7/10. Government decision 112, 1951.

8. In 1945, a political party, KATAK (Association of the Turkish Minority of the Island of Cyprus), was founded. Under the leadership of Fazil Kutchuk, it was renamed CKTP (Cyprus-is-Turkish Party). During the Emergency, after 1956, its objective was partition.

9. CSA/MI/208/1960, p. 8. Ministry of Interior directive to police, immigration and Registration officers, September 27, 1960.

10. CSA/MI/208/1960. Office instruction to all members of government staff, August 15, 1960.

11. CSA/MI/208/1960, p. 7. Ministry of Defence to Ministry of the Interior, April 5, 1962.

12. CSA/MI/208, p. 45. Muftizade to president and attorney general, May 14, 1963.

13. Translation of titles was a painstaking task. The title of "district officer" had been translated into *komiser, kaymakam, idare, memuru, kaza memuru, idare amiri, kaza amiri,* and more. In Turkey, provinces (*vilayet*) are under the charge of a governor (*vali*) and districts (*kaza*) within the provinces are under the charge of district officers (*kaymakam*). After vigorous debates, the district officer of Famagusta decided to adopt the title *kaymakam.* CSA/MI/

208/1960. District officer Famagusta to Ministry of Interior, September 15, 1960; Ministry of Interior, October 24, 1960.

14. CSA/MI/208/1960. Letter from undersecretary to the vice president Muftizade to Pantalides, Ministry of Interior, October 24, 1960.

15. Judicial appointments were considered public service appointments for the purposes of the Ratio clause (Article 123 of the constitution). See CSA/284/1960, p. 8. Report of the committee for the implementation of the 70:30 ratio in the civil service, December 5, 1960.

16. CSA/MI/178/1960/2, p. 47. Minutes by the attorney general of the republic regarding the municipal corporation law.

17. CSA/MI/290/1960, p. 153. Letter from A. K. Anastasiou to the chairman of the Public Service Commission, May 1, 1962.

18. CSA/220/1960, pp. 32–45. Staff list of the Ministry of Interior, 1962.

19. CSA/MI/284/1960, p. 12. Letter from A. D. J. Muftizade, undersecretary for the Vice President to the Minister of Interior, November 1, 1961.

20. CSA/MI/284/1960, pp. 6–7. Report of the committee appointed to make recommendations for the application of the 70:30 ratio in the civil service, Establishment Office, October 3, 1960.

21. CSA/MI/290/1960, pp. 215–268. General form 103, applications and personal records of interchangeable staff.

22. CSA/MI/159/1963/A/1, p. 49. Examination in statute law for assistant district inspectors and administrative assistants.

23. Table compiled from summary of statistical data for 1960–1963. CSA/MI/82/1960, pp. 86–88. In the original data, classification is of Greeks and Turks.

24. Turkish Communal Chamber, *The Turkish Case, 70:30 and the Greek Tactics* (Nicosia: Halkin Sesi Press, 1963).

25. CSA/MI/178/1960/2, p. 42.

26. CSA/MI/178/1960/2, p. 43.

27. Interview with Zaim Nicatigil, former attorney general of the TRNC, Nicosia, June 2012.

28. CSA/ MI/ 20/1964, p. 180. Review of the activities of the Ministry of Interior from the establishment of the republic until December 31, 1965, by the Minister of the Interior, p. 5.

29. Attorney General of the Republic *v.* Mustafa Ibrahim, 1964, CLR 195.

30. The new histories of partition reject the view that the partition of 1947 was the marker of the break between colonial and postcolonial, and unsettle the temporal framework of partition as a singular event. Instead, they demonstrate partition as a social process. See Zamindar (2007), Chatterji (2007), and Ansari (2005).

31. Sir Stafford Cripps, Secretary of State for India in the Labour government speaking for the British government in the House of Commons on March 5, 1947, in the debate on the Indian Independence Bill. Parl. Debates House of Commons, Vol. 434 (x94S47), col. 497–508.

32. NAI HD 32/3/47 ESTS. Notes to the secretariat of the governor general by C. P. Scott on September 6, 1947.

33. The partition committees were given seventy days to arrange the division of assets from British India into the two dominions. For an account of the

organizational logic and negotiation regarding the division of the state see Sengupta (2014).

34. NAI MHA 78/6/48 Admin – starred question no. 51, for the Legislative Assembly of India on July 28, 1948.

35. NAI MHA 170/5/47 ESTS. P. V. R. Rao, Joint Secretary to the Government of India, memo to the Home Department, July 26, 1947.

36. NAI MHA 67/6/7 Public A, p. 4. Office order issued by R. N. Banerjee, secretary to the Government of India, July 21, 1947.

37. NAI MEA 10/8/PV (1)/53. Inquiry on policy for refusal of passport facilities, secretary to the government of Manipur to Ministry of External Affairs, June 30, 1953.

38. NAI MHA 58/16/49 ESTS. Office order, December 17, 1948.

39. NAI MHA 58/16/49 ESTS. Note by U. K. Goshal, March 31, 1949.

40. NAI MHA 58/16/49 ESTS.

41. NAI MHA 16/22/49 ESTS, p. 20.

42. NAI MHA 16/22/49 ESTS, p. 10. Monthly review of the activities of the Ministry of Home Affairs, December 1948.

43. Ibid.

44. NAI MHA 25/78/49 ESTS, p. 1. Minutes of the Assistant Auditor General regarding appointments.

45. NAI MHA 43/00/49 ESTS. Memorandum from August 26, 1947.

46. NAI MHA 25/78/49 ESTS, p. 3. Office memorandum dated October 20, 1948.

47. Historians Gould, Sherman, and Ansari (2013: 248) describe this practice initiated by the Ministry of Home Affairs in Delhi from the perspective of the government of Uttar Pradesh, clarifying that it was not only prevalent in the provinces that were directly affected by partition.

48. NAI MHA 43/12/49. Appointments section, N. L. Nagar, policy clarification from September 25, 1948.

49. NAI MHA 43/12/49. Appointments minutes of U. K. Ghoshal, Deputy Secretary, April 23, 1949.

50. Ibid p. 13.

51. NAI MHA 43/12/49. Appointments section, N. L. Nagar, policy clarification from September 25, 1948.

52. The intense internal negotiations within the ministry, arguing for empathy towards those who had been victims of uncertainty, indecision, or violence, resulted in a limited provision. Those who had migrated before March 31 from Pakistan intending to settle permanently in India were regarded as persons who had never lost their Indian domicile, although they resided in areas that were now in the dominion of Pakistan. MHA 43/20/50 ESTS. Letter from P. V. R. Rao to Govt. Ministries, January 2, 1948.

53. NAI MHA 25/78/49 ESTS, pp. 5–7. Decision of the Ministry of Home Affairs on the termination of services of Mr. S. E. Cooper of the ICS on the grounds of disloyalty and desertion.

54. Ibid.

55. Patel to Govind Malaviya, July 7, 1947, in *Thematic Volumes on Sardar Vallabhbhai Patel: Muslims and Refugees*, ed. Prabha Chopra (Delhi, 2004), 58. Quoted in Gould et al. (2013: 249),

56. MHA 21/13/47 ESTS. Starred question to Patel in the legislative assembly of India on November 29, 1947.

57. MHA 60/25/49 ESTS. Review of the Activities of the Ministry of Home Affairs 1948, Introduction.

58. NAI MHA 45/16/47 ESTS, p. 14. Press Communique of the Government of Sind, June 3, 1947.

59. NAI MHA 45/16/47 ESTS, p. 11. Letter from D. C. Das to the chief secretaries of the governments of Bengal, Punjab, and the Sindh.

60. NAI MHA 60/25/49 ESTS, pp. 1–3. Review of the activities of the Ministry of Home Affairs for the year 1948.

61. NAI MHA 14/1/49 ESTS. Memo on measures taken by the Home Ministry to deal with corruption and nepotism and inefficiency in the police services.

62. Ibid.

63. NAI MHA 14/1/49 ESTS.

64. NAI MHA 60/25/49 ESTS. p. 10.

65. MHA 60/25/49 ESTS, pp. 12–13. Review of the Activities of the Ministry of Home Affairs for the year 1948.

66. NAI MHA 43/8/49 ESTS, p. 7. Home Affairs Resolution 16/10/47 ESTS (R).

67. These articles comprise Part II of the Indian constitution that was brought into effect before the constitution enactment in 1950 to solve issues of status and citizenship.

68. NAI MHA 43/17/47. Resolution no. 16/10/47 ESTS (R), dated August 21, 1947.

69. NAI MHA 43/17/47 ESTS, p. 3. Minutes by P. V. R. Rao on December 2, 1947.

70. NAI MHA 16/22/49 ESTS, p. 10. Monthly report of activities of the Ministry of Home Affairs for December 1948.

71. NAI MHA 10/9/47 APPTS. Copy of domicile questionnaire sent to Mr. S. C. Roy, an applicant to the ICS, by Abdullah Jan, Assistant Secretary to the Government of India on 21 July, 1947.

72. NAI MHA 43/8/49 ESTS. K. N. Subbanna, December 12, 1948.

73. NAI MHA 43/8/49 ESTS. Note of C. B. Gulati at the Ministry of Home Affairs on the case of F. L. Wakefield, October 13, 1948.

74. CZA S19-216. Letter from Gurevitz to the Political Department of the Jewish Agency dated April 23, 1937. Data on the low-tiered officials were given in a letter from April 14, 1938. Gurevitz explains that while the statistics of high-ranking officers appear in the blue books and bulletins, there was little access to mid- and lower-tiered officials.

75. Table compiled from the notes of David Gurevitz, from multiple sources and reports of the Government of Palestine and Jewish Agency statistics for 1937, CZA.

76. Public historian Nathan Braun discovered this episode and I relied heavily upon his initial research for this section as I investigated the state archive.

77. ISA P/990/22. Status of Arab Officers at the end of the mandate. Circular 9, March 15, 1948.
78. ISA G/110/35, p. 13. Emergency plan for organizing government apparatus, February 8, 1948.
79. Ibid.
80. The Jewish Agency increased the numbers of Jews in the government of Palestine through topping up the salaries of civil servants and police who were paid low wages by the Mandate government.
81. ISA G/110/35, p. 34. Protocol of the situation committee on administrative apparatus, March 17, 1948, Jerusalem.
82. ISA G/112/9. Letter from Even Tov to Gertz in the statistics department of the Jewish Agency, June 21, 1948, explains he does not trust the condemnation, despite his support for "cleaning out what is dirty."
83. ISA G/112/9. Letter from the Organization of the Jewish workers in the Mandate government to the histadrut branch of government workers, January 26, 1948.
84. SHAI had experience with surveillance of rival Jewish factions during the Mandate. See Wagner (2008).
85. Palestine Government Employee Ordinance, 1948, Official Gazette 4, Supplement 1, June 9, 1948.
86. Palestine Government Employee Regulations (Investigation Committees) 1948. Official Gazette 9, Supplement 2, July 14, 1948.
87. Haaretz, July 21, 1948.
88. ISA G121/5. Excerpt from a letter of one of the workers in Lyd Airport, sent to the situation committee on April 18, 1948.
89. ISA G 121/.5 Even Tov reporting to Shlomo Kedar, assistant to secretary of Israeli government, December 10, 1948.
90. ISA G 121/5. Alhasid to Golda Meir, Head of the state department of the Jewish Agency.

5 HOW HYBRID BUREAUCRACY AND PERMIT REGIMES MADE CITIZENSHIP

1. This understanding of partition has been termed "the new histories of partition" (Roy 2012), initiated by Zamindar (2007), Ansari (2005), and Chatterji (2007).
2. Sabbagh-Khoury suggests a similar framework of a "long Nakba" as a process that begins during the British Mandate, rather than an event (Sabbagh-Khoury 2021). In Palestinian writing, the Nakba refers to both the historical events of 1948 and the ongoing occupation and colonization of Palestine (Bashir & Goldberg 2018: 1, 33).
3. Himaiti Roy suggests that low- and mid-tier officials produced these categories most prominently in border peripheries and diplomatic missions (Roy 2012: 5).
4. The studies of returnees and refugees as a method to understand the nature of political regimes through their constitution of political membership have been

a productive way to move beyond the historical debates about intentions and ideologies in the national conflicts. Influenced by Arendt's analysis of refugees and the stateless as those who define political membership from its absence, these studies shift the focus from the motivations, intentions, and constraints of the perpetrators of violence to the institutional choices made in the aftermath of that violence. For South Asia, see Zamindar (2007); Sen (2018); Haimanti Roy (2012). For Israel/Palestine, see Robinson (2013); Tatour (2019); Rouhanna & Sabbagh-Khoury (2015).

5. Tatour calls attention to the two components of the first census: the registry of population and the registry of Arab property. She views the first as the baseplate for the prevention of the return of Palestinians to their home and the second as the data that facilitated the confiscation of Palestinian land and property through the absentee property laws (2019: 20). See also Leibler (2004).

6. I do not claim that abolition of the emergency laws was the only cause of the different outcome in Cyprus, because it was part of a set of intertwined political constraints and each one could be seen as a cause for divergence from the other two cases. I see it as a deterministic critical juncture (Slater and Simmons 2010) because it prevented the use of the repertoire for population management against the minority, as it was deployed in Israel and India.

7. In Israel, the Mandatory regulations have the status of primary laws; they apply notwithstanding any law, and they may amend any law with and without modification. They also remain in force with no time limit, and they are valid regardless of whether a state of emergency has been formally declared. See Mehozay (2016) for a comprehensive analysis of Israel's multiple bodies of emergency laws.

8. Article 183 of the Cyprus constitution outlines the state of emergency as one that affords measures to combat political violence. Although the constitution is based on the cooperation of both communities, it contained no safeguards in the event of a refusal of the power-sharing structure itself, which happened in the crisis of 1963 (see Constantinou 2008; Papastylianos 2018: 116; and Lerner 2011: 30–51).

9. The military government over the Palestinians was also called a state within a state by one of its most vocal Palestinian critics (Jar Sabri Jiryis, *Ha-'Aravim Be-Yisrael* [Haifa, 1966]). However, very different from the Turkish Cypriot efforts to establish a provisional administration in the enclaves, the military government did not include any Palestinian representation.

10. Esmeir refers to the separation and proliferation of legal status and institutions as "pervasive legalities" (Esmeir 2015: 22, 32).

11. Quoted in Zamindar (2007), p. 92 n. 126 – source report, May 12, 1948. Delhi State Archives cc 55/48 conference p. 8.

12. TNA pol: col: 131/1 p. Numbers are until April 1949. Press release no. 1194 from the office of the High Commissioner of India in London, issued July 16, 1949.

13. NDM Ministry of Rehabilitation 1949 to 1950. Report on the working of the Ministry of Rehabilitation. New Delhi: Government of India.

14. See Markides (2001: 95–98, n. 157).
15. CSA 290/1690, p. 100. Letter from registration department to the Ministry of Interior on reorganization, November 25, 1961.
16. Chatterji (2002); Chester (2009); Sengupta (2014).
17. Chatterji (1999); Van Schendel (2004).
18. NAI, MHA file, Establishments section 41/1/47. Report on the definition of domicile, regarding requirements for appointment to the civil service following partition.
19. The committee recommended that partition should not impose changes in nationality and restrict freedom of movement, besides restrictions on entry into the public service, which I discuss in Chapter 2. On July 7, 1947, the steering committee wrote a note to the Expert Committee on Domicile: "The committee came to the conclusion that partition by itself will affect no change in nationality and calls for no immediate action by the petition committee except in regard to the public service ... if it is desired to restrict entry into the public service in the manner indicated but not otherwise."
20. The motivation for the Pakistani permit regime was economic; officials wanted to halt the arrival of poor Muslim refugees, which the East Bengal government strongly opposed. The Ministry of Interior in Pakistan thought that the permit regime was the most effective way to keep the undesirable poor refugees out of Pakistan. The ministries argued between them on the best technique to deter refugees. The market logic that guided the Pakistani permit regime was entirely different from the justifications in India, where the threat was framed not as a political security threat but an economic one.
21. IOR/L/PJ/7/12537. Extract from secret telegram of High Commissioner to Pakistan to Commonwealth Relations' Office, November 19, 1948, announcing that the permit regime will be extended to East Bengal.
22. The East Bengal government initially objected to the extension of the permit system to its borders, even though it had agreed to it during the first round of provincial discussions. Its premier argued that the initial agreement had been acceded to primarily threaten India into withdrawing its permit system, but its actual position was that the permit regime was opposed to "our people's needs."
23. IOR/L/PJ/7/12537. Secret telegram from High Commissioner to Pakistan.
24. IOR/L/PJ/7/12209 Opdom 29. Telegram from High Commissioner of the UK in India from April 18, 1948. The telegram reports that over 45,000 Muslim have returned to India in the last three weeks due to lack of accommodation and occupation.
25. NAI MHA Political External Branch file 10/11/47. Correspondence with Government of West Bengal and Intelligence Bureau, July 1947–March 1949.
26. Source: Frances Pritchett's Website at MESAAS, Columbia University.
27. NAI MHA 10/11/47, Singh to West Bengal Government, p. 23.
28. NAI MHA 10/11/47. Deputy Secretary G. V. Bedekar writes on April 29, 1948, to R. N. Banerjee, the Home Minister's secretary.
29. Ibid. Summary of discussions with Intelligence Bureau, Fateh Singh, p. 44.
30. Ibid. Banerjee to Bedekar, minute from May 12, 1948.
31. Ibid. Fateh Singh, December 18, 1948.

32. Ibid. B. Shukla to Fateh Singh and R. N. Banerjee on February 28, 1949.

33. Estimates on the extent of migration, displacement, and death vary. Over four million Hindus fled to the western border, and five million Muslims fled to Pakistan. There is an estimate of 180,000 to 500,000 deaths from communal violence. See Aiyar (1998).

34. Zamindar (2007: note 126).

35. NAI MEA 6/19/56 PSP. Minutes to Intelligence Bureau, R. P. Sharma, January 17, 1956.

36. NAI MEA 646/56, pp. 7–9. Note of deputy secretary of the Home Department from August 21, 1956. Fateh Singh explains how the permit system worked, focusing on resettlement permits for those that had fled to Pakistan. The resettlement permits became long-term visas for categories of returnees, which would be renewed from year to year. A similar system existed in Israel, in which people would get certificates of residency that would be renewed from year to year (A/5); after a number of years, they could apply for citizenship, which would be granted or not dependent upon recommendations of the police and secret service.

37. MHA 35/78/49 ESTS, P. 6–7. Many government servants, who had decided to work for the new Pakistan Government, left their families in India. The opposite was also true, and civil servants with families in Pakistan were usually categorized as those of dubious loyalty because of that fact, as we saw in Chapter 4.

38. NAI MEA 646/56. File on the case of Mr. Godfrey Edward Airan. The file is an inquiry of Jawaharlal Nehru, prime minister of India, into the case of an engineer who had been denied permits to enter India and was denied a visa or resettlement after the citizenship acts. The intervention of the prime minister brought about a flurry of administrative activity that revealed the discretion used in the past to delineate suspects from those deserving permits.

39. Section 3 of the Foreigners Act 1946 titled "the power to make orders" enabled Home Ministry officials to impose any restriction on movement.

40. NAI MEA/41(61)55 PSP.

41. Ibid.

42. Ibid.

43. NAI MEA 646/56, pp. 5–6. Letter from Prime Minister's secretary to the Home Ministry, August 8, 1956.

44. NMML B. N. Rau Private Papers, p. 4. Letter from Jawaharlal Nehru to constitutional adviser B. N. Rau, January 30, 1949.

45. For analysis of Israel's goals in relation to the Palestinian minority at the inception of the state, and their fuzzy articulation by the leaders of the Yishuv, see Lustick (1980).

46. While political scientists such as Ian Lustick and others agree on this point, some scholars challenge the absence of a master plan. For instance, historian Yair Bäumel claims that, because Israeli political leadership had a distinctive set of principles that guided its policies towards the Arab minority, which were set apart from Jewish policy, and that these principles were followed in general by officials, there is no need to recruit evidence for a master plan, since this government perspective served in its

stead (see Bäumel 2007: 391). My interest in the interplay between administrative practice, institutional logics, and classifications of populations demands an inquiry into the existence of plans, large and small, and their implementation.

47. The military government based its authority formally on the Defence (Emergency) Regulations retroactively, only a year and half after it began operation, following a special committee of inquiry.

48. The entire area of the military regime was declared a closed zone requiring a permit for both exit and entry from all but military and police officials and the Custodian's officials. Within this zone, the governors could declare specific areas closed zones. They were required to review their decision to close the area every few months, and see if the reasons for closure remained intact.

49. Section 3, Foreigners Act 1946.

50. IDFA, 68/55–81, Unnumbered. "For the Inquiry Committee," handwritten testimony of Immanuel Mor.

51. IDFA. Emanuel Mor to Yehoshua Palmon, sent February 1951.

52. IDFA, 243/52/6, unnumbered. Summary of a Meeting of the Secondary Coordination Committee, September 8, 1949.

53. IDFA, 243/52/6, unnumbered. Summary of a Meeting of the Secondary Coordination Committee, March 22, 1950. Statistical tables detailing "estimated military potential of the Arab population in the territories of the military regime, divided by areas and ethnicities," together with their brief explanatory notes, question the loyalty of the entire population on the grounds of "the strong familial and ethnic bonds this population has with the refugees who are pressing on the Israeli borders."

54. IDFA, 243/52/6, unnumbered. Summary of a Meeting of the Secondary Coordination Committee, September 8, 1949.

55. IDFA. Letter from police headquarters on registration of population with special "registration units," January 27, 1950.

56. IDFA File 243/52/6/aleph. Letter from Palmon to the military government and Ministry of Interior regarding the relevant dates of return to the distribution of temporary permits, February 19, 1950. Those that had returned before June 1, 1949, would receive temporary residency permits. Those that had returned after that date had to request from a special intra-ministry committee that applied severe scrutiny to every permit request. See letter 89/4659 dated December 6, 1949.

57. Jenin was under Jordanian rule at the time.

58. Following resolution 194 of the UN general assembly, in a 1949 conference in Lausanne, Israel committed to the repatriation of 100,000 refugees.

59. IDFA file 243/52/6. Hartglass to General Director of the Ministry of Interior, August 7, 1949, PZ/YOM/1706.

60. IDFA file 243/52/6 "directives to military governors." Letter from Palmon to the legal advisers of Ministries of Justice and Interior, September 2, 1949. Ref. 89/1/603.

61. Ibid., and IDFA 1/4/212/2/YM. The response of the head of Legislation Department October 12, 1949.

62. One could argue that the administration of the permit regime was the outcome of an inter-agency battle. It was the reaction of the Ministry of Minorities and the military government to the inaction of the Ministry of Interior that had not promulgated an amendment to the population registration ordinance.

63. IDFA file 243/52/6. Hartglass to General Director of the Ministry of Interior, August 7, 1949. PZ/YOM/1706.

64. IDFA file 243/52 "Directives to Military Governors." Letter from Palmon to the legal advisers of Ministries of Justice and Interior, September 2, 1949. Ref. 89/1/603.

65. IDFA 243/52/6. Hartglass to General Director of the Ministry of Interior, August 7, 1949, PZ/YOM/1706Hartglass.

66. IDFA 243/52/6. Major Lavy to head of the military government branch, September 5, 1950.

67. IDFA 243/52/6. Palmon to registration office of Ministry of Interior, June 29, 1949, 89/13467.

68. 243/52/6. Palmon to registration office of Ministry of Interior, June 29, 1949, 89/13467.

69. IDFA, 243/52/6, unnumbered. "Temporary Residency Permits."

70. IDFA 68/55/81. Letter correspondence (89/4/625) from Head of military government Emanuel Mor to Yehoshua Palmon on directive to military governors regarding restrictions on movement and differentiation between infiltrators and permit holders, February 19, 1951.

71. IDFA, 243/52/6, unnumbered. Summary of a Meeting of the Coordination Committee, October 6, 1950.

72. IDFA, 68/55–81, letter number 1910. "The Detention of Infiltrators from Enemy Territories," October 10 1949.

73. IDFA, 68/55–81, unnumbered. "For the Inquiry Committee," handwritten testimony of Emanuel Mor. See also Degani (2015: 5).

74. These allegations of corruption and violence toward the civilian population, from local leadership as well as Members of Knesset of the opposition on the left from Maki, the communist party, and from the revisionist right, led by Menachem Begin, grew into committees of inquiry about the peculiar and uneven practices of the military government

75. IDFA, 68/55–82, unnumbered. "Opinion," from a meeting on the December 14, 1949.

76. IDFA, 68/55–82, unnumbered. "Protocol of a meeting in the legal status of the military regime," December 14, 1949.

77. The Israeli Law of Return, 1950, 4 L.S.I. 114 (1949–50).

78. The production of "motherland" nationalism was an active effort of Turkish Cypriot leadership, as an answer to the irredentist Greek nationalism. For an account of the development of Turkish Cypriot institutions, see Bryant & Hatay (2020: 9). For a relational account of the development of Greek irredentist nationalism, see Kitromilides (1990; 2019).

79. Article 183 of the Cyprus constitution.

80. CSA 208/60. Note of Attorney General Tornaritis, August 19, 1960, and responses from the districts, in minutes.

81. CSA 208/60. Office instruction to staff, District officer of Limassol, August 1960.

82. CSA 208/60. Undersecretary Mustesarligi to undersecretary to Pantelides, Ministry of Interior, October 24, 1960

83. Ibid.

84. CSA MI 208/60. Pantelides to Muftizadeh, undersecretary to the vice president, October 12, 1960.

85. CSA 208/60. District officer Famagusta to Ministry of Interior, September 15, 1960.

86. CSA 44/61. Ministry of Interior to Council of minister – Restriction of public vehicles. Supplies and Services (Transitional powers) (continuation) Law, January 17, 1961.

87. CSA 208/60. Office instruction to staff, District officer of Limassol, August 1960.

88. Article 173 of the constitution of the Republic of Cyprus. For the centrality of the municipal issue to the constitutional collapse in Cyprus, see Markides (1998).

89. TNA CO 926/805. Letter of Turkish Cypriot leadership to Foreign Office, February 27, 1959.

90. Interview with Zaim Nicatigil, former attorney general of the TNRC/ Occupied North Cyprus, and Minister of justice in the Temporary Turkish Cypriot Administration 1963–1968, Nicosia, June 2, 2012.

91. CSA 201/1964. Review of the activities of the Ministry of Interior until December 31, 1965, p. 12, section 5–6, "registration of the population" and "lands and surveys department."

92. Interview with Rustem Tatar, former Auditor General of Cyprus 1960–3, and Minister of Finance of the Temporary Turkish Cypriot Administration 1967–1976. Nicosia, June 2, 2012.

93. Interview with Zaim Nicatigil, former attorney general of the TNRC/ Occupied North Cyprus, and Minister of Justice in the Temporary Turkish Cypriot Administration 1963–8, Nicosia, June 2, 2012.

94. Interview with Zaim Nicatigil, former attorney general of the "TNRC"/ Occupied Cyprus, and Minister of Justice in the Turkish Cypriot Administration 1963–8, Nicosia, May 31, 2012.

95. CSA 167/959/1, p. 33 Letter from High Commissioner Ashiotis to Director General, Ministry of Foreign Affairs, January 24, 1967.

Bibliography

Agamben, G. (1995). *Homo sacer*. Turin: Einaudi.

Aiyar, S. (1998). "August anarchy": The partition massacres in Punjab, 1947. In D. A. Low and H. Brasted (eds.), *Freedom, Trauma, Continuities: Northern India and Independence*. New Delhi: Sage, pp. 15–38.

Akoijam, A. B. and Tarunkumar, T. (2005). Armed Forces (Special Powers) Act 1958: Disguised war and its subversions. *Eastern Quarterly* 3(1), 5–19.

Al-Hout, B. N. (1979). The Palestinian political elite during the mandate period. *Journal of Palestine Studies*, 9(1), 85–111.

Amara, A. (2018). Civilizational exceptions: Ottoman law and governance in late Ottoman Palestine. *Law and History Review*, 36(4), 915–941.

Anderson, B. (2006). *Imagined Communities: Reflections on the Origin and Spread of Nationalism*. London: Verso.

Anderson, D. M. (1993). Policing and communal conflict: The Cyprus Emergency, 1954–60. *The Journal of Imperial and Commonwealth History*, 21(3), 177–207.

Anderson, D. M. and Killingray, D. (2017). Consent, coercion and colonial control: Policing the empire, 1830–1940. In D. M. Anderson and D. Killingray (eds.), *Policing the Empire*. Manchester: Manchester University Press, pp. 1–17.

Anghie, A. (2005). The war on terror and Iraq in historical perspective. *Osgoode Hall Law Journal*, 43, 45–66.

Anghie, A. (2007). *Imperialism, Sovereignty and the Making of International Law*. Cambridge Studies in International and Comparative Law Vol. 37. New York: Cambridge University Press.

Ansari, S. F. (2005). *Life after Partition: Migration, Community and Strife in Sindh, 1947–1962*. Karachi: Oxford University Press.

Appadurai, A. (1993). Number in the colonial imagination. In C. A. Breckenridge and P. Van Der Veer (eds.), *Orientalism and the Postcolonial Predicament: Perspectives on South Asia*. Philadelphia: University of Pennsylvania Press, pp. 314–340.

Arendt, H. (1951). *The Origins of Totalitarianism*. New York: Harcourt, Brace.

Arendt, H. (1970). *On Violence*. New York: Houghton Mifflin Harcourt.

Ashcraft, K. L. (2001). Organized dissonance: Feminist bureaucracy as hybrid form. *Academy of Management Journal*, 44: 1301–1322.

Atran, S. (1989). The surrogate colonization of Palestine, 1917–1939. *American Ethnologist*, 16(4), 719–744.

Axelrod, R. (1997). The dissemination of culture: A model with local convergence and global polarization. *Journal of Conflict Resolution*, 41(2), 203–226.

Aymes, M. (2013). *A Provincial History of the Ottoman Empire: Cyprus and the Eastern Mediterranean in the Nineteenth Century*. Abingdon: Routledge.

Azoulay, A. and Ophir, A. (2012). *The One-State Condition: Occupation and Democracy in Israel/Palestine*. Stanford, CA: Stanford University Press.

Balibar, É. (2009). *We, the People of Europe? Reflections on Transnational Citizenship*. Translation/Transnation Vol. 18. Princeton, NJ: Princeton University Press.

Ballas, I. (2020). Fracturing the "exception": The legal sanctioning of violent interrogation methods in Israel since 1987. *Law & Social Inquiry*, 45(3), 818–838.

Ballas, I. (2021). Boundaries, obligations and belonging: The reconfiguration of citizenship in emergency criminal regimes. *Theoretical Criminology*, 26(2), 183–201. https://doi.org/10.1177/13624806211025918.

Banerjee, S. B., Chio, V. C., and Mir, R. (eds.) (2009). *Organizations, Markets and Imperial Formations: Towards an Anthropology of Globalization*. Northampton, MA: Edward Elgar Publishing.

Banko, L. (2012). The creation of Palestinian citizenship under an international mandate: Legislation, discourses and practices, 1918–1925. *Citizenship Studies*, 16(5–6), 641–655.

Banko, L. (2016). *The Invention of Palestinian Citizenship, 1918–1947*. Edinburgh: Edinburgh University Press.

Barakat, R. (2019). Reading Palestinian agency in mandate history: The narrative of the Buraq Revolt as anti-relational. *Contemporary Levant*, 4(1), 28–38.

Baring, E., Earl of Cromer. (1908a). The government of subject races. *Edinburgh Review*, 207, 1–27.

Baring, E., Earl of Cromer. (1908b). *Modern Egypt*. New York: The Macmillan Company.

Baring, E., Earl of Cromer. (1912). *Speeches and Miscellaneous Writings, 1882–1911*. Edinburgh: R. & R. Clark.

Baring, E., Earl of Cromer. (2010). *Modern Egypt*. New York: Cambridge University Press.

Barkey, K. (2005). Islam and toleration: Studying the Ottoman imperial model. *International Journal of Politics, Culture, and Society*, 19(1–2), 5–19.

Barkey, K. (2008). *Empire of Difference: The Ottomans in Comparative Perspective*. New York: Cambridge University Press.

Barkey, K. and Gavrilis, G. (2016). The Ottoman millet system: Non-territorial autonomy and its contemporary legacy. *Ethnopolitics*, 15(1), 24–42.

Baruah, S. (2014). Routine emergencies: India's armed forces special powers act. In A. Sundar and N. Sundar (eds.), *Civil Wars in South Asia: State, Sovereignty, Development*. New Delhi: Sage, pp. 189–211.

Bashir, B. and Goldberg, A. (2018). Introduction. The Holocaust and the Nakba: A new syntax of history, memory, and political thought. In B. Bashir and A. Goldberg (eds.), *The Holocaust and the Nakba*. New York: Columbia University Press, pp. 1–42.

Bashkin, O. (2020). Solidarity in the Galilee. *The American Historical Review*, 125(2), 554–558.

Bauman, Z. (2000). *Modernity and the Holocaust*. Ithaca, NY: Cornell University Press.

Bäumel, Y. (2007). *Blue and White Shadow: The Israeli Establishment Policy and Action, the Formative Years (1958–1968)*. Haifa: Pardes [Hebrew].

Bäumel, Y. (2011). The military government. In N. N. Rouhana and A. Sabbagh-Khoury (eds.), *The Palestinians in Israel: Readings in History, Politics and Society*. Haifa: Mada al-Carmel–Arab Center for Applied Social Research, pp. 47–57.

Baxi, U. (2003). The colonialist heritage. In P. Legrand and R. J. Munday (eds.), *Comparative Legal Studies: Traditions and Transitions*. Cambridge: Cambridge University Press, pp. 46–58.

Bayly, C. A. (1999). *Empire and Information: Intelligence Gathering and Social Communication in India, 1780–1870*. Cambridge Studies in Indian History and Society Vol. 1. Cambridge: Cambridge University Press.

Behar, C. (1998). Qui compte? "Recensements" et statistiques démographiques dans l'Empire ottoman, du XVIe au XXe siècle. *Histoire & Mesure*, 13(1–2), 135–145.

Bendix, R. (1956). *Work and Authority in Industry*. Berkeley, CA: University of California Press.

Bendix, R. (1964/2017). *Nation-Building and Citizenship: Studies of Our Changing Social Order*. London: Routledge.

Ben-Natan, S. (2021). The dual penal empire: Emergency powers and military courts in Palestine/Israel and beyond. *Punishment & Society*, 23(5), 741–763.

Benton, L. (1999). Colonial law and cultural difference: Jurisdictional politics and the formation of the colonial state. *Comparative Studies in Society and History*, 41(3), 563–588.

Benton, L. (2002). *Law and Colonial Cultures*. Cambridge: Cambridge University Press.

Benton, L. (2009). *A Search for Sovereignty: Law and Geography in European Empires, 1400–1900*. New York: Cambridge University Press.

Ben-Youssef, N. and Tamari, S. S. (2018). Enshrining discrimination: Israel's nation-state law. *Journal of Palestine Studies*, 48(1), 73–87.

Berda, Y. (2013). Managing dangerous populations: Colonial legacies of security and surveillance. *Sociological Forum*, 28(3), 627–630.

Berda, Y. (2017). *Living Emergency: Israel's Permit Regime in the Occupied West Bank*. Stanford, CA: Stanford University Press.

Berda, Y. (2020). Managing "dangerous populations": How colonial emergency laws shape citizenship. *Security Dialogue*, 51(6), 557–578.

Berger, M. (1957). *Bureaucracy and Society in Modern Egypt*. Princeton, NJ: Princeton University Press.

Best, J. (2012). Bureaucratic ambiguity. *Economy and Society*, 41(1), 84–106.

Bhagat, R. B. (2006). Census and caste enumeration: British legacy and contemporary practice in India. *Genus*, 62(2), 119–134.

Bhagavan, M. (2003). *Sovereign Spheres: Princes, Education and Empire in Colonial India*. Oxford: Oxford University Press.

Bhambra, G. K. (2014). A sociological dilemma: Race, segregation and US sociology. *Current Sociology*, 62(4): 472–492.

Bhambra, G. K. (2015). Citizens and others: The constitution of citizenship through exclusion. *Alternatives*, 40(2), 102–114.

Bhambra, G. K. (2016). Comparative historical sociology and the state: Problems of method. *Cultural Sociology*, 10(3), 335–351.

Bhandar, B. (2018). *Colonial Lives of Property*. Durham, NC: Duke University Press.

Bivona, D. (1998). *British Imperial Literature 1870–1940: Writing and the Administration of Empire*. Cambridge: Cambridge University Press.

Blecher, R. (2005). Citizens without sovereignty: Transfer and ethnic cleansing in Israel. *Comparative Studies in Society and History*, 47(4), 725–754.

Blum, B. (2017). The hounds of empire: Forensic dog tracking in Britain and its colonies, 1888–1953. *Law and History Review*, 35(3), 621–665.

Bose, S. (2007). *Contested Lands: Israel-Palestine, Kashmir, Bosnia, Cyprus, and Sri Lanka*. Cambridge, MA: Harvard University Press.

Bourdieu, P. (1994). Rethinking the state: Genesis and structure of the bureaucratic field. Trans. L. J. D. Wacquant and S. Farage. *Contemporary Sociological Theory*, 12(1), 1–18.

Bourdieu, P. (2000). *Pascalian Meditations*. Stanford, CA: Stanford University Press.

Bracha, O. (1997). Unfortunate or perilous: The infiltrators, the law and the supreme court 1948–1954. *Tel Aviv University Law Review.*, 21, 333.

Braun, N. (2008). The bitterness that did not fade: The purification committees for British Mandate government workers in the transition to Israel. In Bar On and Hazan (eds.), *A People at War (Am Bemilhama): Research on Civil Society in the War of Independence*. Jerusalem: Yad Yitzhak Ben Zvi.

Brown, M. (2001). Race, science and the construction of native criminality in colonial India. *Theoretical Criminology*, 5(3), 345–368.

Brown, N. J. (1995). Law and imperialism: Egypt in comparative perspective. *Law and Society Review*, 29, 103.

Brubaker, R. (1992). *Citizenship and Nationhood in France and Germany*. Cambridge, MA: Harvard University Press.

Brubaker, R. (2010). Migration, membership, and the modern nation-state: Internal and external dimensions of the politics of belonging. *Journal of Interdisciplinary History*, 41(1), 61–78.

Brubaker, R. (2014). Beyond ethnicity. *Ethnic and Racial Studies*, 37(5), 804–808.

Brubaker, R. and Cooper, F. (2000). Beyond "identity." *Theory and Society*, 29(1), 1–47.

Burra, A. (2010). The Indian Civil Service and the nationalist movement: Neutrality, politics and continuity. *Commonwealth & Comparative Politics*, 48(4), 404–432.

Bryant, R. (2003). Bandits and "bad characters": Law as anthropological practice in Cyprus, c. 1900. *Law and History Review*, 21(2), 243–270.

Bryant, R. (2004). *Imagining the Modern: The Cultures of Nationalism in Cyprus*. London: IB Tauris.

Bryant, R. (2012). Partitions of memory: Wounds and witnessing in Cyprus. *Comparative Studies in Society and History*, 54(2), 332–360.

Bryant, R. and Hatay, M. (2020). *Sovereignty Suspended: Political Life in a So-Called State*. Philadelphia: University of Pennsylvania Press.

Butalia, U. (2017). *The Other Side of Silence: Voices from the Partition of India*. New Delhi: Penguin UK.

Byron, R. A. and Roscigno, V. J. (2019). Bureaucracy, discrimination, and the racialized character of organizational life. In M. E. Wooten (ed.), *Race, Organizations, and the Organizing Process*. Bingley, UK: Emerald Publishing.

Campos, M. (2010). *Ottoman Brothers: Muslims, Christians, and Jews in Early Twentieth-Century Palestine*. Stanford, CA: Stanford University Press.

Campos, M. (2014). Between others and brothers. *International Journal of Middle East Studies*, 46(3), 585–588.

Carswell, G., Chambers, T., and De Neve, G. (2019). Waiting for the state: Gender, citizenship and everyday encounters with bureaucracy in India. *Environment and Planning C: Politics and Space*, 37(4), 597–616.

Carthill, A. L. (1924). *The Lost Dominion*. Edinburgh: William Blackwood.

Cecil, E. (1921). *The Leisure of an Egyptian Official*. Kilkerran: Hardinge Simpole.

Cell, J. W. (2002). *Hailey: A Study in British Imperialism, 1872–1969*. Cambridge: Cambridge University Press.

Chakrabarty, D. (1995). Modernity and ethnicity in India: A history for the present. *Economic and Political Weekly*, 3373–3380.

Chakrabarty, D. (2009). *Provincializing Europe*. Princeton, NJ: Princeton University Press.

Chatterjee, P. (1993). *The Nation and its Fragments: Colonial and Postcolonial Histories*. Princeton, NJ: Princeton University Press

Chatterjee, P. (2004). *The Politics of the Governed: Reflections on Popular Politics in Most of the World*. New York: Columbia University Press.

Chatterji, A. P., Hansen, T. B., and Jaffrelot, C. (eds.) (2019). *Majoritarian State: How Hindu Nationalism Is Changing India*. New York: Oxford University Press.

Chatterji, J. (1999). The fashioning of a frontier: The Radcliffe line and Bengal's border landscape, 1947–52. *Modern Asian Studies*, 33(1), 185–242.

Chatterji, J. (2002). *Bengal Divided: Hindu Communalism and Partition, 1932–1947*. Cambridge: Cambridge University Press.

Chatterji, J. (2007). *The Spoils of Partition: Bengal and India, 1947–1967*. Cambridge:Cambridge University Press.

Chatterji, J. (2009). New directions in partition studies. *History Workshop Journal*, 67(1), 213–220.

Chatterji, J. (2012). South Asian histories of citizenship, 1946–1970. *The Historical Journal*, 55(4), 1049–1071.

Chawla, S. et al. (2020). Who is a citizen in contemporary India? *Epicenter* (Weatherhead blog, Harvard University), February 11, https://epicenter .wcfia.harvard.edu/blog/who-citizen-contemporary-india.

Chenoy, A. M. and Chenoy, K. A. M. (2010). *Maoist and Other Armed Conflicts*. New Delhi: Penguin Random House India.

Chester, L. P. (2009). *Borders and Conflict in South Asia: The Radcliffe Boundary Commission and the Partition of Punjab*. Manchester: Manchester University Press.

Christopher, A. J. (2005). Race and the census in the Commonwealth. *Population, Space and Place*, 11(2), 103–118.

Clawson, D. (1980). *Bureaucracy and the Labor Process*. New York: Monthly Review Press.

Clegg, S. (2008). Bureaucracy, the Holocaust and techniques of power at work. *Management Revue*, 20(4), 326–347.

Clemens, E. S. and Cook, J. M. (1999). Politics and institutionalism: Explaining durability and change. *Annual Review of Sociology*, 25(1), 441–466.

Cohen, H. (2015). *Year Zero of the Arab-Israeli Conflict 1929*. The Schusterman Series in Israel Studies. Waltham, MA: Brandeis University Press.

Cohen, H. (2018). The two faces of the War of 48. *Hazman Haze* [online journal, Hebrew].

Cohen, J. (1975). De-Parsonizing Weber: A critique of Parsons' interpretation of Weber's sociology. *American Sociological Review*, 40, 229–241.

Cohen, Y. (2002). From haven to heaven: Changes patterns of immigration to Israel. In D. Levy and Y. Weiss (eds.), *Challenging Ethnic Citizenship: German and Israeli Perspectives on Immigration*. New York: Berghahn Books, pp. 36–56.

Cohen, Y. and Gordon, N. (2018). Israel's biospatial politics: Territory, demography, and effective control. *Public Culture*, 30(2), 199–220.

Cohn, S. B. (1989). Law and the colonial state in India. In J. Starr and J. F. Collier (eds.), *History and Power in the Study of Law*. Ithaca, NY: Cornell University Press, pp. 131–152.

Cohn, S. B. (2004a). The study of Indian society and culture. In *The Bernard Cohn Omnibus*. New Delhi: Oxford University Press, pp. 136–171.

Cohn, S. B. (2004b). From Indian status to British contract. In *The Bernard Cohn Omnibus*. New Delhi: Oxford University Press, pp. 463–482.

Cohn, S. B. (2004c). Some notes on law and change in North India. In *The Bernard Cohn Omnibus*. New Delhi: Oxford University Press, pp. 554–574.

Comaroff, J. L. (1998). Reflections on the colonial state, in South Africa and elsewhere: Factions, fragments, facts and fictions. *Social Identities*, 4(3), 321–361.

Comaroff, J. L. (2001). Colonialism, culture, and the law: A foreword. *Law & Social Inquiry*, 26(2), 305–314.

Comaroff, J. and Comaroff, J. L. (eds.) (2008). *Law and Disorder in the Postcolony*. Chicago: University of Chicago Press.

Condos, M. (2017). *The Insecurity State: Punjab and the Making of Colonial Power in British India*. Cambridge: Cambridge University Press.

Constantinou, C. M. (2008). On the Cypriot states of exception. *International Political Sociology*, 2(2), 145–164.

Constantinou, C. M. and Richmond, O. P. (2005). The long mile of empire: Power, legitimation and the UK bases in Cyprus. *Mediterranean Politics*, 10(1), 65–84.

Cooke, B. (2003). The denial of slavery in management studies. *Journal of Management Studies*, 40, 1895–1918.

Cooper, F. (2011). From Chief to Technocrat: Redefining Colonial Authority in Post-World War II Africa. Paper presented at Empires & Bureaucracy, a Colloquium Exploring the Comparative History of European Empires from Late Antiquity to the Modern World. Trinity College, Dublin, June 16–18, 2011.

Cooper, F. and Stoler, A. L. (eds.) (1997). *Tensions of Empire: Colonial Cultures in a Bourgeois World*. Berkeley, CA: University of California Press.

Corrigan, P. and Sayer, D. (1985). *The Great Arch: English State Formation As Cultural Revolution*. Oxford: Blackwell.

Courpasson, D. and Clegg, S. (2006). Dissolving the iron cages? Tocqueville, Michels, bureaucracy and the perpetuation of elite power. *Organization*, 13 (3), 319–343.

Courpasson, D. and Dany, F. (2003). Indifference or obedience? Business firms as democratic hybrids. *Organization Studies*, 24, 123–160.

Crozier, Michel. (1964). *The Bureaucratic Phenomenon*. Chicago: University of Chicago Press.

Curzon, G. N. (1909). *The Place of India in the Empire: Being an Address Delivered before the Philosophical Institute of Edinburgh*. London: J. Murray.

Darweish, M., and Sellick, P. (2017). Everyday resistance among Palestinians living in Israel 1948–1966. *Journal of Political Power*, 10(3), 353–370.

Das, V. (2006). *Life and Words: Violence and the Descent into the Ordinary*. Berkeley: University of California Press.

Das, V., and Poole, D. (2004). Anthropology in the margins of the state. *PoLAR: Political and Legal Anthropology Review*, 30(1), 140–144.

Davis, G. F., and Greve, H. R. (1997). Corporate elite networks and governance changes in the 1980s. *American Journal of Sociology*, 103(1), 1–37.

Dayan, H. (2009). Regimes of separation: Israel/Palestine and the shadow of apartheid. In A. Ophir, M. Givoni, and S. Hanafi (eds.), *The Power of Inclusive Exclusion: Anatomy of Israeli Rule in the Occupied Palestinian Territories*. New York: Zone Books, pp. 281–322.

De, R. (2012). Emasculating the executive: The Federal Court and civil liberties in late colonial India: 1942–1944. In *Fates of Political Liberalism in the British Post-Colony: The Politics of the Legal Complex*. New York: Cambridge University Press, pp. 59–90.

De, R. (2018). *A People's Constitution*. Princeton, NJ: Princeton University Press.

Degani, A. Y. (2015). The decline and fall of the Israeli Military Government, 1948–1966: A case of settler-colonial consolidation? *Settler Colonial Studies*, 5 (1), 84–99.

Degani, A. (2020). On the frontier of integration: The Histadrut and the Palestinian Arab citizens of Israel. *Middle Eastern Studies*, 56(3), 412–426.

Deringil, S. (2003). "They live in a state of nomadism and savagery": The late Ottoman Empire and the post-colonial debate. *Comparative Studies in Society and History*, 45(2), 311–342.

Desrosières, A. (1998). *The Politics of Large Numbers: A History of Statistical Reasoning*. Cambridge, MA: Harvard University Press.

Devji, F. (1992). Hindu/Muslim/Indian. *Public Culture*, 5(1), 1–18.

Devji, F. (2007). A shadow nation: The making of Muslim India. In K. Grant, P. Levine, and F. Trentmann (eds.), *Beyond Sovereignty*. London: Palgrave Macmillan, pp. 126–145.

Devji, F. (2013). *Muslim Zion*. Cambridge, MA: Harvard University Press.

De Vries, D. (1997). National construction of occupational identity: Jewish clerks in British-ruled Palestine. *Comparative Studies in Society and History*, 39(02), 373–400.

De Vries, D. (2004). British rule and Arab–Jewish coalescence of interest: The 1946 civil servants' strike in Palestine. *International Journal of Middle East Studies*, 36(4), 613–638.

DiMaggio, P. J. and Powell, W. W. (1983). The iron cage revisited: Institutional isomorphism and collective rationality in organizational fields. *American Sociological Review*, 48(2), 147–160.

DiMaggio, P. J. and Powell, W. W. (eds.) (1991). *The New Institutionalism in Organizational Analysis*. Chicago: University of Chicago Press.

Dobbin, F. (1994). Cultural models of organization: The social construction of rational organizing principles. In D. Crane (ed.), *Sociology of Culture: Emerging Theoretical Responsibility*. Oxford: Basil Blackwell, pp. 117–141.

Drohan, B. (2018). *Brutality in an Age of Human Rights: Activism and Counterinsurgency at the End of the British Empire*. Ithaca, NY: Cornell University Press.

Droussiotis, M. (2005). *The First Partition, Cyprus 1963–1964*. Nicosia: Alfadi [Greek].

Dubnov, A. and Robson, L. (2019). *Partitions: A Transnational History of Twentieth-Century Territorial Separatism*. Stanford, CA: Stanford University Press.

Dubois, L. (2005). *Avengers of the New World*. Cambridge, MA: Harvard University Press.

Du Gay, Paul. (2000). *In Praise of Bureaucracy: Weber, Organization, Ethics*. London: Sage Publications.

Edwards, R. C. (1979). *Contested Terrain: The Transformation of the Workplace in the Twentieth Century*. New York: Basic Books.

El Rifai, Y., Yaser, D., and Jarrar, A. (2017). Tegart's modern legacy: The reproduction of power, a timeless paradox. *Jerusalem Quarterly*, 69, 78.

Emigh, R. J., Riley, D., and Ahmed, P. (2015). The racialization of legal categories in the first US census. *Social Science History*, 39(4), 485–519.

Emigh, R. J., Riley, D., and Ahmed, P. (2016). *Changes in Censuses from Imperialist to Welfare States: How Societies and States Count*. New York: Palgrave Macmillan.

Emilianides, A. C. (2019). *Constitutional Law in Cyprus*. The Hague: Kluwer Law International BV.

Esmeir, S. (2012). *Juridical Humanity: A Colonial History*. Stanford, CA: Stanford University Press.

Esmeir, S. (2015). On the coloniality of modern law. *Critical Analysis of Law*, 2 (1), 19–41.

Evans, I. (1997). *Bureaucracy and Race*. Berkeley, CA: University of California Press.

Ewing, A. (1984). The Indian Civil Service 1919–1924: Service discontent and the response in London and in Delhi. *Modern Asian Studies*, 18(1), 33–53.

Farazmand, A. (2009). *Bureaucracy and Administration*. New York: CRC Press.

Feagin, J. (2013). *Systemic Racism: A Theory of Oppression*. New York: Routledge.

Feldman, I. (2008). *Governing Gaza*. Durham, NC: Duke University Press.

Feldman, I. (2018). *Life Lived in Relief: Humanitarian Predicaments and Palestinian Refugee Politics*. Oakland, CA: University of California Press.

Feldman, K. P. and Medovoi, L. (2016). Race/religion/war: An introduction. *Social Text*, 34(4), 1–17.

Ferguson, J. and Gupta, A. (2002). Spatializing states: Toward an ethnography of neoliberal governmentality. *American Ethnologist*, 29(4), 981–1002.

Fisher, J. (2007). Official responses to foreign travel at the British Foreign and India Offices before 1914. *The English Historical Review*, 122(498), 937–964.

Fisher, M. H. (1993). The office of Akhbār Nawīs: The transition from Mughal to British forms. *Modern Asian Studies*, 27(1), 45–82.

Fisher, M. H. (1998). *Indirect Rule in India: Residents and the Residency System, 1764–1858*. New Delhi: Oxford University Press.

Forman, G. and Kedar, A. (2003). Colonialism, colonization and land law in Mandate Palestine: The Zor al-Zarqa and Barrat Qisarya land disputes in historical perspective. *Theoretical Inquiries in Law*, 4(2), 491–539.

Foucault, M. (2007). *Security, Territory, Population: Lectures at the Collège de France, 1977–78*. Houndmills, Basingstoke: Palgrave Macmillan.

Frantzman, S. J., Levin, N., and Kark, R. (2014). Counting nomads: British census attempts and tent counts of the Negev Bedouin 1917 to 1948. *Population, Space and Place*, 20(6), 552–568.

Fraser, T. G. (1984). *Partition in Ireland India and Palestine: Theory And Practice*. London: Macmillan.

French, D. (2015). *Fighting EOKA: The British Counter-insurgency Campaign on Cyprus, 1955–1959*. New York: Oxford University Press.

Frenkel, M. and Shenhav, Y. (2006). From binarism back to hybridity: A postcolonial reading of management and organization studies. *Organization Studies*, 27(6), 855–876.

Friedland, R. and Alford, R. R. (1991). Bringing society back in: Symbols, practices, and institutional contradictions. In P. J. DiMaggio and W. W. Powell (eds.), *The New Institutionalism in Organizational Analysis*. Chicago: University of Chicago Press, pp. 232–263.

Friedrichsmeyer, S., Lennox, S., and Zantop, S. (eds.) (1998). *The Imperialist Imagination: German Colonialism and Its Legacy*. Ann Arbor: University of Michigan Press.

Fuller, B. (1913). *The Empire of India*. London: Sir Isaac Pitman & Sons.

Fuller, C. J. and Harriss, J. (2000). For an anthropology of the state in India. In C. J. Fuller and V. Bénéï (eds.), *The Everyday State and Society in Modern India*. New Delhi: Social Science Press, pp. 1–30.

Furnivall, J. S. (1939). The training for civil administration in Netherlands India. *Journal of the Royal Central Asian Society*, 26(3), 415–439.

Furnivall, J. S. (1948). *Colonial Policy and Practice: A Comparative Study of Burma and Netherlands India*. Cambridge: Cambridge University Press.

Furnivall, J. S. (1974). *Experiment in Independence: The Philippines*. Manila: Solidaridad Publishing House.

Galanter, M. and Krishnan, J. (2000). Personal law and human rights in India and Israel. *Israel Law Review*, 34, 101.

Gavison, R. (2003). Constitutions and political reconstruction? Israel's quest for a constitution. *International Sociology*, 18(1), 53–70.

Ghosh, D. (2017). *Gentlemanly Terrorists: Political Violence and the Colonial State in India 1919–1947*. Cambridge: Cambridge University Press.

Gilmartin, D. (2017). 4. Imperial sovereignty in Mughal and British forms. *History and Theory*, 56(1), 80–88.

Gingeras, R. (2016). *Fall of the Sultanate: the Great War and the End of the Ottoman Empire, 1908–1922*. Oxford: Oxford University Press.

Go, J. (2008). Global fields and imperial forms: Field theory and the British and American empires. *Sociological Theory*, 26(3), 201–229.

Go, J. (2011). *Patterns of Empire: The British and American Empires, 1688 to the Present*. New York: Cambridge University Press.

Go, J. (2013). For a postcolonial sociology. *Theory and Society*, 42(1), 25–55.

Go, J. (2018). Relational sociology and postcolonial theory: Sketches of a "postcolonial relationalism." In F. Dépelteau (ed.), *The Palgrave Handbook of Relational Sociology*. Cham:Palgrave Macmillan, pp. 357–373.

Go, J. (2020). Race, empire, and epistemic exclusion: Or the structures of sociological thought. *Sociological Theory*, 38(2), 79–100.

Goh, D. P. (2008). From colonial pluralism to postcolonial multiculturalism: Race, state formation and the question of cultural diversity in Malaysia and Singapore. *Sociology Compass*, 2(1), 232–252.

Gorsky, Philip S. (2005). The Protestant ethic and the bureaucratic revolution: Ascetic Protestantism and administrative rationalization in early modern Europe. In C. Charles, P. Gorsky, and D. Trubek (eds.), *Max Weber's "Economy and Society."* Stanford, CA: Stanford University Press, pp. 267–296.

Gould, W. (2010). *Bureaucracy, Community and Influence in India: Society and the State, 1930s–1960s*. London: Routledge.

Gould, W., Sherman, T., and Ansari, S. (2013). The flux of the matter: Loyalty, corruption and the "everyday state" in the post-partition government services of India and Pakistan. *Past & Present*, 219(1), 237–279.

Gouldner, A. (1954). *Patterns of Industrial Bureaucracy*. New York: Free Press.

Graeber, D. (2015). *The Utopia of Rules: On Technology, Stupidity, and the Secret Joys of Bureaucracy*. London: Melville House.

Guha, S. (2003). The politics of identity and enumeration in India c. 1600–1990. *Comparative Studies in Society and History*, 45(1), 148–167.

Guillen, Mauro F. (1994). *Models of Management: Work, Authority, and Organization in a Comparative Perspective*. Chicago: University of Chicago Press.

Gupta, A. (1998). *Postcolonial Developments: Agriculture in the Making of Modern India*. Durham, NC: Duke University Press.

Gupta, A. (2012). *Red Tape: Bureaucracy, Structural Violence, and Poverty in India*. Durham, NC: Duke University Press.

Gupta, A. (2013). Messy bureaucracies. *HAU: Journal of Ethnographic Theory*, 3 (3), 435–440.

Gutiérrez, R. A. (2004). Internal colonialism: An American theory of race. *Du Bois Review*, 1(02), 281–295.

Gutman, D. (2016). Travel documents, mobility control, and the Ottoman state in an age of global migration, 1880–1915. *Journal of the Ottoman and Turkish Studies Association*, 3(2), 347–368.

Haan, M. (2005). Numbers in Nirvana: How the 1872–1921 Indian censuses helped operationalise "Hinduism." *Religion*, 35(1), 13–30.

Hacker, J. S., Pierson, P., and Thelen, K. (2015). Drift and conversion: Hidden faces of institutional change. In J. Mahoney and K. Thelen (eds.), *Advances in Comparative-Historical Analysis*. Cambridge: Cambridge University Press, pp. 180–208.

Hacking, I. (2007). Kinds of people: Moving targets. *Proceedings of the British Academy*, 151, 285–318.

Hall, H. L. (1937). *The Colonial Office: A History (Vol. 13)*. London: Published for the Royal Empire Society by Longmans, Green.

Halliday, T. C., Karpik, L., and Feeley, M. M. (eds.) (2012). *Fates of Political Liberalism in the British Post-colony: The Politics of the Legal Complex*. New York: Cambridge University Press.

Hansen, T. B. and Steputat, F. (2006). Sovereignty revisited. *Annual Review of Anthropology*, 35, 295–315.

Haque, M. S. (2007). Theory and practice of public administration in Southeast Asia: Traditions, directions, and impacts. *International Journal of Public Administration*, 30(12-14), 1297–1326.

Harel-Shalev, A. (2010). *The Challenge of Sustaining Democracy in Deeply Divided Societies: Citizenship, Rights, and Ethnic Conflicts in India and Israel*. Washington, DC: Lexington Books.

Hareuveni, Y. (1993). *The Mandate Government in Palestine – A Historical and Political Analysis*. Jerusalem: Bar Ilan University Press [Hebrew].

Haveman, H. A. and Rao, H. (1997). Structuring a theory of moral sentiments: Institutional and organizational coevolution in the early thrift industry. *American Journal of Sociology*, 102(6), 1606–1651.

Hay, D. and Craven, P. (eds.) (2005). *Masters, Servants, and Magistrates in Britain and the Empire, 1562–1955*. Chapel Hill: University of North Carolina Press.

Herzfeld, M. (1992). *The Social Production of Indifference*. Chicago: Chicago University Press.

Heussler, R. (1963). *Yesterday's Rulers: The Making of the British Colonial Service*. Syracuse, NY: Syracuse University Press.

Hillyard, P. (1993). *Suspect Community: People's Experience of the Prevention of Terrorism Acts in Britain*. London: Pluto Press.

Hind, R. J. (1984). The internal colonial concept. *Comparative Studies in Society and History*, 26(03), 543–568.

Hirschman, C. (1987). The meaning and measurement of ethnicity in Malaysia: An analysis of census classifications. *The Journal of Asian Studies*, 46(3), 555–582.

Honig, B. (2009). *Emergency Politics*. Princeton, NJ: Princeton University Press.

Honig, B. (2017). *Public Things: Democracy in Disrepair*. New York: Fordham University Press.

Hopkins, B. D. (2015). The frontier crimes regulation and frontier governmentality. *The Journal of Asian Studies*, 74(2), 369–389.

Horowitz, I. L. (1982). *Taking Lives: Genocide and State Power*. New Brunswick, NJ: Transaction Books.

Hughes, M. (2009). The banality of brutality: British armed forces and the repression of the Arab revolt in Palestine, 1936–39. *The English Historical Review*, 124(507), 313–354.

Hughes, M. (2019). *Britain's Pacification of Palestine: The British Army, the Colonial State, and the Arab Revolt, 1936–1939*. Cambridge: Cambridge University Press.

Hull, M. S. (2012). Documents and bureaucracy. *Annual Review of Anthropology*, 41, 251–267.

Hussain, N. (2003). *The Jurisprudence of Emergency: Colonialism and the Rule of Law*. Ann Arbor: University of Michigan Press.

Hussain, N. (2007). Hyperlegality. *New Criminal Law Review*, 10(4), 514–531.

Hussain, N. (2019). *The Jurisprudence of Emergency: Colonialism and the Rule of Law*. With new foreword and preface. Ann Arbor: University of Michigan Press.

Hussin, I. (2014). Circulations of law: Cosmopolitan elites, global repertoires, local vernaculars. *Law and History Review*, 32(4), 773–795.

India (1913). *Census of India, 1911: Volume VI City of Calcutta*. Calcutta: Bengal Secretariat Book Depot.

Iyer, L. (2010). Direct versus indirect colonial rule in India: Long-term consequences. *The Review of Economics and Statistics*, 92(4), 693–713.

Jabareen, H. and Bishara, S. (2019). The Jewish nation-state law. *Journal of Palestine Studies*, 48(2), 43–57.

Jacobs, D. (1998). The determinants of deadly force: A structural analysis of police violence 1. *American Journal of Sociology*, 103(4), 837–862.

Jacobson, A. (2011). *From Empire to Empire: Jerusalem between Ottoman and British Rule*. Syracuse, NY: Syracuse University Press.

Jalal, A. (2002). *Self and Sovereignty: Individual and Community in South Asian Islam since 1850*. Abingdon: Routledge.

Jamal, A. (2007). Nationalizing states and the constitution of "hollow citizenship": Israel and its Palestinian citizens. *Ethnopolitics*, 6(4), 471–493.

Jamal, A. (2019). Israel's new constitutional imagination: The nation state law and beyond. *Journal of Holy Land and Palestine Studies*, 18(2), 193–220.

Jayal, N. G. (2013). *Citizenship and Its Discontents: An Indian History*. Cambridge, MA: Harvard University Press.

Jayal, N. G. (2019). Reconfiguring citizenship in contemporary India. *South Asia: Journal of South Asian Studies*, 42(1), 33–50.

Jiryis, Ş. (1976). *The Arabs in Israel*. New York: Monthly Review Press.

Johnston, R. (1973). *Sovereignty and Protection: A Study of British Jurisdictional Imperialism in the Late Nineteenth Century*. Durham, NC: Duke University Press.

Jones, R. (2014). The false premise of partition. *Space and Polity*, 18(3), 285–300.

Joyce, P. and Mukerji, C. (2017). The state of things: State history and theory reconfigured. *Theory and Society*, 46(1), 1–19.

Kalberg, S. (1980). Max Weber's types of rationality: Cornerstones for the analysis of rationalization processes in history. *American Journal of Sociology*, 85(5), 1145–1179.

Kalhan, A. (2010). Constitution and "extraconstitution": Colonial emergency regimes in postcolonial India and Pakistan. In V. V. Ramraj and A. K. Thiruvengadam (eds.), *Emergency Powers in Asia: Exploring the Limits of Legality*. Cambridge: Cambridge University Press, pp. 89–120.

Kalhan, A., Conroy, G. P., Kaushal, M., and Miller, S. S. (2006). Colonial continuities: Human rights, terrorism, and security laws in India. *Columbia Journal of Asian Law*, 20, 93.

Kaminsky, A. P. (1986). *The India Office, 1880–1910*. Westport, CT: Greenwood Publishing Group.

Kanter, R. M. (1977). *Men and Women of the Corporation*. New York: Basic Books.

Karlsson, B. T. and Subba, T. B. (eds.) (2006). *Indigeneity in India*. London: Kegan Paul.

Kasaba, R. (2011). *A Moveable Empire: Ottoman Nomads, Migrants, and Refugees*. London: University of Washington Press.

Kattan, V. (2018). The empire departs: The partitions of British India, Mandate Palestine, and the dawn of self-determination in the Third World. *Asian Journal of Middle Eastern and Islamic Studies*, 12(3), 304–327.

Kaur, R. (2007). *Since 1947: Partition Narratives among Punjabi Migrants of Delhi*. New Delhi: Oxford University Press.

Kaviraj, S. (1984). On the crisis of political institutions in India. *Contributions to Indian Sociology*, 18(2), 223–243.

Kedar, A. (2014). Expanding legal geographies. In I. Braverman, N. Blomley, D. Delaney, and A. Kedar (eds.), *The Expanding Spaces of Law: A Timely Legal Geography*. Stanford, CA: Stanford University Press, pp. 95–119.

Kelman C. H. (1973). Violence without moral restraint. *Journal of Social Issues*, 29, 29–61.

Kemp, A. (2004). Dangerous populations: State territoriality and the constitution of national minorities. In J. Migdal (ed.), *Boundaries and Belonging States and Societies in the Struggle to Shape Identities and Local Practices*. New York: Cambridge University Press, pp. 73–98.

Khalidi, R. (2007). *The Iron Cage: The Story of the Palestinian Struggle for Statehood*. Boston, MA: Beacon Press.

Khalidi, W. (2005). Why did the Palestinians leave, revisited. *Journal of Palestine Studies*, 34(2), 42–54.

Khalili, L. (2010). The location of Palestine in global counterinsurgencies. *International Journal of Middle East Studies*, 42(3), 413–433.

Khalili, L. (2012). *Time in the Shadows*. Stanford, CA: Stanford University Press.

Khalili, L. (2015). Counterterrorism and counterinsurgency in the neoliberal age. In A. Ghazal and J. Hanssen (eds.), *The Oxford Handbook of Contemporary Middle-Eastern and North African History*. Oxford: Oxford University Press, pp. 365–383.

Khan, Y. (2017). *The Great Partition*. New Haven, CT: Yale University Press.

Khan Bangash, Y. (2021). Implementing partition: Proceedings of the Punjab Partition Committee, July–August 1947. *Modern Asian Studies*, 1–43.

Kim, J. (2016). *Contested Embrace*. Stanford, CA: Stanford University Press.

Kim, S. H. (2012). Max Weber. In E. N. Zalta (ed.), *The Stanford Encyclopedia of Philosophy*, https://plato.stanford.edu/.

Kimmerling, B. (1977). Sovereignty, ownership, and "presence" in the Jewish-Arab territorial conflict: The case of Bir'im and Ikrit. *Comparative Political Studies*, 10(2), 155–176.

Kinder, D. R. and Sanders, L. M. (1996). *Divided by Color: Racial Politics and Democratic Ideals*. Chicago: University of Chicago Press,.

Kiser, E. and Sacks, Audrey. (2011). Assessing decentralized and privatized tax administration. *The Annals of the American Academy of Political and Social Science*, 36, 129–149.

Kitromilides, P. M. (1990). Greek irredentism in Asia minor and Cyprus. *Middle Eastern Studies*, 26(1), 3–17.

Kitromilides, P. M. (2019). *Insular Destinies: Perspectives on the History and Politics of Modern Cyprus*. Abingdon: Routledge.

Kliot, N., and Mansfield, Y. (1997). The political landscape of partition: The case of Cyprus. *Political Geography*, 16(6), 495–521.

Kolsky, E. (2005). Codification and the rule of colonial difference: Criminal procedure in British India. *Law and History Review*, 23(3), 631–683.

Kolsky, E. (2010). *Colonial Justice in British India*. Cambridge: Cambridge University Press.

Kolsky, E. (2015). The colonial rule of law and the legal regime of exception: Frontier "fanaticism" and state violence in British India. *The American Historical Review*, 120(4), 1218–1246.

Korn, A. (2003). From refugees to infiltrators: Constructing political crime in Israel in the 1950s. *International Journal of the Sociology of Law*, 31(1), 1–22.

Kothiyal, T. (2016). *Nomadic Narratives: A History of Mobility and Identity in the Great Indian Desert*. New Delhi: Cambridge University Press,

Krasniqi, G. (2019). Contested states as liminal spaces of citizenship: Comparing Kosovo and the Turkish Republic of Northern Cyprus. *Ethnopolitics*, 18(3), 298–314.

Laidlaw, Z. (2013). *Colonial Connections, 1815–45: Patronage, the Information Revolution and Colonial Government*. Manchester: Manchester University Press.

Lange, M. (2009). *Lineages of Despotism and Development: British Colonialism and State Power*. Chicago: University of Chicago Press.

Lee, C. K., and Strang, D. (2006). The international diffusion of public-sector downsizing: Network emulation and theory-driven learning. *International Organization*, 60(4), 883–909.

Legg, S. (2008). *Spaces of Colonialism: Delhi's Urban Governmentalities.* Malden, MA: Blackwell.

Legg, S. (2011) Introduction. In *Spatiality, Sovereignty and Carl Schmitt: Geographies of the Nomos.* London: Routledge.

Leibler, A. E. (2004). Statisticians' ambition: Governmentality, modernity and national legibility. *Israel Studies*, 9(2), 121–149.

Leibler, A. and Breslau, D. (2005). The uncounted: Citizenship and exclusion in the Israeli census of 1948. *Ethnic and Racial Studies*, 28(5), 880–902.

Lerner, H. (2011). *Making Constitutions in Deeply Divided Societies.* Cambridge: Cambridge University Press

Levitt, B. and March, J. G. (1988). Organizational learning. *Annual Review of Sociology*, 14(1), 319–338.

Li, D. (2018). From exception to empire: Sovereignty, carceral circulation, and the "Global War on Terror." In C. McGranahan and J. F. Collins (eds.), *Ethnographies of US Empire.* Durham, NC: Duke University Press, pp. 456–476.

Likhovski, A. (2009). Argonauts of the eastern Mediterranean: Legal transplants and signaling. *Theoretical Inquiries in Law*, 10(2), 619–651.

Lippmann, S. and Aldrich, H. E. (2016). A rolling stone gathers momentum: Generational units, collective memory, and entrepreneurship. *Academy of Management Review*, 41(4), 658–675.

Locher-Scholten, E. (2012). Imperialism after the Great Wave: The Dutch Case in the Netherlands East Indies, 1860–1914. In M. Fitzpatrick (ed.), *Liberal Imperialism in Europe.* New York: Palgrave Macmillan, pp. 25–46.

Loevy, K. (2021). The Balfour Declaration's territorial landscape: Between protection and self-determination. *Humanity: An International Journal of Human Rights, Humanitarianism, and Development*, 12(2), 138–158.

Loizides, N. G. (2007). Ethnic nationalism and adaptation in Cyprus. *International Studies Perspectives*, 8(2), 172–189.

Loizides, N. (2015). Settlers, mobilization, and displacement in Cyprus: Antinomies of ethnic conflict and immigration politics. In O. Haklai and N. Loizides (eds.), *Settlers in Contested Lands: Territorial Disputes and Ethnic Conflicts.* Stanford, CA: Stanford University Press, pp. 168–191.

Loizos, P. (1976). Notes on future anthropological research on Cyprus. *Annals of the New York Academy of Sciences*, 268(1), 355–362.

Lokaneeta, J. (2021). Rule of law, violence and exception: Deciphering the Indian State in the Thangjam Manorama inquiry report. *Law, Culture and the Humanities*, 17(1), 71–91.

Loveman, M. (2005). The modern state and the primitive accumulation of symbolic power. *American Journal of Sociology*, 110(6), 1651–1683.

Loveman, M. (2014). *National Colors: Racial Classification and the State in Latin America.* New York: Oxford University Press.

Lowe, L. (2015). *The Intimacies of Four Continents.* Durham, NC: Duke University Press.

Lucassen, L. and Willems, W. (2003). The weakness of well-ordered societies: Gypsies in Western Europe, the Ottoman Empire, and India, 1400–1914. *Review (Fernand Braudel Center)*, 26(3), 283–313.

Lugard, F. J. D. (1922). *The Dual Mandate in British Tropical Africa.* Edinburgh and London: William Blackwood and Sons.

Lustick, I. (1980). *Arabs in the Jewish State: Israel's Control of a National Minority.* Austin: University of Texas Press.

Macklin, A. (2007). Who is the citizen's other? Considering the heft of citizenship. *Theoretical Inquiries in Law*, 8(2), 333–366.

Maheshwari, S. (1996). *The Census Administration under the Raj and After.* New Delhi: Concept Publishing Company.

Mahmud, T. (1998). Colonialism and modern constructions of race: A preliminary inquiry. *University of Miami Law Review*, 53, 1219.

Mahoney, J. (2003). Long-run development and the legacy of colonialism in Spanish America. *American Journal of Sociology*, 109(1), 50–106.

Mahoney, J. (2010). *Colonialism and Postcolonial Development: Spanish America in Comparative Perspective.* New York: Cambridge University Press.

Mahoney, J. and Thelen, K. A. (2010). A Theory of Gradual Institutional Change. In J. Mahoney and K. A. Thelen, *Explaining Institutional Change: Ambiguity, Agency, and Power.* Cambridge University Press, pp. 1–37.

Mahmud, T. (1998). Colonialism and modern constructions of race: A preliminary inquiry. *University of Miami Law Review*, 53, 1219.

Major, A. J. (1999). State and criminal tribes in colonial Punjab: Surveillance, control and reclamation of the "dangerous classes." *Modern Asian Studies*, 33 (3), 657–688.

Makdisi, U. (2000). Corrupting the sublime sultanate: The revolt of Tanyus Shahin in nineteenth-century Ottoman Lebanon. *Comparative Studies in Society and History*, 42(01), 180–208.

Malkki, L. H. (1995). Refugees and exile: From "refugee studies" to the national order of things. *Annual Review of Anthropology*, 24(1), 495–523.

Mamdani, M. (1996). *Citizen and Subject: Contemporary Africa and the Legacy of Late Colonialism.* Princeton, NJ: Princeton University Press.

Manasse, E. M. (1947). Max Weber on race. *Social Research Quarterly*, 14(2), 191–221.

Mantena, K. (2010). *Alibis of Empire.* Princeton, NJ: Princeton University Press.

March, J. G. and Simon, H. A. (1958). *Organizations.* New York: John Wiley.

March, J. G. and Olsen, J. P. (1976). *Ambiguity and Choice in Organizations.* Bergen, Norway: Universitetsforlaget.

Markides, D. (1998). The issue of separate municipalities in Cyprus 1957–1963: An overview. *Journal of Mediterranean Studies*, 8(2), 177–204.

Markides, D. W. (2001). *Cyprus 1957–1963: From Colonial Conflict to Constitutional Crisis: The Key Role of the Municipal Issue.* Minneapolis: University of Minnesota.

Markides, D. and Georghallides, G. S. (1995). British attitudes to constitution-making in post-1931 Cyprus. *Journal of Modern Greek Studies*, 13(1), 63–81.

Marshall, T. H. (1950). *Citizenship and Social Class.* New York: Cambridge University Press.

Marsot, A. L. al.-S. (1999). The British occupation of Egypt from 1882. In A. Porter (ed.), *The Oxford History of the British Empire: The Nineteenth Century*. Oxford: Oxford University Press, pp. 651–664.

Martin, A. W., et al. (2013). Against the rules: Synthesizing types and processes of bureaucratic rule-breaking. *Academy of Management Review*, 38(4), 550–574.

Masalha, N. (1997). *A Land Without a People: Israel, Transfer and the Palestinians 1949–96*. London: Faber and Faber.

Masalha, N. (2003). *The Politics of Denial: Israel and the Palestinian Refugee Problem*. London: Pluto Press.

Mathur, N. (2016). *Paper Tiger*. New Delhi: Cambridge University Press.

Mathur, N. (2017). Bureaucracy. In *The Cambridge Encyclopedia of Anthropology*, www.anthroencyclopedia.com/entry/bureaucracy.

Mattar, P. (1992). *The Mufti of Jerusalem: Al-Hajj Amin al-Husayni and the Palestinian National Movement*. New York: Columbia University Press.

Mawani, R. (2014). Law as temporality: Colonial politics and Indian settlers. *University of California Irvine Law Review*, 4, 65.

Mawani, R. (2015). Law and colonialism: Legacies and lineages. In A. Sarat and P. Ewick (eds.), *The Handbook of Law and Society*. Chichester: John Wiley and Sons, pp. 417–432.

Mawani, R. (2018). *Across Oceans of Law*. Durham, NC: Duke University Press.

Mbembe, A. (2001). *On the Postcolony*. Berkeley: University of California Press.

McClure, A. (2018). Sovereignty, law, and the politics of forgiveness in colonial India, 1858–1903. *Comparative Studies of South Asia, Africa and the Middle East*, 38(3), 385–401.

McGranahan, C., and Collins, J. F. (eds.) (2018). *Ethnographies of US Empire*. Durham, NC: Duke University Press.

Mehozay, Y. (2016). *Between the Rule of Law and States of Emergency: The Fluid Jurisprudence of the Israeli Regime*. Albany: State University of New York Press.

Merton, R. K. (1963/1939). Bureaucratic structure and personality. *Social Forces*, 18, 560.

Minkoff, D. C. (1994). From service provision to institutional advocacy: The shifting legitimacy of organizational forms. *Social Forces*, 72(4), 943–969.

Mintz, S. W. (1985). *Sweetness and Power: The Place of Sugar in Modern History*. New York: Viking.

Mir, Raza A., Mir, A. and Punya, U. A. (2003). Toward a postcolonial reading of organizational control. In A Prasad (ed.), *Postcolonial Theory and Organizational Analysis: A Critical Engagement*. New York: Palgrave Macmillan, pp. 48–73.

Misra, B. B. (1977). *The Bureaucracy in India*. Delhi: Oxford University Press.

Mitchell, T. (1991a). The limits of the state: Beyond statist approaches and their critics. *American Political Science Review*, 85(1), 77–96.

Mitchell, T. (1991b). *Colonizing Egypt*. Berkeley: University of California Press.

Mitchell, T. (2002). *Rule of Experts: Egypt, Techno-Politics, Modernity*. Berkeley: University of California Press.

Mommsen, W. (1959/1984). *Max Weber and German Politics 1890–1920*. Chicago: University of Chicago Press.

Mommsen, W. (1974). *The Age of Bureaucracy: Perspectives on the Political Sociology of Max Weber*. New York: Harper & Row Publishers.

Mongia, R. V. (2003). Race, nationality, mobility: A history of the passport. In S. D. Pennybacker, H. Streets, S. Ward, and A. Curthoys (eds.), *After the Imperial Turn: Thinking with and through the Nation*. Durham, NC: Duke University Press, pp. 196–214.

Mongia, R. (2018). *Indian Migration and Empire*. Durham, NC: Duke University Press.

Moore, R. J. (1999). Imperial India, 1858–1914. In A. Porter (ed.), *The Oxford History of the British Empire: The Nineteenth Century*. Oxford: Oxford University Press, pp. 422–446.

Mora, G. C. (2014). Cross-field effects and ethnic classification: The institutionalization of Hispanic panethnicity, 1965 to 1990. *American Sociological Review*, 79(2), 183–210.

Morgan, G. 1986. *Images of Organization*. Thousand Oaks, CA: Sage.

Morgan, K. J. and Orloff, A. S. (2017). Introduction: The many hands of the state. In *The Many Hands of the State: Theorizing Political Authority and Social Control*. New York: Cambridge University Press, pp. 1–32.

Mukherjee, M. (2010). *India in the Shadows of Empire*. Oxford: Oxford University Press.

Nadan, A. (2018). Revisiting the anti-mushā' reforms in the levant: Origins, scale and outcomes. *British Journal of Middle Eastern Studies*, 47(4), 595–611.

Nandi, S. (2010). Constructing the criminal: Politics of social imaginary of the" Goonda." *Social Scientist*, 38(3/4), 37–54.

Nasasra, M. (2020). Two decades of Bedouin resistance and survival under Israeli military rule, 1948–1967. *Middle Eastern Studies*, 56(1), 64–83.

Navaro-Yashin, Y. (2006a). De-ethnicizing the ethnography of Cyprus. In Y. Papadakis, N. Peristianis, and G. Welz (eds.), *Divided Cyprus: Modernity, History, and an Island in Conflict*. Bloomington: Indiana University Press, pp. 84–99.

Navaro-Yashin, Y. (2006b). Affect in the civil service: A study of a modern state-system. *Postcolonial Studies*, 9(3), 281–294.

Navaro-Yashin, Y. (2007). Make-believe papers, legal forms and the counterfeit: Affective interactions between documents and people in Britain and Cyprus. *Anthropological Theory*, 7(1), 79–98.

Neocleous, M. (2006). The problem with normality: Taking exception to "permanent emergency." *Alternatives*, 31(2), 191–213.

Neocleous, M. (2007). From martial law to the war on terror. *New Criminal Law Review*, 10(4), 489–513.

Neocleous, M. (2011). The police of civilization: The war on terror as civilizing offensive. *International Political Sociology*, 5(2), 144–159.

Neumann, F. (1963/1942). *Behemoth*. New York: Harper Books.

Nkomo, S. M. (1992). The emperor has no clothes: Rewriting "Race in Organizations." *Academy of Management Review*, 17, 487–513.

Norris, J. (2013). *Land of Progress: Palestine in the Age of Colonial Development, 1905–1948.* Oxford: Oxford University Press.

Nuriely, B. (2005). Foreigners in national space: Jews and Arabs in the Lod Ghetto, 1950–1959. *Theory and Criticism,* 26, 13–42.

Nuriely, B. (2019). The hunger economy: The military government in the Galilee, Ramle, and Lydda, 1948–1949. *Arab Studies Journal,* 27(2), 64–84.

O'Leary, B. (2007). Analysing partition: Definition, classification and explanation. *Political Geography,* 26(8), 886–908.

Olick, J. K., and Robbins, J. (1998). Social memory studies: From "collective memory" to the historical sociology of mnemonic practices. *Annual Review of Sociology,* 24(1), 105–140.

Onurkan-Samani, M. (2018). The Legislative Council and its historical/political implications in Cyprus (1882–1931). In T. Kyritsi and N. Christofis (eds.), *Cypriot Nationalisms in Context.* Cham: Palgrave Macmillan, pp. 75–92.

Orton, D. J. and Weick, K. E. (1990). Loosely coupled systems: A reconsideration. *Academy of Management Journal,* 15(2), 203–223.

Ouchi, W. G. (1980). Markets, bureaucrats and clans. *Administrative Science Quarterly,* 25, 129–141.

Owen, R. (2004). *Lord Cromer: Victorian Imperialist, Edwardian Proconsul.* Oxford: Oxford University Press.

Pandey, G. (2001). *Remembering Partition: Violence, Nationalism and History in India.* Cambridge: Cambridge University Press.

Papadakis, Y. (2005). Locating the Cyprus problem: Ethnic conflict and the politics of space. *Macalester International,* 15(1), 11.

Papastylianos, C. (2018). The Cypriot doctrine of necessity within the context of emergency discourse: How a unique emergency shaped a peculiar type of emergency law. *The Cyprus Review,* 30(1), 113–143.

Parmar, P. (2015). *Indigeneity and Legal Pluralism in India: Claims, Histories, Meanings.* New York: Cambridge University Press.

Patrick, R. A. and Bater, J. H. (1976). *Political Geography and the Cyprus Conflict, 1963–1971.* Department of Geography Publication Series No. 4. Waterloo, Canada: University of Waterloo.

Peabody, N. (2001). Cents, sense, census: Human inventories in late precolonial and early colonial India. *Comparative Studies in Society and History,* 43(4), 819–850.

Pedersen, S. (2016). The impact of league oversight on British policy in Palestine. In R. Miller (ed.), *Britain, Palestine and Empire: The Mandate Years.* London: Routledge, pp. 39–66.

Peled, Y. (1992). Ethnic democracy and the legal construction of citizenship: Arab citizens of the Jewish state. *American Political Science Review,* 86(2), 432–443.

Percival, D. A. (1949). Some features of a peasant population in the Middle East: Drawn from the results of the census of Cyprus. *Population Studies,* 3(2), 192–204.

Peristianis, N. (2008). Between nation and state: Nation, nationalism, state, and national identity in Cyprus. Unpublished doctoral dissertation, Middlesex University.

Plonski, S. (2017). *Palestinian Citizens of Israel: Power, Resistance and the Struggle for Space*. London: Bloomsbury Publishing.

Pollis, A. (1973). Intergroup conflict and British colonial policy: The case of Cyprus. *Comparative Politics*, 5(4), 575–599.

Poole, E. D. and Regoli, R. M. (1980). Race, institutional rule breaking, and disciplinary response: A study of discretionary decision making in prison. *Law and Society Review*, 14, 931–946.

Porter, A. N. (1973). Sir Alfred Milner and the press, 1897–1899. *The Historical Journal* 16(02), 323–339.

Porter, A. and Stockwell, A. J. (1989). *British Imperial Policy and Decolonization, 1938–64: Volume 2: 1951–64*. New York: Springer.

Potter, D. (1973). Manpower shortage and the end of colonialism: The case of the Indian Civil Service. *Modern Asian Studies*, 7, 47–73.

Prakash, G. (2019). *Emergency Chronicles*. Princeton, NJ: Princeton University Press.

Prasad, A. (2003). *Postcolonial Theory and Organizational Analysis: A Critical Engagement*. New York: Springer.

Ram, M. (2015). Colonial conquests and the politics of normalization: The case of the Golan Heights and Northern Cyprus. *Political Geography*, 47, 21–32.

Raman, B. (2008). The familial world of the Company's kacceri in early colonial Madras. *Journal of Colonialism and Colonial History*, 9(2).

Raman, B. (2012). *Document Raj: Writing and Scribes in Early Colonial South India*. Chicago: University of Chicago Press.

Raman, B. (2017). Law and identity in colonial South Asia. *Law & Social Inquiry*, 42(4), 1210–1214.

Raman, B. (2018). Law in times of counterinsurgency. In A. Balachandran, R. Pant, and B. Raman, (eds.), *Iterations of Law: Legal Histories from India*. New Delhi: Oxford University Press, pp. 121–146.

Ramnath, K. (2021). Histories of Indian citizenship in the age of decolonisation. *Itinerario*, 45(1), 152–173.

Rappas, A. (2008). The elusive polity: Imagining and contesting colonial authority in Cyprus during the 1930s. *Journal of Modern Greek Studies*, 26 (2), 363–397.

Rath, S. K. (2011). Census of India 2011 and the issues of national security: A dangerous gambit. *Revista de Cercetare și Intervenție Socială*, 33, 91–113.

Ray, V. (2019). A theory of racialized organizations. *American Sociological Review*, 84(1), 26–53.

Reynolds J. (2012). The political economy of states of emergency. *Oregon Review of International Law*, 14(1), 85–130.

Riles, A. (2005). A new agenda for the cultural study of law: Taking on the technicalities. *Buffalo Law Review*, 53, 973.

Rishmawi, M. (1987). Planning in whose interest? Land use planning as a strategy for Judaization. *Journal of Palestine Studies*, 16(2), 105–116.

Robinson, S. N. (2013). *Citizen Strangers*. Stanford, CA: Stanford University Press.

Robson, L. (2011). *Colonialism and Christianity in Mandate Palestine*. Austin: University of Texas Press.

Robson, L. (2017). *States of Separation*. Oakland: University of California Press.

Rouhana, N. N. (1997). *Palestinian Citizens in an Ethnic Jewish State: Identities in Conflict*. New Haven, CT: Yale University Press.

Rouhana, N. N. and Sabbagh-Khoury, A. (2015). Settler-colonial citizenship: Conceptualizing the relationship between Israel and its Palestinian citizens. *Settler Colonial Studies*, 5(3), 205–225.

Rouhana, N. N. and Sabbagh-Khoury, A. (2019). Memory and the return of history in a settler-colonial context: The case of the Palestinians in Israel. *Interventions*, 21(4), 527–550.

Roy, A. (2010). *Mapping Citizenship in India*. New Delhi: Oxford University Press.

Roy, A. and Singh, U. K. (2009). The ambivalence of citizenship: The IMDT Act (1983) and the politics of forclusion in Assam. *Critical Asian Studies*, 41(1), 37–60.

Roy, H. (2012). *Partitioned Lives: Migrants, Refugees, Citizens in India and Pakistan, 1947–65*. Oxford: Oxford University Press.

Rozin, O. (2016). Infiltration and the making of Israel's emotional regime in the state's early years. *Middle Eastern Studies*, 52(3), 448–472.

Rudolph, L. I. and Rudolph, S. H. (1979). Authority and power in bureaucratic and patrimonial administration: A revisionist interpretation of Weber on bureaucracy. *World Politics*, 31(2), 195–227.

Rutherford, D. (2012). *Laughing at Leviathan*. Chicago: University of Chicago Press.

Saban, H. (2011). Theorizing and tracing the legal dimensions of a control framework: Law and the Arab-Palestinian minority in Israel's first three decades (1948–1978). *Emory International Law Review*, 25, 299.

Sabbagh-Khoury, A. (2011). The internally displaced Palestinians in Israel. *The Palestinians in Israel: Readings in History, Politics and Society*, 1, 27–46.

Sabbagh-Khoury, A. (2021). Tracing settler colonialism: A genealogy of a paradigm in the sociology of knowledge production in Israel. *Politics and Society*, 0032329221999906.

Sa'di, A. H. (2003). The Koenig Report and Israeli policy towards the Palestinian minority, 1965–1976: Old wine in new bottles. *Arab Studies Quarterly*, 25(3), 51–61.

Sa'di, A. H. (2016). *Thorough Surveillance: The Genesis of Israeli Policies of Population Management, Surveillance and Political Control towards the Palestinian Minority*. Manchester: Manchester University Press.

Sa'di, A. H. (2019). The nation state of the Jewish People's basic law: A threshold of elimination? *Journal of Holy Land and Palestine Studies*, 18(2), 163–177.

Sadiq, K. (2008). *Paper Citizens: How Illegal Immigrants Acquire Citizenship in Developing Countries*. New York: Oxford University Press.

Sadiq, K. (2017). Postcolonial citizenship. In A. Shachar et al. (eds.), *The Oxford Handbook of Citizenship*. Oxford: Oxford University Press, pp. 178–191.

Said, E. W. (1992). *The Question of Palestine*. New York: Vintage.

Samaddar, R. (2006). Law and terror in the age of colonial constitution making. *Diogenes*, 53(4), 18–33.

Saumarez Smith, R. (1985). Rule-by-records and rule-by-reports: Complementary aspects of the British Imperial rule of law. *Contributions to Indian Sociology*, 19 (1), 153–176.

Schleneur, C. (1970). *The Twisted Road to Auschwitz*. Urbana: University of Illinois Press.

Schmitt, C. (2003). *The Nomos of the Earth*. Trans. G. L Ulmen. New York: Telos Press.

Scott, J. C. (1998). *Seeing Like a State: How Certain Schemes to Improve the Human Condition Have Failed*. New Haven, CT: Yale University Press.

Scott, J. C. (2009). *The Art of Not Being Governed*. New Haven, CT: Yale University Press.

Scott, R. W. (2003). *Organizations: Rational, Natural, and Open Systems*. Upper Saddle River, NJ: Prentice Hall.

Scott, R. and Meyer, J. (1994). *Institutional Environments and Organizations*. Thousand Oaks: Sage.

Seikaly, S. (2015). *Men of Capital: Scarcity and Economy in Mandate Palestine*. Stanford, CA: Stanford University Press.

Sen, S. (2013). Unfinished conquest: Residual sovereignty and the legal foundations of the British Empire in India. *Law, Culture and the Humanities*, 9(2), 227–242.

Sen, U. (2018). *Citizen Refugee: Forging the Indian Nation after Partition*. Cambridge: Cambridge University Press.

Sengupta, A. (2014). Breaking up: Dividing assets between India and Pakistan in times of partition. *The Indian Economic & Social History Review*, 51(4), 529–548.

Shachar, A. (1998). Group identity and women's rights in family law: The perils of multicultural accommodation. *Journal of Political Philosophy*, 6(3), 285–305.)

Shafir, G. (1996). *Land, Labor and the Origins of the Israeli-Palestinian Conflict, 1882–1914*. Berkeley: University of California Press.

Shafir, G. (2018). From overt to veiled segregation: Israel's Palestinian Arab citizens in the Galilee. *International Journal of Middle East Studies*, 50(1), 1–22.

Shafir, G. and Peled, Y. (1998). Citizenship and stratification in an ethnic democracy. *Ethnic and Racial Studies*, 21(3), 408–427.

Shafir, G. and Peled, Y. (2002). *Being Israeli: The Dynamics of Multiple Citizenship*. Cambridge: Cambridge University Press.

Shamir, R. (1996). Suspended in space: Bedouins under the law of Israel. *Law and Society Review*, 30, 231–257.

Shamir, R. (2000). *The Colonies of Law: Colonialism, Zionism and Law in Early Mandate Palestine*. Cambridge: Cambridge University Press.

Shani, O. (2017). *How India Became Democratic: Citizenship and the Making of the Universal Franchise*. Cambridge: Cambridge University Press.

Shany, Y. (2005). How supreme is the supreme law of the land? Comparative analysis of the influence of international human rights treaties upon the interpretation of constitutional texts by domestic courts. *Brooklyn Journal of International Law*, 31, 341.

Sharma, A. and Gupta, A. (eds.) (2009). *The Anthropology of the State: A Reader*. Hoboken, NJ: John Wiley & Sons.

Shaw, W. (1930). *Report of the Commission on the Palestine Disturbances of August, 1929* (Cmd. (Great Britain. Parliament); 3530). London: H.M.S.O.

Shenhav, Y. (1994). Manufacturing uncertainty and uncertainty in manufacturing: Managerial discourse and the rhetoric of organizational theory. *Science in Context*, 7(2), 275–305.

Shenhav, Y. (1999) *Manufacturing Rationality: The Engineering Foundations of the Managerial Revolution*. Oxford: Oxford University Press.

Shenhav, Y. (2003). The historical and epistemological foundations of organization theory: Fusing sociological theory with engineering discourse. In H. Tsoukas and C. Knudsen (eds.), *The Oxford Handbook of Organization Theory* . Oxford: Oxford University Press, pp. 183–203.

Shenhav, Y. (2012). Imperialism, exceptionalism and the contemporary world. In M. Svirsky and S. Bignall (eds.), *Agamben and Colonialism*. Edinburgh: Edinburgh University Press, pp. 17–31.

Shenhav, Y. (2013). Beyond "instrumental rationality": Lord Cromer and the imperial roots of Eichmann's bureaucracy. *Journal of Genocide Research*, 15 (4): 339–359.

Shenhav, Y., and Berda, Y. (2009). The colonial foundations of the racialized theological bureaucracy: Juxtaposing the Israeli occupation of Palestinian territories with colonial history. In A. Ophir, M. Givoni, and S. Hanafi (eds.), *The Power of Inclusive Exclusion: Anatomy of Israeli Rule in the Occupied Palestinian Territories*. Boston, MA: Zone Books, pp. 337–374.

Sherman, T. C. (2011). Migration, citizenship and belonging in Hyderabad (Deccan), 1946–1956. *Modern Asian Studies*, 45(1), 81–107.

Shlaim, A. (2005). The Balfour Declaration and its consequences. In W. R. Louis and W. R. Louis (eds.), *Yet More Adventures with Britannia: Personalities, Politics and Culture in Britain*. London: IB Tauris, pp. 251–270.

Silvestri, M. (2019). *Policing "Bengali Terrorism" in India and the World: Imperial Intelligence and Revolutionary Nationalism, 1905–1939*. Cham: Springer.

Simmons, B. A. and Elkins, Z. (2004). The globalization of liberalization: Policy diffusion in the international political economy. *American Political Science Review*, 98(1), 171–189.

Sinanoglou, P. (2016). The Peel Commission and partition, 1936–1938. In R. Miller (ed.), *Britain, Palestine and Empire: The Mandate Years*. London: Routledge, pp. 119–140.

Sinclair, G. (2006). "Get into a Crack Force and earn £20 a Month and all found . . . ": The influence of the Palestine police upon colonial policing 1922–1948. *European Review of History: Revue européenne d'histoire*, 13(1), 49–65.

Sinclair, G. (2017). *At the End of the Line: Colonial Policing and the Imperial Endgame 1945–80*. Manchester: Manchester University Press.

Sinclair, G. and Williams, C. A. (2007). "Home and away": The cross-fertilisation between "colonial" and "British" policing, 1921–85. *Journal of Imperial and Commonwealth History*, 35(2), 221–238.

Singh, U. K. (2007). *The State, Democracy and Anti-terror Laws in India.* New Delhi: Sage.

Singha, R. (2000). Settle, mobilize, verify: Identification practices in colonial India. *Studies in History,* 16(2), 151–198.

Singha, R. (2003). Colonial law and infrastructural power: Reconstructing community, locating the female subject. *Studies in History,* 19(1), 87–126.

Singha, R. (2015). Punished by surveillance: Policing "dangerousness" in colonial India, 1872–1918. *Modern Asian Studies,* 49(2), 241–269.

Singhi, Narendra Kumar. (1974). *Bureaucracy: Positions and Persons.* New Delhi: Abhinav Publications.

Skocpol, T. and Somers, M. (1980). The uses of comparative history in macrosocial inquiry. *Comparative Studies in Society and History,* 22(2), 174–197.

Slater, D. and Simmons, E. (2010). Informative regress: Critical antecedents in comparative politics. *Comparative Political Studies,* 43(7), 886–917.

Smith, P. A. (1986). The Palestinian diaspora, 1948–1985. *Journal of Palestine Studies,* 15(3), 90–108.

Smooha, S. and Hanf, T. (1992). The diverse modes of conflict-regulation in deeply divided societies. *International Journal of Comparative Sociology,* 33 (1-2), 26–47.

Somers, M. (2005). Citizenship troubles: Genealogies of struggle for the soul of the social. In J. Adams, L. Clemens, and A. Orloff (eds.), *Remaking Modernity.* Durham, NC: Duke University Press, pp. 438–469.

Sriraman, T. (2018). *In pursuit of proof: A history of identification documents in India.* Oxford University Press.

Spangenberg, B. (1976). *British Bureaucracy in India.* Delhi: South Asia Books.

Stein, K. W. (1984). The Jewish National Fund: Land purchase methods and priorities, 1924–1939. *Middle Eastern Studies,* 20(2), 190–205.

Steinmetz, G. (ed.). (1999). *State/Culture: State-Formation after the Cultural Turn.* Ithaca, NY: Cornell University Press.

Steinmetz, G. (2008a). *The Devil's Handwriting: Precoloniality and the German Colonial State in Qingdao, Samoa, and Southwest Africa.* Chicago: University of Chicago Press.

Steinmetz, G. (2008b). The colonial state as a social field: Ethnographic capital and native policy in the German overseas empire before 1914. *American Sociological Review,* 73(4), 589–612.

Steinmetz, G. (2014). The sociology of empires, colonies, and postcolonialism. *Annual Review of Sociology,* 40, 77–103.

Steinmetz, G. (2016). Social fields, subfields and social spaces at the scale of empires: Explaining the colonial state and colonial sociology. *The Sociological Review,* 64(2_suppl), 98–123.

Stoler, A. L. (2002). Colonial archives and the arts of governance: On the content in the form. In C. Hamilton, V. Harris, M. Pickover, G. Reid, R. Saleh, and J. Taylor (eds.), *Refiguring the Archive.* Dordrecht: Springer, pp. 83–102.

Stoler, A. L. (2008). Epistemic politics: Ontologies of colonial common sense. *The Philosophical Forum,* 39(3), 349–361.

Stoler, A. L. (2010a). Considerations on imperial comparisons. In I. Gerasimov, J. Kusber, and A. Semyonov (eds.), *Empire Speaks Out*. Leiden: Brill, pp. 33–55.

Stoler, A. L. (2010b). *Along the Archival Grain*. Princeton, NJ: Princeton University Press.

Stoler, A. L. (2012). Colony. *Political Concepts: A Critical Lexicon*, 1, www.politicalconcepts.org/issue1/colony/.

Stoler, A. L. (2016). 3. A deadly embrace: Of colony and camp. In *Duress: Imperial Duarbilities in Our Time*. Durham, NC: Duke University Press, pp. 68–121.

Stoler, A. L. and Cooper, F. (1997). Between metropole and colony. In F. Cooper and A. L. Stoler (eds.), *Tensions of Empire: Colonial Cultures in a Bourgeois World*. Berkeley: University of California Press, pp. 1–56.

Stoler, A. L., McGranahan, C., and Perdue, P. C. (2007). *Imperial Formations*. Santa Fe, NM: SAR Press.

Stone, J. (1979). Introduction: Internal colonialism in comparative perspective. *Ethnic and Racial Studies*, 2(3) 255–259.

Stone, J. (1995). Race, ethnicity, and the Weberian legacy. *American Behavioral Scientist*, 38(3), 391–406.

Strang, D. (1991). Adding social structure to diffusion models: An event history framework. *Sociological Methods & Research*, 19(3), 324–353.

Strang, D., and Meyer, J. W. (1993). Institutional conditions for diffusion. *Theory and Society*, 22(4), 487–511.

Strong, P. N. (1999). The economic consequences of ethno-national conflict in Cyprus: the development of two siege economies after 1963 and 1974. Unpublished doctoral dissertation, The London School of Economics and Political Science.

Subrahmanyam, S. (2006). A tale of three empires: Mughals, Ottomans, and Habsburgs in a comparative context. *Common Knowledge*, 12(1), 66–92.

Subramaniam, V. (2009). Indian legacy of bureaucracy and administration. In A. Farmazand (ed.), *Bureaucracy and Administration*. Boca Raton, FL: CRC Press, 53–64.

Suchman, M. C. and Edelman, L. B. (1996). Legal rational myths: The new institutionalism and the law and society tradition. *Law & Social Inquiry*, 21(4), 903–941.

Sutton, D. (2009). *Other Landscapes: Colonialism and the Predicament of Authority in Nineteenth-Century South India*. Copenhagen: NIAS Press.

Sutton, D. (2011). Imagined sovereignty and the Indian subject: Partition and politics beyond the nation, 1948–1960. *Contemporary South Asia*, 19(4), 409–425.

Swedberg, R. (2003). The changing picture of Max Weber's sociology. *Annual Review of Sociology*, 29, 283–306.

Swedberg, R. (2005). *The Max Weber Dictionary*. Stanford, CA: Stanford University Press.

Swidler, A. (1986). Culture in action: Symbols and strategies. *American Sociological Review*, 51(2), 273–286.

Sundar, N. (1997). *Subalterns and Sovereigns: An Anthropological History of Bastar, 1854–1996*. New Delhi: Oxford University Press.

Sundar, N. (2000). Caste as census category: Implications for sociology. *Current Sociology*, 48(3), 111–126.

Sundar, N. (2011). Interning insurgent populations: The buried histories of Indian democracy. *Economic and Political Weekly*, 46(6), 47–57.

Tamari, S. (2000). Jerusalem's Ottoman modernity: The times and lives of Wasif Jawhariyyeh. *Jerusalem Quarterly*, 9, 5–27.

Tatour, L. (2019). Citizenship as domination: Settler colonialism and the making of Palestinian citizenship in Israel. *Arab Studies Journal*, 27(2), 8–39.

Tawil-Souri, H. (2011). Colored identity: The politics and materiality of ID cards in Palestine/Israel. *Social Text*, 29(2), 67–97.

Thornton, P. H., and Ocasio, W. (1999). Institutional logics and the historical contingency of power in organizations: Executive succession in the higher education publishing industry, 1958–1990. *American Journal of Sociology*, 105(3), 801–843.

Tilly, C. (1995). The emergence of citizenship in France and elsewhere. *International Review of Social History*, 40(S3), 223–236.

Tinker, H. (1977). *The Banyan Tree: Overseas Emigrants from India, Pakistan, and Bangladesh*. Oxford: Oxford University Press.

Titunik, Regina F. 2005. Democracy, domination, and legitimacy in Max Weber's political thought. In C. Camic, P. Gorsky, and D. Trubek (eds.), *Max Weber's "Economy and Society."* Stanford, CA: Stanford University Press, pp. 143–163.

Tomlins, C. (2006) Framing the fragments – Police: Genealogies, discourses, locales, principles. In M. D. Dubber and M. Valverde (eds.), *The New Police Science: The Police Power in Domestic and International Governance*. Stanford, CA: Stanford University Press, pp. 248–294.

Tomlins, C. (2008). Necessities of state: police, sovereignty, and the constitution. *Journal of Policy History*, 20(1), 47–63.

Tomlins, C. (2010). *Freedom Bound: Law, Labor, and Civic Identity in Colonizing English America, 1580–1865*. New York: Cambridge University Press.

Tompson, J. D. (1967). *Organizations in Action*. New York: McGraw-Hill.

Torpey, J. (1998). Coming and going: On the state monopolization of the legitimate "means of movement." *Sociological Theory*, 16(3), 239–259.

Torpey, J. C. (2000). *The Invention of the Passport: Surveillance, Citizenship and the State*. Cambridge: Cambridge University Press.

Trimikliniotis, N. (2009). Nationality and citizenship in Cyprus since 1945: Communal citizenship, gendered nationality and the adventures of a post-colonial subject in a divided country. In R. Bobock and B Perchinig (eds.), *Citizenship Policies in the New Europe*. Amsterdam: Amsterdam University Press, pp. 263–291.

Tsoukas, H., and Knudsen, C. (2003). Introduction: The need for meta-theoretical reflection in organization theory. In H. Tsoukas and C. Knudsen (eds.), *The Oxford Handbook of Organization Theory*. Oxford: Oxford University Press, pp. 1–36.

Turner, B. S. (1990). Outline of a theory of citizenship. *Sociology*, 24(2), 189–217.

Valverde, M. (2006). "Peace, order, and good government": Policelike powers in postcolonial perspective. In M. D. Dubber and M. Valverde (eds.), *The New*

Police Science: The Police Power in Domestic and International Governance. Stanford, CA: Stanford University Press, pp. 73–106.

Van Schendel, W. (2004). *The Bengal Borderland.* London: Anthem Press.

Varnava, A. (2010). The state of Cypriot minorities. *The Cyprus Review,* 22(2), 205–218.

Varnava, A. (2017). *British Imperialism in Cyprus, 1878–1915: The Inconsequential Possession.* Manchester: Manchester University Press.

Vlieland, C. A. (1932). *British Malaya: A Report on the 1931 Census and on Certain Problems of Vital Statistics.* Singapore: Government Publication.

Wagner, S. (2008). British intelligence and the Jewish resistance movement in the Palestine Mandate, 1945–46. *Intelligence and National Security,* 23(5), 629–657.

Wallach, Y. (2011). Creating a country through currency and stamps: State symbols and nation-building in British-ruled Palestine. *Nations and Nationalism,* 17(1), 129–147.

Wallerstein, I. M. (1961). *Africa: The Politics of Independence and Unity.* Lincoln: University of Nebraska Press.

Wasserstein, B. (1977). "Clipping the claws of the colonisers": Arab officials in the government of Palestine, 1917–48. *Middle Eastern Studies,* 13(2), 171–194.

Weber, M. (1949). *On the Methodology of the Social Sciences.* Glencoe, IL: The Free Press.

Weber, M. (1978). *Economy and Society: An Outline of Interpretive Sociology, Vol. 1.* Berkeley: University of California Press.

Weick, K. E. (1976). Educational organizations as loosely coupled systems. *Administrative Science Quarterly,* 21, 1–19.

West, R. (1900). Recent changes in Egypt. *Journal of the Society of Comparative Legislation,* 2(3), 495–503.

Whetstone, T. J. (2002). Personalism and moral leadership. *Business Ethics,* 11(4), 385–392.

Wimmer, A. (1997). Who owns the state? Understanding ethnic conflict in post-colonial societies. *Nations and Nationalism,* 3(4), 631–666.

Xydis, S. G. (1973). *Cyprus: Reluctant Republic.* Near and Middle Eastern Monographs Vol. 11. Berlin: De Gruyter.

Yacobi, H. (2015). *Israel and Africa: A Genealogy of Moral Geography.* Abingdon: Routledge.

Yadgar, Y. (2020). *Israel's Jewish Identity Crisis: State and Politics in the Middle East.* Cambridge: Cambridge University Press.

Yahaya, N. (2020). *Fluid Jurisdictions: Colonial Law and Arabs in Southeast Asia.* Ithaca, NY: Cornell University Press.

Yiftachel, O. (2009). Ghetto citizenship: Palestinian Arabs in Israel. In N. Rouhana and A. Sabbagh (eds.), *Palestine and Israel : Key Terms.* Haifa: Mada Center for Applied Research, pp. 177–208.

Young, C. (1994). *The African Colonial State in Comparative Perspective.* New Haven, CT: Yale University Press.

Zamindar, V. F. Y. (2007). *The Long Partition and the Making of Modern South Asia: Refugees, Boundaries, Histories.* New York: Columbia University Press.

Zuckerman, E. W. (2012). Construction, concentration, and (dis) continuities in social valuations. *Annual Review of Sociology,* 38, 223–245.

Zureik, E. (1979). *The Palestinians in Israel: A Study in Internal Colonialism.* Abingdon: Routledge.

Zureik, E. (2001) Constructing Palestine through surveillance practices. *British Journal of Middle Eastern Studies*, 28(2), 205–227.

Zureik, E. (2003). Theoretical and methodological considerations for the study of Palestinian society. *Comparative Studies of South Asia, Africa and the Middle East*, 23(1), 152–162.

Index

Adivasis, 78, 223n20
administrative detention, 91, 99, 104, 108
administrative flexibility and discretion, 21, 35, 49–51
administrative memory, 22–25, 127–130
  automatic cognition, 23
  concept of, 22
administrative toolkit of emergency, 112–113
administrative toolkit of suspicion, 207
adopters, 61
aftermath of partition, 17–18
aloofness, 47
Anastasiou, A.K., 137
anticolonial struggle, 5, 9, 88, 95, 112
anticolonial violence, 72
Arab civil servants, 152, 154–155
Arab Executive Committee, 84
archival research, 218n13
Arendt, Hannah, 2, 19, 20, 31, 33, 47, 56
Armed Forces Ordinance, 110
Armed Forces Special Powers Act (AFSPA), 99, 110–112
Assam Disturbed Areas Act, 229n63
Assam Maintenance of Public Order Act, 111, 229n63
axis of suspicion, 15, 18, 25, 62, 80
  bureaucratic toolkit of emergency, 124
  classification, 25–26, 92, 99, 112, 113, 118, 121, 123, 151, 158, 174, 183, 206, 208
  hybrid bureaucracy, 130
  infiltrators, 167

inherited, 16, 130, 142, 158
legacy, 128, 141
permit regime, 169–173, 177
trajectories of civil servants, 133, 147

Balfour Declaration, 63, 81–83, 88
Banerjee, R. N., 172
Baring, Evelyn, 219n1
Bäumel, Yair, 238n46
Bedouin tribes, 67
Bengal Criminal Law Amendment Ordinance, 109
Bengal Special Powers Amendment Ordinance, 107
Benton, Lauren, 19, 96, 225n3
Bhambra, Gurminder, 9
blacklists, 99–102
border
  control, 94, 102, 169, 173, 218n13
  India's eastern, 110, 163, 171, 173
  India's western, 163, 170, 173, 213, 238n33
border crossings, 172
Bourdieu, Pierre, 10
Braun, Nathan, 234n76
Brigandage Commissions, 42
British civil servants, 152–153
British civil service, 155
British colonial administration, 64–65
British colonial bureaucracy, 3–6, 20, 25, 34, 56, 65
British colonial rule, 7, 11
British Empire, 43–45

suspicion (cont.)
  administrative toolkit of, 207
  axis of, 25
  bureaucratic logics of, 167–169
  classifying populations, 13–15, 59–60
  colonial bureaucrats, 58
  corruption, 148–149
  diffusion, horizontal circuits of, 60–62
  enumeration, 69, 81, 88
  forms of, 26
  governmentality as power, 58
  graded classification, 183
  inheriting colonial bureaucracy, 131–134
  mobility of civil servants, 144–148
  Mughal and Ottoman empire legacies, 65
  of British civil servants, 152–153
  population management, 57
  Refugee Census (India), 79–81
  rigid classification, 183
  rule by ratio, 134–136
suspicious affinities, 144
suspicious civilians, 102–104
synthetic model of hybrid bureaucracy, 34, 56
systematizers, 47
systemic creation of exceptions, 21, 35,
    51–52

taksim, 72, 135
Tatar, Rustem, 241n92
Tatour, Lana, 179, 188, 236n5
tautological reasoning, 52
Tegart, Charles, 115
teleological reasoning, 52
territorial separation, 8, 134, 139, 161, 169,
    198
Torpey, John, 108
transnational histories of partition, 9–12
  ad hoc solutions, 10
  counterinsurgency, 11
  de facto, 11
  ethnoreligious majoritarianism, 10

  field theory, 10
  political outcomes, 11
  Zionist movement, 10
tribals/original inhabitants, 77
Trump, Donald, 204
Turkish Cypriots
  citizenship, 199, 208
  civil servants, 134, 135, 139
  civil service, 74, 133, 134, 158, 195
  de facto state, 199
  district officer, 194
  enclaves, 12, 18, 74, 128, 139, 140, 161,
    190, 195–198, 236n9
  minorities, 73, 74
  mobility regime, 191
  rebels, 195

uncertainty, 47, 53–54, 131, 146, 147, 174,
    183, 194, 214, 222n22, 233n52
  governing through uncertainty, 155
United Provinces Disturbed Areas, 229n64
universalism, 37–38

Vaadat Hamatzav, 154

Weber, Max, 3, 5, 18, 20, 31, 32, 33, 38, 47,
    50, 54, 217n12
Weberian model of rational-legal
    bureaucracy, 5, 18, 31
withheld violence, 16

Yashin, Yael Navaro, 139, 201
Yeatts, M.W.M., 78–79

Zamindar, Vazira, 9, 17, 144, 161, 170,
    216n4
Zionist industrial complex, 83
Zionist movement, 10, 81, 83
zone of lawlessness, 96, 132
zones, dangerous, 91, 107–108, 210
Zvi, Yitzhak Ben, 86